Donald Wesling
Perceiving-Thinking-Writing: Merleau-Ponty and Literature

Donald Wesling

Perceiving-Thinking-Writing: Merleau-Ponty and Literature

—

ISBN 978-83-67405-96-6
e-ISBN (PDF) 978-83-67405-95-9

This work is licensed under the Creative Commons Attribution-NonCommercial-NoDerivs 4.0 License. For details go to http://creativecommons.org/licenses/by-nc-nd/4.0/.

Library of Congress Cataloging-in-Publication Data
A CIP catalog record for this book has been applied for at the Library of Congress.

© 2024 Donald Wesling
Cover design: Sciendo
Cover art: Tihany 1954 by István Komlós
Edited by: Donald E. Morse
Copy edited by: Kálmán Matolcsy

Funding for this book has been provided by the Faculty of the Humanities, the Institute of English and American Studies, and the University of Debrecen.

Co-published by Debrecen University Press and Sciendo, De Gruyter Brill's electronic publishing subsidiary
https://sciendo.com/book/

Books by Donald Wesling:
Animal Perception and Literary Language
Joys and Sorrows of Imaginary Persons: On Literary Emotions
Bakhtin and the Social Moorings of Poetry
The Scissors of Meter: Grammetrics and Reading
Literary Voice: The Calling of Jonah with Tadeusz Sławek
The New Poetries: Poetic Form Since Wordsworth and Coleridge
The Chances of Rhyme: Device and Modernity
Wordsworth and the Adequacy of Landscape

Edited, co-edited, and translated books by Donald Wesling:
Internal Resistances: The Poetry of Edward Dorn
John Muir, *To Yosemite and Beyond: Writings from the Years 1863 to 1875*; co-edited with Robert Engberg
Bakhtin and the Nation; special issue of *The Bucknell Review* 43.2 (2000); member of editorial collective

Translation by Donald Wesling of a long poem in Russian: Alexei Parshchikov, *I Lived on the Battlefield of Poltava*

Contents

List of Abbreviations of Texts by Merleau-Ponty	1
Preface	2
Introduction	3
Philosophy and Literature in a Relation of Constructive Interference	3
Perceiving-Thinking-Writing	3
On defining phenomenology	5
Origin and scope of the argument	9
Stories that help to explain the argument's leading terms	10
Why Merleau-Ponty?	16
Chapter 1: The Prodigious Search of Appearance	18
The search of appearance as a first (and continuous) move to initiate a philosophy	18
Merleau-Ponty's great Preface of 1945	28
Chapter 2: Eye and Mind in Painting and Writing	32
The primacy of perception	34
Eye and Mind in painting and writing	43
"Cézanne's Doubt" (1945)	47
"The Indirect Language," chapter 3 of *The Prose of the World* (written 1952; posthumous publication)	50
"Eye and Mind" (originally published both in *Art de France* and *Les Temps Modernes* in 1961)	54
Just as	56
Chapter 3: *Ineinander*: Energies of Interference	58
Oneinanother	58
Polemical thesis: Nothing in Merleau-Ponty is ever taken by itself	58
Structures of relation: The dialectic and (not versus) quantum superposition	61
Verbal art as interference	70
Moving toward writing	74
Chapter 4: Recovering the Subject in the Act of Speaking—and Writing	76
On thinking from and of the body	76
On perceiving-thinking-writing, previous to phenomenology	77
Perceptual content of the English sentence: The trial with Henry James	84
Interference as a metaphor for structure of mind	87
Modes of Attention	89

Powers of Attention ... 90
Late essays/notes on recovering the subject in the act of speaking/writing ... 91
On style ... 96

Chapter 5: Energies of Attention: Syntax in Depth ... 100
From perceiving and thinking to writing—and back ... 100
The skills of attention and the forms of energy that connect us to the world and other people ... 100
Energies of attention: Syntax in sentences and sequences of sentences ... 110

Chapter 6: Modes and Powers of Attention: Nine Terms from Merleau-Ponty ... 124
Modes of Attention ... 125
Movement ... 125
Depth ... 126
Chiasm ... 126
Reversibility ... 128
Non-coincidence ... 129
Rhythm ... 130
Powers of Attention ... 131
Interrogation ... 131
Description ... 133
Disclosure ... 134
Toward a trial of reading with the nine terms ... 136

Chapter 7: Reading Poems and a Novel with the Nine Terms ... 138
Sentence and scene in poems by W. C. Williams, Ange Mlinko, and Robert Burns ... 138
Sentence and scene in Henry James's *The Ambassadors* (1903) ... 151

Chapter 8: Ordinary Creativity ... 160
The birth of meaning ... 160
Ordinary creativity ... 165
The co-creativity of those who understand ... 171
"Co-," the prefix of mutuality ... 171
Co-creativity ... 172
Those who understand ... 173
On the freedom of the reader ... 175
Using our freedom ... 176

Bibliography ... 179
Acknowledgments ... 187
Note on the author ... 189

For the other members of the 2020–2023 Pandemic Mondays Lunch Group in Pacific Beach, California.

List of Abbreviations of Texts by Merleau-Ponty

Page citations refer to the editions listed in the Bibliography.

"CD"	"Cézanne's Doubt," *The Merleau-Ponty Reader*
"EM"	"Eye and Mind," *The Merleau-Ponty Reader*
"ILVS"	"Indirect Language and the Voices of Silence," *The Merleau-Ponty Reader*
"Primacy"	"The Primacy of Perception and Its Philosophical Consequences," *The Merleau-Ponty Reader*
"Shadow"	"The Philosopher and His Shadow," *Signs*
AD	*Adventures of the Dialectic*
HLP	*Husserl at the Limits of Phenomenology*
HT	*Humanism and Terror*
IP	*Institution and Passivity*
IPP	*In Praise of Philosophy and Other Essays*
MPR	*The Merleau-Ponty Reader*
N	*Nature*
PLS	*Phenomenology, Language and Sociology*
PP	*Phenomenology of Perception*
PW	*The Prose of the World*
S	*Signs*
SB	*The Structure of Behavior*
SNS	*Sense and Non-Sense*
VI	*The Visible and the Invisible*

Preface

The research questions I have set for myself in this book include: what is the relation of perception to cognition, and how do these embodied skills do their work in human language? Assuming Maurice Merleau-Ponty is correct and *perception already stylizes*, why does it, and what terms might we borrow, or invent, to describe how this happens?

Briefly, my argument is that once we speculatively suspend our naïve but necessary experience of visible-audible-touchable appearance, we can rehabilitate the physical world of things and persons for thought. Perception is in a reciprocal and constructive sort of relationship with cognition both in ordinary experience and in our everyday as well as literary approach to language.

How might we justify writing and reading about these issues, in a time of pandemic—the deadly Covid-19 virus plague that began to spread worldwide in February 2020 and still continues? I will offer an answer after two more two questions: *why* did Maurice Merleau-Ponty make the search of appearance half a century ago; why do we do so now? *Why* consider how our senses get embodied and then inscribed? *Because* we have immense gratitude for the body-world-language we live within, and *because* perception is political in the sense that no class of persons has more or less of it or is better or worse at having it. No one, no class of perceiving persons, should ever, but especially now, be separated out for sacrifice. (It will long be remembered that in March 2020 the lieutenant governor of Texas went on Fox News to say that he and other grandparents would rather die than see public health measures damage the United States economy.)

The Coronavirus pandemic means invisible death droplets beyond the doorsteps of the many; it means stasis; it means the breakdown of bonds; it means the loss of persons and ideas of value. (Philosophers and literary writers, multiplying perspectives, know the irony that the virus is also seeking survival on Earth.)

Perception as the humanism of the many means the registration of movement in time; it means life; it means that creative achievement always remains a possible but uncertain contingency.

Donald Wesling / Pacific Beach, California / 2024

Introduction

Philosophy and Literature in a Relation of Constructive Interference

Perceiving-Thinking-Writing

A constructive relation of interference exists between cognition and perception in Maurice Merleau-Ponty's late writings, as I will insist throughout this book. Of course, I am thinking, in the first instance, of quantum interference in physics, taking "interference" as metaphor to describe a kind of embodied mind that does not relegate thinking or perceiving but keeps them at play (at work) in full indetermination.

I have chosen the triple phrasing in the title with its repeating in-between hyphen to convey through present participles that philosophy in Merleau-Ponty is an in-process activity. The advantage of the Hyphen as a constitutive metaphor is that it brings in a feature of writing to stand for the activity of thinking. Also, it exemplifies, in little, the book's approach, namely, philosophy and literature invading-appreciating each other both ways, and it gives a metaphor to the process disclosed in the book's eight chapters. This three-in-one in "perceiving-thinking-writing" is the kind of effect Merleau-Ponty liked, and he borrowed from German the term *Ineinander* [oneinanother] to describe concepts on the level in their chiastic, interwoven, in-tension relation with each other, with no vector gaining victory.

The *Oxford English Dictionary* says that the word "hyphen," Greek in origin, means *together, in one*; the hyphen of the Greek grammarians was a little sign placed under a two-word unit, to indicate that it was not to be read as two words. Among other usages the *OED* cites Ben Jonson in 1636 asking "What a sight it is, to see writers committed together by the ears, for ceremonies, syllables, points, colons, commas, hyphens, and the like?" Since in writing what we see is also what we hear in our inner speech, Jonson, always a poet, is clever to say "committed together by the ears." To explain my chapter's title, Jonson's sentence about writers helps me to circumscribe my overall argument concerning in-betweenness. I would here banish all hints in the official definitions of "hyphen" that would mention a relation of compounding or alternation of the entities. Once in the unit-joined-by-hyphen, they are *committed together*!

One-in-another, two-in-one, in-between, Merleau-Ponty.

Since the whole argument to follow concerns perceiving-thinking-writing in their relation of propulsion and feedback, to introduce it I will move sideways from the title's actual triplet of terms into the more general thesis, which I call "philosophy in hyphens," where the hyphen will stand for several other metaphors. The two most prominent of these metaphors are Quantum Interference, to describe a kind of embodied mind that does not relegate either thinking or perceiving but keeps them at play in full indetermination; and the Search of Appearance, which is my attempt to rename for explicitness and clarity The Reduction, the key term Merleau-Ponty takes from Edmund Husserl. (In the first chapter, I describe how the reduction initiates this kind of philosophy.)

The metaphor is the perfect figure for combined relation and indetermination. For writers, writers-as-philosophers, philosophers, and philosophers-as-writers, the metaphor is the primary trope with which to think. Scientists and historians of science also think with metaphor when they are creating and describing the natural world. Charis Anastopoulos, typical of many such as Neils Bohr, Richard Feynman, and Karen Barad, who in the past century also described the achievement of quantum physics, says about metaphor in his 2008 book with the indeterminate title *Particle or Wave*,

> What we call the "rational" approach for the description of nature is based on a very important ability in the human intellect: the ability to transfer familiar concepts, ideas, and descriptions into a new context, completely unrelated to the initial one. We call this process metaphor (a transfer). Metaphors make possible the description of things that lie beyond our immediate experience through a comparison with things that are well known and understood. . . . Indeed, the things we know can lead us—after strenuous efforts of will and intellect—to concepts that refer to a world beneath and beyond anything we perceive through our senses. (11-12)

Particle and *wave* are metaphors, and their relation of *interference* is also a metaphor. As Anastopoulos says, "[l]anguage is steeped in metaphor" (12). Many, if not all, metaphors take one or the other side of the transfer (the tenor or the vehicle), from what perception infers from the outer world. Essential to this kind of insight is what Merleau-Ponty maintained eloquently in his late writings: you do not get beneath and beyond the senses, or from the visible to the invisible, without having and using the senses as they are mounted within and expressed through the embodied mind. *Embodied mind*, as the undeniable-forgettable two-in-one, is the foundational metaphor in phenomenology. It derives from the fact of actual biological life (this upright front-facing mind-body, these sense organs, binocular vision, fish-gills evolved into voice-boxes), which before Husserl and Merleau-Ponty many professional philosophers and scientists found useful to forget. It is the active assignment of phenomenology to disclose how a buzzing and flashing world exists, bodied against our senses. For Husserl and Merleau-Ponty, the outer world exists and exists in relation to our minds, mediated by our perceptions. That is why Merleau-Ponty always refers to the *primacy* of perception. By this he means not victory over the other skills but a necessary undeniable firstness.[1]

---

[1] Here at the start, and to condition all that follows, it is necessary to admit that phenomenology, as philosophy, has itself largely forgotten that perception may be lost or impaired in the disabled body. Merleau-Ponty has a page or two on phantom limbs and ansognosia (denial of illness and specifically paralysis), but that is far short of a full recognition. This essay is also guilty of ableism

On defining phenomenology

Here are the kinds of issues that arise when a stranger hopeful to gain new insights first encounters Husserl and his tribe: why does phenomenology, a subset that proposes to rebuild philosophy, have an altogether more rebarbative label than other disciplinary names with similar construction, like biology and anthropology? The study of phenomena seems pitched at too high a level of generality to be helpful, at last, because all other disciplines do *that*, that is, study phenomena, and what is the value of washing out a specific method or signature topic? Also: tally up all the phenomenologists (after Husserl) who ever lived and made a name, and the number (in hundreds) is barely enough to constitute a disciplinary cohort—even when you add in Edith Stein, Jean-Paul Sartre, James J. Gibson, Claude Lefort, Hubert Dreyfus, and more recent major scholars like Paul Ricoeur, Charles Taylor, Alphonso Lingis, Lawrence Lawlor, Louise Westling, Lawrence Hass, Dermot Moran, Judith Butler, Renaud Barbaras, Ted Toadvine, Annabelle Dufourcq, Kelly Oliver, Jessica Wiskus, Andrew Inkpin, and Claude Romano.[2] A standard student introduction lists the field's arguments against scientific psychology, and in favor of Gestalt psychology, and explains one prominent concern to be "to provide an account of the structures that make a shared, objective world intelligible" (Käufer and Chemero 2). Although that explanation wrongly assumes that we already know the meanings of "structures," "shared," "objective," "world," and also "intelligible," it does put into relation all the pertinent elements—except, of course, perception, the central value discussed in the chapters that follow.

Somewhere, one has to start the inquiry into the commonalities and research priorities. We do need the summaries for students, the introductions to the translations, the essays in the *Cambridge Companion to Merleau-Ponty* (2005), all such aids to knowledge. Also, rereading the works of the principals increases our mental grasp

---

and the avoidance of impairment and suffering. In 2024, phenomenology as a subset of philosophy trying to become all of philosophy remains an ableist thinking, as if perception is difficult and rich enough as an inquiry—but there is now work to be done to complete phenomenology's mission by a full recognition of disabled perception in all its variety and severity. This project would do well to begin with scholarship on the topic in the last thirty years, especially with the book by Tobin Siebers, *Disability Theory* (2008). His critique of theories of social constructivism in the heroic figures of the 1970s-1980s, Judith Butler and Michel Foucault, on biopower and their way of missing the actual body when they talk about the constructed one, shows how they miss actual suffering. Siebers always confronts suffering and takes as his assignment the forcing of theory to admit suffering. (Michael Davidson's 2008 review of Siebers's book discusses this topic and many related topics.) Disability theory may trouble the theory of social construction, but it also troubles the standard procedures of phenomenology.

2 For works by these writers, here listed randomly, please consult the Bibliography. The two-year Covid shutdown of libraries has limited the list. As to quality, the named writers are magnificent! Nearly all I have to say is a refinement upon, or development from, their writings.

of the linkages. It is not an option to stop using the term "phenomenology," since the name is already part of the disciplinary landscape, but if my experience is typical, the term for the field itself is a dragon crouching in the gate, warning off readers.

In this book, I have two ways of addressing the essential assignment of field-definition. Starting with the basics, I go back to the two Greek words behind the invented term, in the faith learned from Martin Heidegger, that philology is always already philosophy: a necessary but never sufficient starting phase. In subsequent chapters, I will specify and imply further and (I trust) richer explanations of phenomenological practice, as those emerge from stages of the overall argument.

The components of the word "phenomenology" are *phainomenon* and *logos*. *Phainomenon* is a present passive participle. Its root, *phaino*, derives from the Indo-European *bha-*, which has to do with "light." The transitive version of the verb means "bring to light" or "make to appear"; the middle-voice version, *phaenesthai*, is prevalent in all periods and means "come to light" or "appear." Very common is the adverb *phainomenōs*, which means "apparently." The word can also have, in a judicial setting, a pejorative sense, meaning "(appear to) denounce." In the Platonic dialogues, the third person singular—*phainetai*—can merely signify a weak positive reply, as in the common English language phrase "it would appear so."

The word "logos" is more telling yet because Merleau-Ponty so often finds a use for it and always uses it thus, in transliterated form. In its first signification, it means merely "the word by which the inward sense is expressed." Unlike the relatively starved sense of "word" in English, logos reaches into other semantic realms thanks to its verbal root, *legein*, whose foundational meaning is "lay in order, arrange," and, therefore, "pick up, collect," hence (in the middle voice), "pick out, choose, reckon, count," hence "recount, relate," and hence "mean, refer to, reason out." Logos, therefore, easily comes to mean "reason, law," and, most notably in this context, "speech."

In Heidegger's Introduction to *Being and Time*, he provides a tutorial in the extended meanings of the classical Greek terms behind that compound word, that internally interfering two-in-one, phenomenology.[3] He says that the quick-summary motto "To the things themselves!" is a misleading commonplace of Husserl commentary. We must get to the Greek, to the verb meaning "to show itself . . . the self-showing, the manifest . . . to bring into daylight, to place in brightness . . . that is, that within which something can become . . . visible in itself" (27). This first-stage self-showing turns out to be a "good that looks like—but . . . is not what it gives itself out to be" (27). Further, "[a]ppearance, as the appearance 'of something,' . . . precisely does not mean that something shows itself; rather, it means that something which does not show itself announces itself through something that does show itself" (28). The upshot of this explanation, a half-page later, is that phenomena are *never* appearances, but

---

[3] Quotations here are taken from chapter 2, section 7.

every appearance is dependent upon phenomena (see 28-29). I interpret Heidegger as saying that self-showing manifests itself at a higher level, and as something of value, once we've accepted the brute, wild, uninterpreted results of our experience in the world as indispensable. Value comes from our realizing that the experience is presuppositionless and that this realization is the way we start disclosing what are our presuppositions.

Heidegger goes on to say that if we define logos as "discourse," we have to validate this literal translation by defining what discourse (in German, *Rede*) itself means, involving also the extended senses of "reason, judgment, concept, definition, ground, relation" (30). So discourse really means what is talked about in discourse, "and indeed *for* the speaker . . . or for those who speak with each other" (31). Furthermore, says Heidegger, "because *logos* lets something be seen, it can *therefore* be true or false" (31). With this meaning, there always exists the possibility of covering up, concealment. However, the Greek concept of truth is of a simple, straightforward letting of things to be apprehended. That meaning, more favorable to disclosure than to concealment, is what is conveyed in the other extended senses: logos as *reason*, logos as *relationship*.

Addressing one of my previous concerns, Heidegger in this preliminary account of the concept says that titles like "biology" designate "the objects of the respective disciplines in terms of their content. 'Phenomenology' neither designates the object nor is it a title that describes their content. . . . Here description does not mean a procedure like that of, say, botanical morphology. The term rather has the sense of a prohibition" (32-33). This takes us back to the earlier distinction between revelation and concealment, and Heidegger is judging the revelation side "vulgar" (35) and the concealment side fully philosophical: "manifestly [phenomenon] is something that does not show itself initially" (33). What's concealed, covered up, disguised "is not this or that being, but rather . . . the *being* of beings," a move to the meta-level (33). Phenomenology is needed because "phenomena are initially and for the most part *not* given" (34). As explanation of the topic with which this paragraph began, and as placement of the new method within the philosophical discipline, Heidegger concludes, "As far as content goes, phenomenology is the science of the being of beings—ontology" (35), and the method of phenomenological description is interpretation.

As Husserlian interpreters Heidegger and Merleau-Ponty both address themselves to the way human beings inadvertently and also deliberately forget, obscure, deny, block, and badmouth the temporality of being-toward-death of Dasein, and the corporeality of thinking/writing. More explicitly and massively for Merleau-Ponty than for Heidegger, however, bodily perception is a condition of thought and language. With the French thinker we need to "dis-close"—to relearn, to restore—our systems of perception, including our experiences of community, of the other—whether human or nonhuman—and of the nature of time. When Merleau-Ponty is writing he very often uses Logos at crucial turning points, as in the course notes from the late '50s collected as *Nature*, where he says that "[t]he life of language reproduces perceptual structures at another level.... There is a Logos of the natural esthetic world, on which the Logos of language relies" (212). Here are phrases from the posthumous "Working Notes" at the end of *The Visible and the Invisible*: "Logos also as what is realized in man, but nowise as his *property*"; "and we do not take Logos and truth in the sense of the Word .... [the Logos] is neither logic, nor teleology of consciousness but a study of the language that has man" (274). To paraphrase: we inhabit the spectacle, our bodies are geared to the material surround, and language *has man* rather than us having it because in speech the body becomes the thought.

Recent testimony as to the stakes involved comes from French thinker Claude Romano, who in 2015 published an analytical hymn to a Merleau-Pontian "bighearted reason" that might be on the horizon: a program for us in the 21st century "to *reunite* a reason cut off from its corporeal and experiential roots" (527). Writing from outside Romano's discipline, I agree with his conclusions, most particularly:

> We should replace the *linguistic turn* by an "experiential turn," ... since language has its roots in our prelinguistic openness to the world, as the dimension of our sensible and embodied existence, and draws from its very possibility ... [P]henomenology holds both ends of a chain extending from the second naïveté of our immersion into the world to the refined products of history and culture. It is probably the only philosophical option that is able to embrace and intertwine these two dimensions. If all this makes sense, phenomenology is not a dead possibility ... only belonging to documentary ... history, but a living possibility, born of a living investigation. (527)

Yes, and in more ancient phrasing that I take from Herakleitos, these studies are urgent because they help us show in gritty sensory detail how a human person is an organic continuation of the Logos.

In 2024 phrasing, Herakleitos's organic continuation of the Logos is the embodied mind, and the embodied mind is built of ineluctable links both ways, between sensing and thinking. For my purposes, these meanings open onto my pursuit of *the search of appearance* as an early stage, the prototypical move, of phenomenological philosophy; and these meanings justify my emphasis on the relation between thought and language as a unity, an always already constructive interference, cognitive and aesthetic, before these forces get differentiated.

For Merleau-Ponty's purposes, as his kind of phenomenologist, reason unaided by the senses is impossible. That is why he needs to keep up the interference between perception and cognition. For him in his tradition, and for Romano and for us in his line, the question becomes: how do we get from sense to reason, from reason to sense, from perception to writing, from writer's coding of perception to reader's decoding? How do we get from phenomenalism to phenomenology?[4]

---

4 In a 2003 essay, Erazim Kohák explains the difference between the two terms. "Phenomenology can be a phenomeno*logy* and not mere phenomenalism precisely because it focuses not on individual

As to intent, topic, and method, I need to bring perceptual content back into the center of literary study, and I need to use what I know of literature to colonize philosophy. I need to give a rationale for using the English sentence as a primary unit, as I take perception into cognition through sentence structure. In the practical-critical parts of this book, where I read poems and a novel, I propose to think through the Merleau-Pontian categories of perceiving perception and attending to attention. Along the way, playing my part in the constructive interference between disciplines, I will be telling a style-story of how the French thinker presents his thought.

Origin and scope of the argument

This argument began as a proposal to use nine of Merleau-Ponty's terms to help readers of literary (and other) works appreciate how perception gets into writing. At that stage, the essay was a foray outside literature, my home territory, to bring new analytical tools back into the mystery. Then, after reading a condescending ironic essay by Richard Rorty on "Philosophy as a Kind of Writing," everything became more complicated, and I spent two false starts trying to think two disciplines in one thought. It became clear to me that Merleau-Ponty, barely worth a mention within Rorty's restricted frame, wrote consciously and creatively about being a philosopher-writer, and he admired literary storytellers as wild thinkers who got to his core concept, the primacy of perception, long before professional philosophers like him. Tacked above my computer, his phrase "perception already stylizes" became the answer to my research question: the task of this book is to explain why and how that happens.

This book is now in its broadest intent a study of the relationship of constructive interference between philosophy and literature as disciplines. That is the aim of all the specific kinds of interference, and of entities in interference, that I describe in chapters to follow. Earlier drafts were limited to working out the lessons for language and literature of Merleau-Ponty's major book *Phenomenology of Perception*, published in 1945 at the end of World War II and sixteen years before his death in 1961. He was enormously productive after that book, and I wish to describe, and use, his changes of attitude, topic, and emphasis in the published books, course-notes, and draft manuscripts from the late 1940s to the year of his death. These writings represent the way he changed emphasis, became more exploratory with his core concepts in phenomenology, the kind of creativity, he might have said, that concerns the living, real, and original relation between the elements of the world as registered by the embodied mind. I do not plan to avoid *Phenomenology of Perception*, but the emphasis

---

empirical instantiations but rather on principles, on the eidetic structures of life's functioning. The move from empirical ways of knowing to phenomenology is in part a shift from the *naiveté* as a set of space-time objects in causal relations to approaching it as a system of interlocking roles" (23-24).

here is on how Merleau-Ponty, without denying anything of record, developed more (and more eloquent) capaciousness in his ideas of the role of others in our perceptions and in our language use, the meanings of the search of appearance, the role of perception in relation to cognition, and especially the core concept of interference. He learned the interference-term and concept of *Ineinander* from his heroic, prolific, flawed predecessor-mentor Edmund Husserl and increasingly, during the 1950s, put that quantum relation into the center of his version of phenomenology.

Stories that help to explain the argument's leading terms

To prepare for the chapters that follow, I will set down my reasons for making Maurice Merleau-Ponty the writer who stands for philosophy as a discipline. And I need to offer, to readers in general and especially those with philosophical and literary interests, my own interpretations of the terms I have selected to parcel out the argument: namely, the search of appearance, cognitive-aesthetic interference, and co-creativity.

Indirectly as allegory, the French philosopher's system of thought, and the working vocabulary of my own argument, will be disclosed in the following story of a high-summer Monday in the time of Covid-19 lockdown. The day begins at 5 a.m. exactly, with the sound of *The New York Times*, in its blue plastic cover, hitting the front screen door. At about 7:30 the he who is I takes out the US flag to put it in the metal holder on the porch post, as a way to convey, to the few who walk and the thousands who drive by, the message "We're here." At 9 a.m. the marmalade cat noses the bag that contains the flea comb and the rubber-nubble mitten, so there begins the ritual of getting off her back the daily handful of fur; she preens and purrs in ecstasy. There is then the interval of performing scholarship on his topics when libraries are all shut down and he must rely on the hundreds of books he already has plus, on occasion, books purchased online. Lunch is at the neighbor's house, where he and wife meet with three others, all middle- and high-school teachers, in a neighborhood pod where they practice social distance but, as healthy senior citizens, don't need their masks. Then more scholarship, watching with Scotch a political commentator on MSNBC at 5 p.m., taking in the flag at twilight, and during the long hot evening watching several international fictional stories by streaming, on TV. He turns on the air conditioning in the bedroom at 9 p.m. when the peak-charge hours for electricity are over, and it produces a rumble that is audible through the structure of the bed, before sleep enhanced by a gummy of melatonin.

By this allegory, phenomenology would be, in Merleau-Pontian terms, a project of thinking about how perception occurs as the exercise of a body-mind that is sensitive to change in time and space. For the French thinker, the indispensable category, meant literally and then symbolically as an infinite series that ends only with the death of the individual experiencer, is *movement*. A phenomenology of the registration of movement would turn us "away from a retrospective philosophy which would convert the world and history into a universal past in advance" and toward an "idea of the central function of the temporal present" with this purpose: "to record this passage of meaning rather than to take it as an accomplished fact" ("In Praise of Philosophy," *IPP* 9). Thus time markers include sights, touches, sounds, colors; descriptive details, with lots of adjectives; and notations of change and passage as the prime directive, even before intellectual recognition.

By this allegory, *the search of appearance* would be the first moment of an infinite, unfinalizable sequence of noticings that revealed, from the facts of the scene, the hidden assumptions that make the scene possible. In philosophical discourse, this involves reference to, indeed practice of, the cogito of René Descartes, where we would start a project of thought by doubting our own existence and the existence of the world outside ourselves (before reconstructing everything by understanding that there must be a thinking entity, the self, for there to be a thought). We may also refer to Edmund Husserl's bracketing or suspension of all perceptual experience, named by him "The Reduction," wherein what he calls the natural attitude (of ordinary body-centered sensing and also the whole gathering of facts which is contemporary science) is kept in mind but also kept apart, to see what's left in its absence, or hollowed out behind it. Merleau-Ponty's title-phrase from a posthumous book, *The Visible and the Invisible*, is the even-handed, reversible, short explanation of the search of appearance that is the reduction.

By the lockdown allegory, what is appearance, and thus suspended, is what is told in the day-in-the-life story, namely, a list of actions and names along a line of time. What is disclosed must be all the days that precede this day, as preparation for this one in a series and as building the consciousness that will understand such things as circadian rhythms of day and night. Also understood is the throwing of newspapers from a car against a door as deduced from a sound, the decreed protocols of putting out and taking in flags, the invisible presence of a killer virus that keeps a nation indoors for half a year (and shuts down libraries) in fear of receiving or giving infection, the attendant need for social distancing and masks, the existence of television, of whisky with an ice-cube at end of day, of stories both factual and fictional, of an animal in the house that has fleas that require to be combed out, of conversations with friends that occur during lunch, of neighborhoods, streets, and alleys. That is enough to reconstruct a scene, but for context I add the memory of refugee scholar Erich Auerbach, who, in Istanbul without an adequate library during World War II, wrote his canonical study of *Mimesis*, on classic works in Western literature, by working with the texts alone and few secondary materials. This parallel is not to make a comparison of value, but to disclose a hidden similarity in scholarly circumstance.

That is enough, except for one more event in this Monday of the Coronavirus-pandemic summer, which occurs when he and his wife, after lunch with Mary, Kenneth, and Susan at Susan's house at the end of the alley, have started to walk home. Rounding Susan's hedge to go up the alley, they saw two crows, grounded, chasing a rat toward us along Susan's high wood fence. There were perhaps a dozen other squawking crows in trees and wires above: encouragers. The rat tried once to climb the fence, got half-way, fell, and ran again at us. Our presence stopped the attackers, and the rat dodged in the hedge, escaped. That would have been enough, a story rounded off. Crows scattered, quok quok. But then the he that is I went ahead up the path between two fences, and a crow up on a wire from the phone pole on our lot line shat a thick white load on his shoulder, best blue shirt, perfect timing, perfect aim.

What is *that*, as phenomenology of perception? I recount this event of two minutes' duration because the whole summer has organized itself around it. Before getting to Husserl and Merleau-Ponty I call upon James J. Gibson, a cognitive scientist consciously in their line during the 1970-90s period, who in *The Ecological Approach to Visual Perception* spoke of affordances, where things and beings make meanings. Gibson believes the universe beckons to us! Through movement, changes in space and time, bodily position and alignment, across surfaces and with effects of sound, and so on, the world is soliciting us to see and understand. Here, employing his approach, it is hard to escape the strong inference that the meaningful universe was, precisely but through symbol, teaching some kind of lesson. In this case, the surround was Southern California, a summer Monday, but also the condition of a pandemic, caused by an invisible omnipresent killer of hundreds of thousands of Americans (and many more perceiving persons worldwide).

I recount this summer day in order to place into context *interference* and *co-creativity*, the two other terms that organize this book. The movement of perception into thinking and writing is the whole-career issue for Husserl and Merleau-Ponty. For Husserl the first act to suspend the natural attitude is to bracket the world, and for him this bracketing does not mean any loss of perceiving or knowing, or of the particulars of what is outside the self, but rather is a mental doubt-experiment. Merleau-Ponty, learning from Husserl's original move and increasingly becoming troubled by some of the one-sided-rational implications of Husserl's pursuit of the argument, would say *yes* to the suspension: but for this French follower in phenomenology, we cannot discount either the world or the sensing subject, because if we do, we lose the principle of constructive perceptual-cognitive interference. For Merleau-Ponty interference is the core position that philosophy must keep.

I have already mentioned the relation between philosophy and literature, disciplines advancing together insofar as they share an interest in how perception gets into thought and language and in how perception is influenced by thought in a feedback system (action in both directions with no punctual start and no ending to the process). In this book, I highlight philosophical terms mostly from Merleau-Ponty that help us read for perceptual content in all forms of writing. The reciprocity occurs when Donald Wesling starts in literature and Maurice Merleau-Ponty starts in philosophy, and *we each inquire into and with the other kind of discourse*. In this book, the task (from my literary side of the interference) is to find new perception-terms that may illuminate storytelling of all sorts. Equally, the task is to study the way philosophical works are, after all, writing and must submit to the constraints of writing such as hierarchies of presentation, dialogism, sentencing, and deployment (or not) of the pronoun I.

Terms from the philosopher himself and from his commentators—reciprocity, encroachment, reversibility, chiasm, expression, flesh, non-coincidence—have sharpened my ideas about his core positions, but here I am proposing a new term for the systematic shape of his mind: *cognitive-perceptual interference*, and, since "aesthetic" (by the root in classical Greek) means perceptual, more specifically we shall refer to *cognitive-aesthetic interference*. Later I will explore the metaphors that help to explain the relation of interference, analogies from dialectic in philosophy and quantum indeterminacy in physics. Here let us affirm provisionally that the recovery of appearance at another level in late Merleau-Ponty shows that perception is not an illusion but a creative act, in ordinary experience and in art, and this recognition is true both pre-propositionally and pre-eminently in thinking. Ordinary perception is foundational for all of language, all of writing. Ordinary perception is creative. Ordinary perception is co-creative with the capacities of other humans and animals who also perceive-think; it is also co-creative in the interference-structures of the languages of painting, literature, and philosophy.

Interference means "not one without the other." More specifically, it means that each of the two entities in the non-dual whole is trying to reduce the other to matter and failing, and over-emphasis on one side or the other is loss of meaning for thinking and writing. Self-world loss of meaning on one side leads to an isolated idealism, self-world loss of meaning on the other side leads to an isolated materialism. Interference, when it is working well, has entities counter-posed against, and blending with, each other at the highest pitch of indeterminacy.

What are those entities-in-relation? Ranged below the most general, philosophy-literature relation, there are many. My literary example of cognitive-aesthetic interference is the traditional poem in rhyme and meter, where meter and grammar both seamlessly inhabit the same stretch of writing and are thought together by those who know how to read, where sentence scissors line and line scissors sentence to make the poem. At any given point, that scissoring simultaneity is the interference. Along the developing utterance, that scissoring is continuously sutured by the performance of tacit perceptions, which is the action of reading.[5] This clarification is to re-state, by an unfamiliar route, something obvious: through colons and dashes and periods

---

5 This is more fully argued in my book *The Scissors of Meter: Grammetrics and Reading* (1995). I will mention the book on meter early in this study, because I first imagined and worked out the claim of a constructive interference in its pages, and it will become evident that this is central to the argument in *perceiving-thinking-writing*. The point is that because as readers we process the grammar and the meter together in the poem, each system interrupts the other continually but in mappable places.

the hyphen or slash separates and connects two words; also, more generally, through breaking-off and interruption division becomes as essential to literary writing/reading as continuity. What is being scissored and stitched up are the reader's acts of attention, and it will be one of this book's claims that from such action a new force is created out of the near-nothing that—as appearance—is black marks on white paper.

Some of these interference-structures, such as an I that is a he, may be seen in my stories about events in a summer day and about crows chasing a rat. Even when I read Husserl and Merleau-Ponty in English translations, the designs of propositional sentencing and of exposition show patterns of interference-entanglement in the larger logic and the relations of sentences; these evidences are broad enough so as not to need reference to the original German and French, which in any event are unavailable. (And yet it is striking to see how Husserl eschews such ground-level effects and Merleau-Ponty exploits a wide range.)

Rather than take examples from those sources, I shall plunge fully into literature-as-phenomenology with a paragraph on a late-nineteenth-century summer twilight. This paragraph is from Henry James's *The Tragic Muse* (1890), and Nick Dormer, who has just been elected MP for Harsh and has proposed marriage to his patroness, the wealthy widow Julia, is going for a solitary evening walk in deep rural England. The experience, says James through the consciousness of Nick, is so retro that the lead-in sentence just above this following passage reads "It might as well be 1830," that is, sixty years ago:

> All this would be a part of the suggestion of leisure that invariably descended upon him at Beauclere—the image of a sloping shore where the tide of time broke with a ripple too faint to be a warning. But there was another admonition that was almost equally sure to descend upon his spirit in a summer hour, in a stroll about the grand abbey; to sink into it as the light lingered on the rough red walls and the local accent of the children sounded soft in the churchyard. It was simply the sense of England—a sort of apprehended revelation of his country. The dim annals of the place appeared to be in the air (foundations bafflingly early, a great monastic life, wars of the Roses, with battles and blood in the streets, and then the long quietude of the respectable centuries, all cornfields and magistrates and vicars), and these things were connected with an emotion that arose from the green country, the rich land so infinitely lived in, and laid on him a hand that was too ghostly to press and yet somehow too urgent to be light. It produced a throb that he could not have spoken of, it was so deep, and that was half imagination, and half responsibility.... (147)[6]

Orchestrate that with Ralph Vaughan Williams's "The Lark Ascending"! The paragraph calls forth plangent, lyrical place-affection, with a throat-catch at its best, beautifully earned moment, that "throb that he could not have spoken of, it was so deep." James, like Proust, imagined *avant la lettre* several of the premises

---

6 Another novel by James, *The Ambassadors* (1903), will be my example in chapter 7 for an expanded set of Merleau-Pontian terms, to think about perceptual content in fiction.

of phenomenology and set them into the perceptions of fictional characters in the very terms of later philosophers. The passage is phenomenology in its conveyed impressions, and it does phenomenology with its chosen words. It begins with an image that carries temporality, "the tide of time," and this is an "admonition" very like James J. Gibson's affordance, a direct meaning from the scene delivered to Nick Dormer, James's own fictional-person guise in a fine mind well placed to register red brick walls and the actual local accent of nearby children. History, Merleau-Ponty's preoccupation as a Marxist in the '40s-'50s and as a philosopher of temporality, is inferred from the scene, back centuries, and then "connected with an emotion that arose from the green country": connected by the sense of touch, in a Gibsonian "appeal" to someone who will now represent (as Member for Harsh) the very scene he walks within, and on a national stage. This captured moment is the phenomenology of national feeling as projected onto the immemorial scene, which might even "have a love for him and expect something of him" (147). In sentences omitted at the bottom of this passage, the main character is left with questions, both buoyed by the emotion of the scene and tasked by it, in a "grand kind of reciprocity" (147), which I am reading as the interference of then and now, the outward and inward scenes, the obscure soreness (of the prospect of all the coming political-marital responsibilities) over and against the balms of indifference (meaning: his true vocation as a painter).

This effect is what my own paragraphs on Covid-19 lockdown and aggressive crows would aspire to as writing; if only I had thought about the American nation far enough, through to "throb," that verb. As a writer of an Introduction, in my role as one who frames and explains, my phenomenology is aspirational and my storytelling is in the service of commentary on deceased writers (Husserl, Merleau-Ponty, Auerbach, James). This circumstance makes me a latecomer, but in no sense secondary because a dead writer needs a living reader. Russian theorist of dialogism, Mikhail Bakhtin, gave the topic of my final chapter when he explained this in an offhand note of 1970:

> To understand a given text as the author himself understood it. But our understanding can and should be better. Powerful and profound creativity is largely unconscious and polysemic. Through understanding it is supplemented by consciousness, and the multiplicity of its meanings is revealed. Thus, understanding supplements the text: it is active and also creative by nature. Creative understanding continues creativity, and multiplies the artistic wealth of humanity. The co-creativity of those who understand. ("From Notes" 141-42)

Merleau-Ponty, who wrote that "[o]ur relationship to the true passes through others" (*IPP* 31), has affinities with Bakhtin in the French philosopher's late-career reckoning-in of other beings to the action of perception, and especially in the heavy conscious use of "co-," the prefix of mutuality.[7]

---

[7] Long ago, Michael Gardiner powerfully described the contours of this affinity in "'A Very Understandable Horror of Dialectics': Bakhtin and Marxist Phenomenology" (2000).

Born within a decade of each other at the beginning of the twentieth century, unaware of each other, they yet would have agreed that the consciousness of the person who understands and responds is inexhaustible, that creativity is always related to a change of sense, and that creativity escapes whatever is readymade and finalized. For both, creativity is another term for freedom in a historical era that has an unavoidable and vexed relation to Marxist politics. What Merleau-Ponty in several places calls "coherent deformation" occasioned by the material medium in painting is exactly, for "those who understand" in Bakhtin, what Bakhtin describes as "a potential infinity of responses, languages, codes. Infinity against infinity" (136). For both thinkers the human being's relation to brute external reality in perception is the same as the relation of reader to writer, with no singular, settled meaning—rather multiple, contestatory, body-in-time-and-space meanings. Bakhtin's *dialogism* is the major component in Merleau-Ponty's late, achieved if patchily delivered, philosophy of cognitive-aesthetic *interference*. And both of their terms for a working method, in our approach to discourse, are synonyms of the term for an even higher value, *creativity*.

Why Merleau-Ponty?

It is Merleau-Ponty and no other because of what Jean-Paul Sartre, fellow-student, co-editor, sometime rival in philosophy, remembered him saying: that he, Merleau-Ponty, had never recovered from an incomparable childhood. Sartre said that as an adult Merleau-Ponty was, like a child, "surprised by everything" (268). The surprise of experience is the singularity of his thought.

He values the body and its perceptions, puts these into the center of his thinking. This move becomes an infinite project for thought. In him, phenomenology is always a philosophy of language and of the way perception and language are indispensable to each other. In him, we humans are part of nature, and animals are in us as well as being next to us. So he caught on early to what will be the future of all thinking in what used to be called the humanities. The phenomenology of perception in his writings avoids the residue of idealism he finds in Edmund Husserl, and, as a material practice, it values the daily ordinariness of perceptual experience—because that experience, as topic and model for this thought, is creative and open-ended. He is a skillful expositor of his particular argument, using careful respectful refutation of predecessors, apt metaphors, choice personal anecdotes, imaginary objections, daring compressions of quotable phrase, and sinuous sentencing.

He wrote a grand scholarly masterpiece in *Phenomenology of Perception*, which was a quiet but devastating response to much in the history of philosophy in its treatment of the human body. Then, after his death, his editor and translator delivered *The Visible and the Invisible* from manuscripts, tantalizing in its incompletion but powerful in its jagged restatement and development of his essential message to the world. Something of the highest importance was left for the rest of us to do. In the posthumous lectures translated as *Nature: Course Notes from the Collège de France*, he showed in his last years a constellation of new interests in intellectual history, in 1950s cutting-edge biological science and quantum theory and in utterances as dialogic address to other minds, human or animal. He developed beside his main work a set of aesthetic principles that apply the methods of disclosure to literature and painting. By making the absent present and the invisible visible, the arts have their role in revealing "the world as strange and paradoxical" (Merleau-Ponty, *PP* lxxvii).

Nearly every one of his many works ends with a chapter or paragraph on what it means, and feels like, to be free. Merleau-Ponty would always historicize when writing about the philosophical, literary, and scientific traditions, and in many of his late-career works, he returned to the theory of history from a Marxist position. After World War II, he co-edited a journal of new thinking with Sartre and kept his name off the title page so he could, if necessary, later, disagree with Sartre on the '40s-'50s role of the Communist Party in Russia and France. In the mid-'50s he saw that the Party had become repressive and called out Sartre's hope to minimize the disaster in *Adventures of the Dialectic*, clever and strong in polemic: Sartre admitted his friend was right. A materialist philosophy of the embodied mind turned out to be profoundly historical and political, and it linked the professional studies in philosophy to the active polemical struggles in historical time then and in France.

Chapter 1: The Prodigious Search of Appearance

The search of appearance as a first (and continuous) move to initiate a philosophy

The founding premise of the kind of thinking pursued in this book is, in the magisterial writings of Edmund Husserl, the return to things—and in our focus-figure Maurice Merleau-Ponty, the derived premise is the primacy of perception in our humAnimal[1] harvesting of wild, primordial experience. For phenomenology, the outside-of-us surround exists, and things and persons in the wild in the world are necessary to philosophy as a discipline. Things exist, but things-in-themselves do not. Facing outside from the body, perception in humans and animals operates on the border between ourselves and the world. Facing inside within the body, perception operates on the border between the brain and the senses. The phenomenology is in these two relationships: the *per-ception* is in the *trans-action*, which is the *inter-fusion* and, indeed, as I will be arguing, the *inter-ference*. So our perception sets about doubling the doubled, as is expressed in the word—perception—itself defined in the *Oxford English Dictionary* as consisting of *per*, "through," and *capere*, "to take, seize, lay hold of," "to take *in* or apprehend with the mind *or* senses" (emphasis added). Along with the detailed, beautifully elaborated description that follows it, this constitutive move is the strong achievement and continuing promise of phenomenology. It is also the target of all the reprimands by such as Michel Foucault, who (in two pages) said the school of Husserl could never connect events with meanings, and Jacques Derrida, who (in three whole books) said there never was any perception.[2]

I am most concerned to study visibility and audibility, as senses in interaction with things and persons in the world, but here at the start let us move sideways to consider smell. All our assignments of making-explicit can begin by attending to a sense that (like touch) takes a percept straight to the brain without needing any obvious organ or any distance from a source. This morning a commentator on National Public Radio interviewed a researcher from England who was reconstructing the historical cityscape of smells in early modern Europe—say between Montaigne and Descartes, between Shakespeare and Pope. One rich smell of that era was gone-off cheese and

---

1 HumAnimal: this non-dual, two-in-one term is not original with me; I learned it from Kalpana Rahita Seshadri's book *HumAnimal: Race, Law, Language* (2012) and have used it often in *Animal Perception and Literary Language* (2019) as well as in this study.

2 Michel Foucault, "Theatrum Philosophicum." In counting three books by Jacques Derrida, I am including his introduction to his translation of Husserl's *Origin of Geometry*, his 1950s dissertation titled *The Problem of Genesis in Husserl's Philosophy*, translated by Marian Hobson (2003), and his 1960s book *Voice and Phenomenon: Introduction to the Problem of the Sign in Husserl's Phenomenology*, translated from the French by Leonard Lawlor (2011).

another was the perfume of civet, which required the murdering of cats to get from them excremental sacs. The clever NPR commentator ended the segment: "So the aim is to achieve a historical Dictionary of Smells, Euuugh!" All the issues of my essay are there in his final exclamation, when historical distancing and taste-smell noticing are transformed from interrelation with the world, and from the research of another, into my written version of an oral interjection. The commentator had to evoke the original experience briefly but pungently; then, I had to imagine how to spell a sound. The process that unfolds between perception and cognition produces understanding and communication, in a relation of mutual interfusion, constructive interference, and forward feedback.

Interfusion and interference will be discussed in chapter 3, while "forward feedback" may be better discussed by dissecting my neologism, *perceiving-thinking-writing*. Obviously, perceiving is informed by thinking and writing and by the reading of writing, or we would not understand what we experience, we would be like babies, requiring years of living with fellow humans, requiring tutoring, and having maybe millions of raw experiences. Life beyond infanthood is a continuous cycling of perception and cognition where these faculties recruit each other endlessly, cutting in, doubling back, learning how to respond to new information, how to construct the world as we move into it. To exist and act, we require this skill of attending. This skill is an ordinary creativity in the human animal, so usual that it is hidden and, in fact, if we were to be insistently conscious of doing it, perhaps we could not act in the moment. Phenomenologists are among the first to have noticed, systematically, how our organs of perception have primacy as the indispensable, embodied linking structures on the interfaces between our selves and our surrounds. If, with Husserl and Merleau-Ponty, we wish to imagine what it might be to be presuppositionless, in contact with the wild and primordial experience of things, the feedback might best face forward from perceiving. Make the cut there and look to forward feedback to thinking and writing as the more derived skills. In growing and grown persons, beyond the delightful confusions of the burgeoning senses of babies, of course, thinking and writing help to constitute perceiving, as perceiving equally helps to constitute those faculties.

In this first chapter, I propose to restate, modestly to update with literary interference, the founding premises of phenomenology with respect to the relation between perception and cognition; in chapter 2, I prolong this opening sketch with the help of Merleau-Pontian statements and examples on the relation of the eye to the mind. My topic is the visible, and I shall follow the French philosopher's own late-career interests in painting, especially the work of Cézanne, as an example of how eye relates to mind. I also follow him in considering painting as like writing in those professions' close engagement with the wild, primordial visible—exemplary because closer than philosophy, thus philosophy can learn specific things from the arts of pigment and storytelling. So we will be thinking about the visible, but only as extended, eventually, into audibility through speaking/writing: at last, here, following German-French phenomenology, I will have something to say about legibility through the virtual speech which is writing. (It is part of the larger point in this way of thinking that we always forget that language, through writing and reading, also relies on perception in direct use of the ear and eye and in tracking movement in the time of expectation.)

Merleau-Ponty wrote a powerful essay touching on Cézanne titled "Eye and Mind," very near the time of his 1961 death. The philosopher had already referred to the painter in earlier writings, notably in the essay "Cézanne's Doubt" shortly after *Phenomenology of Perception* was published in 1945. Between 1945-1961, he addressed painting and writing again, together, in meditations after reading André Malraux's *Voices of Silence*, a three-volume work on art history, a sensation of French and world publishing after the first volume was published in 1947. Merleau-Ponty's essential items on Malraux, which in part consist of correction in the context of grateful admiration, are his (at the time unpublished) long and powerful third chapter of *The Prose of the World* and the related (and published) 50 pages of "Indirect Language and the Voices of Silence." These discussions show a consistent continuing concern in late Merleau-Ponty, as he thinks through the position of philosophy in relation to the arts. The essays are evidence of a growth of phenomenology along a line Husserl never took; but without Husserl's bracketing or reduction, this direction could never have been taken.

*

Husserl's first statement of the reduction came in 1905. He knew that the reduction was his best discovery, as a contribution to a new science within his field. He said as much many times, and notably did so in a short and unusually personal book, *Cartesian Meditations*, based on lectures at the Sorbonne—lectures given in 1929 with Maurice Merleau-Ponty in attendance. The reduction employs the cogito of Descartes while also correcting and complexifying it, dropping the theological premises and multiplying perspectives and internal functions by means of new technical terms. *Bracketing*, *suspension*, and the ugly but precise Greek term *epoché* are some of the synonyms, or extensions, of *transcendental reduction* to revise the systematic doubt behind the original cogito. These and related terms help to build the reduction into the founding gesture of phenomenology. It is an origin that then in all practitioners, indeed ideally in all persons, must continue. Once understood as a way to better attend to attention, reduction performed upon the natural attitude must prolong itself from a punctual, decisive, contextualizing act of thought to an attitude or habitus. Since it is premised in perception and ends only when we die, philosophy as phenomenology is unfinalizable after the first time the engine of imagination is turned over. That inherent attribute is why one 1970s commentator rightly called Husserl the philosopher of infinite tasks.[3]

---

[3] See Natanson, *Edmund Husserl: Philosopher of Infinite Tasks* (1973).

Merleau-Ponty out-thinks Husserl on the arts as recognizers of reduction before and better than philosophy. His late-career commentaries on painting and writing argue for their similarities as modes of investigation into perceptual content, and, thus, for their relevance to philosophy. Also, figures like Cézanne and Valéry, the painter and the poet who are often his examples, can think and be quoted like philosophers, from their side of the disciplinary interference. Finally, too, we need language to appreciate and communicate what a painting is doing, and on their side philosophers are inevitably also writers; and the skills of narrative, rhythm, sentencing, and imagery are (or can be) part of what a philosopher shows. Philosophers, too, like writers, indeed as writers, have auditors at the Sorbonne, and they have single readers tracking their paragraphs under lamps.

Wallace Stevens, who died in 1955, a scant six years before Merleau-Ponty died, seems never to have read or mentioned the philosopher, but Stevens did correspond with Jean Wahl, who described for him the experience of reading Husserl's *Cartesian Meditations*. In my informal scan of all of Stevens's poems written after the early 1930s, I find over a hundred lines or passages where Stevens addresses exactly the concerns of contemporary phenomenology, often with the same technical terms found in the philosophers when they are theorizing appearance and the infinite and treacherous relation of language to meaning. Stevens generated poems from notebooks, in a grouping of adagia, from the 1930s to the 1950s, with pertinences like these: "Things seen are things as seen. . . . To live in the world but outside of existing conceptions of it."

Writing about philosophers rather than about poets, Merleau-Ponty could have made the same statements. On the topics of objects, things, conceptions, perceptions, interrelations, and interactions, the French thinker converges on this American contemporary, taking the same path with the same terms.

Stevens, like Merleau-Ponty but from the literary side, several times took up the relation of modern painting to modern writing. Near the end of "The Relations between Poetry and Painting," which Stevens read at the Museum of Modern Art, NYC in 1951, he referred to French figures like Claude and Poussin and Racine, Simone Weil, Mallarmé and Rimbaud, Cézanne and Valéry. He said that in France after two wars and a German occupation "the theory of poetry is not abstract as it so often is with us . . . , but is a normal activity of the poet's mind in surroundings where he must engage in such activity or be extirpated" (750). He went on phenomenologically to launch a metaphor of "a search in reality or through reality or even a search for some supremely acceptable fiction" (750). Standing in a MOMA gallery reading his talk, in mid-paragraph he arrived at the passage that is the incitement to the chapter you are now reading. He is linking the theory of modern poetry to pictures in a museum of modern art, which "often seem to become in time a mystical aesthetic, a prodigious search of appearance, as if to find a way of saying and of establishing that all things, whether below or above appearance, are one and that it is only through reality, in which they are reflected . . . that we can reach them. Under such stress, reality changes from substance to subtlety . . . " (750).[4] The topic is one Merleau-Ponty takes up on occasion: in the historical shift in aesthetic theory and practice, from classical representation in figures like Poussin and Racine to the ability of painting/writing after Cézanne to "create a new reality, a modern reality" (750). Creativity, as such, is at issue as well as what happened to it in modernity. After the long passage just quoted, Stevens refers to Simone Weil's chapter on decreation in *La Pesanteur et La Grâce*, a book which in my paperback first edition dates 1947: "She says that decreation is making pass from the created to the uncreated, but that destruction is making pass from the created to nothingness. Modern reality is a reality of decreation" (750). I interpret this whole set of interrelated terms, including *prodigious*, *search*, *appearance*, *stress*, *subtlety*, *create*, and *decreation* to be contributions, from the literary side, to a theory of poetry as a theory of phenomenological reduction. This is a constructive interference of disciplines because these synonyms of the epoché expand and clarify its possible meanings.

The action of phenomenology is *prodigious* because it occurs when perception interprets movement, namely, whenever humans and animals are conscious, that is, when awake, which is almost always. This action is a *search of appearance* because informed perception is always seeking to interpret the wild, primordial, spontaneous experience that comes into its ken with movement in the surround. This action puts the natural attitude under *stress* because the immediacy of the visible-audible-tangible is forever making us forget what is hollowed out behind them in the invisible etcetera, so it takes immense effort to maintain the search. The result of this is *subtlety*, a transformation of the readymade substance we encounter in the world, a next-level or many-level nuanced interpretation that makes the world once again exciting. That interpretation is an instance of the ordinary *creativity* of everyday experience if we train ourselves to see the real, as a set of patterns that produces what, in the time of expectation, we see-hear-touch. Rather than destruction-to-nothingness of things in the world as we experience them through such a search, this action is a *decreation*, in the sense intended by Simone Weil and Wallace Stevens, that previous philosophy and religion are stripped away and we are left alone with our senses in a roof-rent reality no longer entirely readymade. (After that comes the assignment of re-engaging the rational, again and again making sense of sensing, and understanding what has happened.) The search of appearance, the best of these synonyms, is our way of living in the world but outside of existing conceptions of it.

So far the plan has been to frame Wallace Stevens by the discourse of phenomenology, but now let us narrowly pursue the phenomenology of the visible under the aegis of Stevens's metaphor in *search of appearance*. The same metaphor

---

[4] "The Relations between Poetry and Painting" is the last essay in Wallace Stevens's book *The Necessary Angel: Essays on Reality and the Imagination*, reprinted in *Stevens: Collected Poetry and Prose* (New York: The Library of America, 1997).

occurs in Merleau-Ponty for the same purpose, but not often. What follows is not a literary correction of philosophy, but rather a clarifying re-emphasis that puts *appearance* where it belongs—in the operating description of a relational process that is open-ended and self-correcting.

*

The advantage of bringing forth the metaphor of search, as an additional synonym, is that *appearance* is made explicit in the conceptual toolbox and that the work done is directly stated as being investigative, descriptive, and a process open and endless. In the phenomenological as addressed to the natural attitude, appearance is appreciated and conserved, and also undergoes, continuously, the conversion of intellectual attention Husserl called the reduction. As one commentator has it, the reduction of appearance is the assimilation of spirit by things, and it is also paradoxically the uncovering of spirit in things (see Husserl, *Husserl ou le retour de les choses*).

One must rely on Husserl's own accounts of the reduction/epoché and on Merleau-Ponty's brilliant summaries and critiques, as well as on several specialists whose books are within reach—for instance, Dermot Moran, Lawrence Lawlor, Mauro Carbone, Maurice Natanson, and Paul Ricoeur. Difficulties exist because of terminology often in Greek or German, and because Husserl changed his mind on definitions and perhaps, if Merleau-Ponty is right, misunderstood his own earlier accounts. More challenging to commentary than obscurity, contention, and inconsistency is the paradox, admitted by Husserl and flagged by Merleau-Ponty, that the reduction occurs when a thinking person understands it is needed—but then it is to be performed ceaselessly forever. Contradictoriness in a major thinker is always fascinating, and since it requires reasons for being, it is also productive. With this hint of trouble constantly in mind, my own exposition has to strive to be reader-friendly.

The single best exposé of the whole topic is Merleau-Ponty's brilliant Preface to *Phenomenology of Perception*, and I cannot imagine rivaling or replacing that, but I will take from it a methodological hint. He says that Heidegger's *Being and Time* is a "making explicit" or "developing" of Heidegger's central meanings, and Merleau-Ponty's translator in a note on this says that *l'explicitation* is rigorously opposed to any method of *explicating* or *explaining*. Those two latter types of work are examples of "objective thought" for Merleau-Ponty, of lesser interest for him, and what I develop will be something other than straight neutral summary. What is next will be a synthesis historical-philological-biographical-writerly, boldly biased, and not without digressions but moving to show why and how the search, that is, phenomenology, proceeds.

In framing phenomenology by literary thinking, by remembering the heritage of the phrase from Stevens, we emphasize the basic action, and we avoid misleading associations. As a new leading term in phenomenology's toolbox, our phrase *search of appearance* performs a reduction upon Husserl's term *reduction*. (But still, in accordance with the basic assumptions about appearances of things in the world, we will keep the X-ed out but legible term.) Thus, searching our search, we follow the German thinker's efforts to defamiliarize the natural attitude.

First, though, let us suspend that suspension and point once again at the literary frame, by showing (by using examples of writing) *what the reduction or epoché feels like* when performed. Neither Paul Valéry nor Peter Coyote have read Husserl on the reduction, and they lived in different places and eras. French formal poet (1871-1945) and American actor and Zen priest (1941-), they come at experience with entirely different formations, but their notebooks have comparable passages. Coyote first, because his memoir re-enacts an original *epoché* encounter; then Valéry, because his 1927 notebook entry records and studies one in a series of encounters:

> The boundaries between "in here" and "out there" disappeared. The world remained recognizable, as it had always been, but completely stripped of descriptive language and concepts. Everything appeared to be a phantom of itself, luminous but without weight or substance. "I" had been replaced. The closest I can come to describing what I felt was as part of an awareness with no physical location, inseparable from the entire universe.[5]
>
> *
>
> Dawn
>
>   Birth of the most delicate pink—I see it first on a house—For a while now the birds have been speaking all at once—the roosters begin.
>   The pink is like a breath—the moon grown transparent, a wash of green—
>   Nothing moves except the Earth—that is, except the light which little by little "takes form."
>   The *depth* that appearance makes us feel, and which is itself only appearance.
>   I feel so strongly at this hour . . . the *depth of appearance* (I can't quite express it) and *that* is poetry. What speechless wonder that everything is, and that I am! At this moment, what we see takes on the symbolic value of the sum of all things. An ordinary landscape is a δU—*It conceals what it implies, demands.* (Valéry, *Idea of Perfection* 310).

Both writers explicitly use forms of the word *appearance*, and both of them abandon the outworn opposition between appearance and reality. It is a non-dualism of subject and object, too, so the barrier has vanished between a self that registers through perception and things of the world that are, as Coyote says, *out there*. Coyote's luminous phantom is Valéry's dawn-light, a stepping-down into *depth*, that term of value shared by Merleau-Ponty. Valéry is much more aware of time, with his

---

[5] Peter Coyote's memoir *The Rainman's Third Cure* is quoted in *Lion's Roar*, a journal of Buddhism, January 2021 (Halifax, Nova Scotia, Canada) 46. One reason for including a passage from a Zen Buddhist source is to suggest that another philosophical tradition has independently arrived at systems of doubt with regard to appearance. In a book on the Great Vehicle tenet systems, Guy Newland summarizes where the Mind Only and Middle Way Consequence systems agree: "All of the afflictions that hold us in cyclic existence are built on the assent to the mistaken appearance of things as distant and cut off from their apprehenders. The non-existence of a difference of entity between subject and object is an ultimate truth, an emptiness; it is the subtlest and most profound emptiness that is realized on the path" (45).

references to dawn and daylight: this notebook entry resonates with many others in his notebooks that register new beginnings by details of pre-dawns, dawns, first-light, early mornings. Valéry's *speechless* is Coyote's admission of a lack of resources to describe an awareness. Both writers feel the need to attempt description through inadequate language, even though their non-dual awareness escapes the net of symbolic structures. Valéry also, starting a math metaphor with *sum of all things*, employs the symbol δU for an infinitesimal part of the universe. Referring to *universe*, their passages end on the speaker being consciously and gratefully folded into a larger scheme. If Valéry, more eloquent, has understood what he has undergone, the landscape surround conceals what it demands, a reduction is an expansion, and the search of appearance is a quest for the invisible behind the visible.

There is on this showing always the possibility that the search of appearance will end in a blousy rhetoric of union with the universe. While my literary writers do show that a reduction may lead toward ecstatic affect, they will not topple into over-large claims. Husserl and his heirs in philosophy are careful never to head toward mystical oneness. Neither the certainty of interiority nor the pure immanence of objects are ever concerns for philosophers who are searching for original evidence in perception.

It is customary to speak of three periods in Husserl's research. In the first phase, up to about 1901 and his early 40s, he is thinking about mathematics and logic, hoping to show the development of field-disciplines as intellectual progress occurs through refinement in language and across historical eras. He is interested in the question of intentionality as it has been launched, earlier and in Germany, as an issue in Brentano. He writes in a critical mode on the problems of contemporary psychology and on mistaken theories of empiricism and historicism. In the second phase, he has recognized the profound discoveries in the Cartesian cogito and found that the skepticism of Descartes can be explored to the bottom and corrected in the form of the intentional reduction: the method of finding in perception a relation between consciousness and its world. Deliberate performance of the reduction, according to structural principles and a gathering of powerful ideas about how the mind and emotions work, becomes for Husserl the basis of a new philosophy—also of a way of living our lives. The rigor and promise of the method become his main preoccupation in the second phase, in the three volumes of *Ideas Pertaining to a Pure Phenomenology*, in a book on time-consciousness, and in *Cartesian Meditations*. Increasingly in the second phase he has come to understand the role of others and of the faculty of empathy in our experience of the world, and inter-subjectivity becomes a central topic in late Merleau-Ponty as it is in late Husserl. In the third phase, in the 1930s, Husserl has registered the threat to Europe of German political changes and has become wary of his student Martin Heidegger. At this time he gives an urgent and remarkably clear overview of his achieved thought in a book published long after his 1938 death, *The Crisis in European Sciences and Transcendental Phenomenology: An Introduction to Phenomenological Philosophy* (1954). In the *Crisis* volume, Husserl opens out an entirely new, third-phase topic: the life-world, or the use of subjective-relative experiences for the objective sciences.

Thus, the second and third periods are explorations of phenomenology in his line, after he has originated and named it. There is also a coda that might be called Husserliana: after the German thinker's death, his notebooks and letters and drafts went to a library in Louvain, where Maurice Merleau-Ponty was a frequent visitor both before and after WWII.

In Husserl's titles he called several of his books "investigations" or "introductions." This labeling choice is typical of a thinker who said *philosopher* was too elevated a term for what he did and who invented a beginner's-mind discourse that is always starting anew with acts of perception. Daniel Christoff notes: "Convinced that consciousness is neither a simplification of what's diverse, nor a generalization from experience, nor yet a construction, [Husserl] did not seek a system in philosophy, but a life" (5).[6] To balance out such praise, it also needs to be admitted that Husserl's late-career preference for the term "transcendental" (as in that title to the *Crisis* book) allowed for ambiguities. The term smacks of theology and was never an aid to readers: does it mean outside-self, or beyond-sense-perception, or does this term confuse those two meanings? Both Heidegger and Merleau-Ponty held reservations about possible idealism in this term, but only the latter man most often avoided it.

Appearance. For Husserl, the first concept of consciousness is appearance. Usually this term means the whole glorious multi-layered show of things outside of us and available to the animal senses. We take it in all day every day and we need to do so. That we need appearance for life is assumed to be of value, as a necessity, and as, so we say, normal. Appearance, as in *apparition* or *it appears*, can mean a seeming or a cover event for something that we call real. This second meaning is also possible for Husserl.

The Natural Attitude. To invent a way of doing philosophy that stays as close as possible to the adventures of experience, Husserl understood that we would need to account for the subject of knowing and the object of the content known—to account for the two sides of meaning and knowing. Phenomenology would need to become the science of the essential correlation between subject and object. In his revision of the cogito as his foundational move, the first concept of consciousness needed to be appearance (*Erscheinung*), in the spatio-temporal forms of things of the world that would be set aside. The new way of thinking would take this founding question: How can we determine the relations between the visible and the invisible? To answer that, and to avoid the mistake of positing an inside reality of an outside appearance, Husserl (after 1906) would rename appearance as *die natürliche Einstellung*, the natural attitude. It was natural both in the meaning that it was a full-time habit, human and usual and in no way pejorative or delusional, and in the meaning that,

---

6 My translation.

in the unity of body and consciousness, perceptual experience has a lining and a depth that we achieve only by methods anti-natural. We would do this by getting beyond, or through or behind, the ordinary visible. The phenomenological attitude has to become an anti-natural attitude by suspending not only everyday ordinary experience, but all of contemporary science, all of propositional knowledge. Also, for Husserl this approach means excluding causal, psychological associations, and all position-taking.

Paradoxically, this suspension is not a sublation, not a negation, since the natural attitude of appearances and causalities and propositions and empirical sciences is appreciated and kept alongside the new practices. Paradoxically, conscious intentional knowing searches for the attributes of pre-reflective knowing; and once we have identified naïve perception, we are already beyond it.

There are for Husserl several kinds of attitudes, and we can change from one to another, say, from natural to phenomenological, by taking thought. The natural attitude is self-concealing, so after the reduction the attitude is a theoretical one, that is, self-aware. As I will argue in my final chapter, this self-awareness is precisely the turnover moment when creativity, and co-creativity, enter into this philosophy's story of consciousness.

The Reduction. Husserl took this awkward term for his version of the Cartesian systematic doubt concerning objects in the world. *Reduction* is apt when we think of obliterating what I have above called the whole glorious multi-layered show of things and sciences, but misleading if we believe we are losing all or most of that. For reasons already given, *the search of appearance* is a better term for this essential foundational move, but in this making-explicit of Husserl let us stick with his invention, which after all is his way to distinguish his proposal for a science from Descartes's cogito and its errors. Other, more helpful synonyms in the discourse are *bracketing* and *suspension*, as applied to natural objects and natural sciences. The main issues to make explicit, from the many pages on the reduction by Husserl and Merleau-Ponty and their commentators, are notably that the reduction, as a purging of presuppositions, does not alter experience for us in any way. It is most important to recognize, from this move, that our entire accomplishment in cognition is grounded in our perceptions as they are tracking movement in the glorious show of the outside-of-us surround. This feat is what we do as rational animals, to live and feel and think, using our embodied minds and our embodied perceptions. Through the bracketing of natural objects we can also more powerfully understand our pre-reflective awareness, so this action expresses our freedom and creativity. When we do this bracketing, we release ourselves from a limitation, a concealment, so the intentional act of reduction leads to a splitting of the ego—Merleau-Ponty calls this variously dehiscence, chiasm, interrogation, disclosure.

For Husserl reduction moves through three successive stages. The *Eidetic Reduction* leads the inquirer to attend to the general features of an experience. (*Eidos* is Greek for *form, idea*: it applies to essential features of acts of consciousness, so phenomenology is the science of essences.) The *Transcendental Reduction*, the next step, leads the inquirer to attend to the *structure of acts* that directs them at objects, rather than the objects themselves. The *Phenomenological Reduction* proper comes as the culmination of the two preparatory steps, eidetic and transcendental together.

The Epoché. This term is a frequent synonym that varies and expands the reach of the phenomenological reduction. Epoché is a cover-word that, for Husserl, means exactly the same thing: bracketing of natural attitudes and objects, done because whatever is natural is not intentional. In most translations and commentaries, the second "e" has a French accent acute to signal a different pronunciation from the first "e" in the word, but the term is from Greek. It is a made-up noun: the substantival version of a common classical verb, *epecho*, whose basic sense relies on the preposition *epi-*, then quickly goes ballistic from "hold out to, offer" to "aim at" to "stand facing" to "hold back" to "adjourn" to "cease" to "suspend judgment." Definitions of the noun start with "check, cessation," move to "suspension of judgment," and end with "stoppage of light" (in astronomy) and "period of vibration" (in music). Most of these offshoots are in the background, so that the main meaning has to be "Cartesian suspension of belief." As an opaque and ugly technical term from a German author, it signals a claim for a signature Husserl meaning that improves upon cogito.[7]

Merleau-Ponty's great Preface of 1945

Merleau-Ponty's Preface to *Phenomenology of Perception* goes to the center of what is essential in Husserl's contribution, which is based in part on knowledge of what the French follower found in the archive of unpublished works. This eloquent disciple is nowhere more quotable than where he says: "The most important lesson of the reduction is the impossibility of a complete reduction" (lxxvii). So Husserl as philosopher is a perpetual beginner; phenomenology is "an ever-renewed experiment of its own beginning" (lxxviii); and its work, modest in rational claims yet infinite in scope, involves "describing, and not explaining or analyzing" (lxxi). (A making-explicit analogue: a marriage is both a few sentences uttered at an instant and an extended afterlife. There is a long lead of preparation, a pledging of troth at a single moment of solemn union under the eyes of others—then, a procession of ever-new days wherein the relation is re-enacted, as perception meets contingency and learns about itself. And the human name of this relation is love.)

Husserl's huge output in writing is centered on the reduction but extends outward from it in many directions that exhibit how consciousness may be described. In him

---

[7] In this philosophical style, German gets cultural capital from Greek; French gets it from German and Latin; English gets it from French. My thanks once again to Kenneth Martin for information and phrasing on Greek origins.

phenomenology is a description of forms and structures, processes and pulsions. His researches have sections or whole books on logic, arithmetic, the history of disciplines, the relation of perception to rational thought, the relation of perception to writing, memory, inter-subjectivity and empathy, emotion, perceptual illusions, the internal time sense and temporality generally, the proposition as a form of thought, the history of philosophy as it relates to mental and mind-world interactions, and other reflections on the predicative and pre-predicative life of consciousness. His reading moves out to developments in several contemporary sciences, including quantum physics.

Among these topics in consciousness, Gestalt psychology has a certain priority for both Husserl and Merleau-Ponty, particularly in the structure of a reversible relation between figure and ground, and in Gestalt discoveries about how the mind makes beginnings and closures. Gestalt theory's discoveries about the time of expectation and of resolution, for a sequence of thinking, influences both thinkers as they face the need to discuss temporality. Both thinkers, Merleau-Ponty learning much from his German mentor, are entirely aware of the difficulties of using rational thought to disclose what it might be to be presuppositionless and of using the sentences of language to reveal how writing relies on perceiving and thinking. Since phenomenology is description, both thinkers also write to resist traditional theories of representation, which, like ideas of perspective in painting, are trapped in the old way of accepting the natural attitude toward appearance.

*

Another passage in Merleau-Ponty's great Preface of 1945, notable and quotable as he praises Husserl at the gateway of his masterwork, is this:

> Reflection does not withdraw from the world toward the unity of consciousness as the foundation of the world; rather, it steps back in order to see transcendences spring forth and it loosens the intentional threads that connect us to the world in order to make them appear; it alone is conscious of the world because it reveals the world as strange and paradoxical. (lxxvii)

I am reckoning this statement as the culmination of the French thinker's early-to-middle career homage to his German master. Accordingly, appearances as revelations are to be valued; transcendences as beyond-the-observer's-body are to be valued; eloignment and making-strange are primary reasons for doing philosophy—as we may learn from our study of the more direct arts of pigment and word. The literary equivalent is Ezra Pound's "Make It New."

There are five other statements from 1952-1961 that I take as late reassessments by Merleau-Ponty of Husserl's legacy. 1) There are the ten pages on Husserl and the related pages on the human body in *Nature*, the course notes from the Collège de France from 1956-60, where he finds that Husserl oscillates between overcoming and conserving the natural, naïve attitude. 2) There are two incisive essays in the collection *In Praise of Philosophy and Other Essays* [Lectures at Collège de France

1952-1960], the first of which is "Philosophy as Interrogation," where he argues that Husserl's "pure interrogation" is "not a residue of metaphysics" but "a means of opening us to the world, to time, to nature" (173). 3) The other lecture in this collection is "Husserl at the Limits of Phenomenology," where one theme is the German philosopher's 1930s idea about the life-world and the earth: "The type of being which our experience of the earth and the body reveals to us is no curiosity of external perception but has a philosophical signification" (190). 4) By the same title as the essay noted in 3) above, in the book *Husserl at the Limits of Philosophy*, we have 70 pages of course-notes on Husserl's late essay, "The Origin of Geometry," along with brilliant summaries and analyses and detailed notes on sources by the editor, Leonard Lawlor. These intellectual fireworks are too rich and too jagged to present in a single sentence, but a number of topics are noteworthy: commentary on Heidegger; passivity and activity; the idea of constitution; the idea of horizon; the recurring topic-term *Ineinander* (one in another); admirable excurses on language, speaking, writing. 5) There are 35 ubiquitous, well-spaced references to Husserl in *The Visible and the Invisible*, the torso of a book Merleau-Ponty was working on at the time of his sudden death in 1961. Some of these pocket-analyses come in the first part of the posthumously published book, where he has four chapter drafts and an appendix on the concepts of interrogation and of "The Intertwining—The Chiasm," but most occur in the wonderful and suggestive "Working Notes," which take up the last 100 pages. Here he excavates themes and terms learnt from Husserl, finding ways to push toward his own original version of the primacy of perception, but there is no analysis that takes more than a page or two. In retrospect, this closing ends the lance of thought begun in the Preface to the *Phenomenology* because Husserl is still always present-to-mind during new forays and explorations.

The tables of contents in books by Husserl, Merleau-Ponty, and their commentators will show type and range of descriptions of consciousness with which phenomenology may concern itself. Perceiving-thinking-writing in the embodied mind is everything in this project, so language is always both medium and topic of study. The interfering inquirer from outside the discipline and the language, in both of these original thinkers, can identify the larger differences between them. Fortunate Merleau-Ponty had before him both Descartes and Husserl as investigators who built the structures he could complete and then fill with life and style. In Merleau-Ponty, the progression-plus-feedback in the triad perceiving-thinking-writing is (in the phrase he used for Heidegger's monumental work of apprenticeship) made-explicit. So, too, is the plan of a way of thinking that is inter-subjective, communal, and social, especially in the French thinker's later writings. Whatever is dialectical-historical, Marxist, and engaged-political is also more directly and consistently faced in Merleau-Ponty and connected back to the professional work on consciousness through the theme of freedom—though this focus of his attention is often not remarked upon by commentators who are centered in the phenomenology of perception. Merleau-Ponty has more self-reference, more examples of perception drawn from everyday life, more direct commentary on pictorial and verbal art, more harvesting of contemporary discoveries in the sciences (especially quantum physics), and also more appreciation of fellow workers in philosophy (in his case, notably Henri Bergson and J. P. Sartre) who do not share his particular set of problems.

Merleau-Ponty is also the better stylist. Except when Husserl is lecturing to a live audience, Beginner's Mind has him often reluctant to condense an exposition or finish the argument. The Kant-conscious German tradition he is writing in requires a highly pitched level of generality, a four-square heavy march of paragraphs, speculative restraint, and solemnity of tone. As writer, Merleau-Ponty opens and closes chapters with gestures strong and graceful; he uses striking images that illustrate an argument and help to make it with perceptual content; he uses compressed technical-philosophical phrasing that reinvigorates terms whether inherited or invented; he is always politely counter-arguing and imagining objections; he varies periodic, hierarchical sentences with short direct sentences. The late lecture notes on Husserl's Geometry book and the "Working Notes" at the end of *The Visible and the Invisible* take us back to his workroom, with evidences that the elegant and armored published works come out of an energy of thought that is daring, prolific, questing for original ideas and turns of phrase. As in his statement "our relation to the true passes through others" (*IPP* 30), he is able to say original things in simple language to make them memorable.

Looking ahead: if I am right in chapter 3, Merleau-Ponty achieved a refinement upon Husserl's thought that is the perfection of it, as original in its way as the founding edifice. Merleau-Ponty never named or proclaimed this discovery of the principle of a cognitive-aesthetic interference, but he made it explicit in nearly every one of his works, published and unpublished, from the late 1940s to the end of his life.

Chapter 2: Eye and Mind in Painting and Writing

The optometrist, a wag, has just sent a reminder postcard for the annual checkup and, on the front, he has printed his teaser: it includes eighteen color-words, but yellow is printed in blue, green in black, and so on. "Look at the chart and say the color not the word." Yes, it is difficult. For each color-printed word, you need to insist each time in a separate decision to get through the ridiculous test without stalling; the optometrist's explanation: left-right conflict. "The reason is because your right brain tries to say the color but your left brain insists on reading the word" ("The Everything Is Off-Topic Thread"). Brain interferes with itself; eye interferes with mind; saying interferes with reading. This minor message is the summary-neurological for the present chapter in its thesis-theoretical.

*

Paul Cézanne, a painter who grew up in Aix-en-Provence near his life-long frenemy, writer Émile Zola—what Gods of French Culture ordained that? Cézanne, who said, "grey alone reigns in nature" (qtd. in Verdi 53).[1] Who said the painter should "render the image of what we see, forgetting everything that existed before us " (15). Who said of the Gulf of Marseille, "the sun here is so tremendous that it seems to me as if the objects were silhouetted not only in black and white but in blue, red, brown and violet. . . . this seems to me to be the opposite of modeling." Who said, "I am the primitive of the way that I have found" (74-75). Who said, and Merleau-Ponty more than once quoted, "C'est effrayante, la vie," *life is terrifying* (196). Who signed 13 of his paintings and left 550 canvases unsigned out of self-doubt. Add that Cézanne is for Merleau-Ponty the painter most valuable for philosophy, because with the painter of Mt. St. Victoire and of *Still Life with Compotier*, his "difficulties are those of the first word" (15)—meaning, I would guess, that to get to an Adamic instance of speaking/writing through perceiving/thinking is the most Godlike/gargantuan of creative actions and also the most ordinary thing in the world.[2]

Paul Valéry, writer, who said, since everybody perceives and since everybody, even the "coarsest and least lyrical souls," can be happy, "[t]o *perceive* does not imply *to make perceptible*—still less: *beautifully perceptible*" ("Problems of Poetry," *The Art of Poetry* 86). Who is several times in several essays quoted by Merleau-Ponty as speaking about the animal of words. Add that, for Merleau-Ponty, Valéry is the poet and aesthetic theorist, Marcel Proust the novelist, most valuable for philosophy.

I have not tallied up the significantly large number of pages Merleau-Ponty devoted to these three representatives of the arts. However, it is clear that a good deal of his later career, as a professional writer on perception, was taken up with the

---

1 See Richard Verdi's heavily illustrated survey of the whole career, *Cézanne* (1992).
2 *Ordinary creativity*, that contradiction, that aporia, that paradox, that catachresis, that oxymoron, is also the result of left brain trying and right brain resisting. On this topic see my last chapter.

problems assigned by modern painting and writing.³ For him, unusually for those in his field, the deceptions and the gifts of the visible were especially productive.⁴

Add that for him, in the late 1940s and the 1950s, the psychological and perceptual assignments of childhood were always productive for thinking. Childhood is where everything starts but also where some illusions and skills of the visible have barely begun.

*

1952 is the year of an unfinished book devoted to a new idea of literary language. Claude Lefort, editor of Merleau-Ponty's posthumous volume *The Prose of the World*, says there is evidence the book was abandoned but was intended to be part of a larger three-book project to be called, overall, The Theory of Truth.⁵ The larger scheme would have been completed had the philosopher lived. Lefort quotes Merleau-Ponty's statement about the *Prose* draft, that it deals with "literary language," and Lefort explains that what was intended was a new idea of *expression* (that technical term in phenomenology) in literary language. Lefort quotes Merleau-Ponty on a unique writerly autonomy: "The writer's thought does not control his language from without; the writer himself is a kind of new idiom, constructing itself, inventing ways of expression. . . . All great prose is also a re-creation of the signifying instrument, henceforth manipulated according to a new syntax" (qtd. in Merleau-Ponty, *PW* xiii). The sixth and last chapter of this half-written book takes the new idea in the direction of another art, and this detour into the topic of "Expression and the Child's Drawing" may help explain why the author hit an impasse with the book. (There is a focus on the productive idea of *expression* that he was exploring here and elsewhere in the early 1950s, but from this a large panorama was beginning to open out. Possibly this made it hard to imagine just what line to take going forward.) In any event, abruptly the philosopher's final sentence in the whole Prose draft, at the end of the chapter on drawing, is, "But these remarks apply to language" (*PW* 152). I am speculating that for him in 1952 painting and writing are becoming identified as similar in their relation to the medium and also entangled as modes of expression. In both painting and writing emerges "*a re-creation of the signifying instrument*" (xiii; emphasis added).

My intention in chapter 2 is to ask: What can philosophy and writing—philosophy *as* writing—learn from painting and, especially, from Cézanne's doubt concerning the sensible? The answer will be that they can learn how to overthrow the relation that has always been made by thought between the eye and the mind. They can learn, further,

---

3 It would not over-simplify to say that there is enough of quality and of quantity of writing after 1945 to make for three careers: on phenomenology of perception; on history, class, and party from a Marxist perspective; and on painting and writing as exemplary address to the surround. That's to leave out *The Phenomenology of Perception*, which prepared for all three of those lines of development.

4 Add that it is reported when Merleau-Ponty died of a heart attack, he had open on his desk in front of him Descartes's book *Dioptics*—to the end inquiring into the relation of eye and mind.

5 See Merleau-Ponty, *PW* xi, xiii.

how to understand more radically the relation of the sensible to language. Husserl and Merleau-Ponty are developing a phenomenology of language that assimilates it toward perception as wild and primordial, even as they acknowledge language as arbitrary sign and impersonal and systematic and historical semiosis.

The primacy of perception

The brief chapter on the child's drawing is a statement that contains—and makes explicit—many of the elements of this thinker's position on perception and expression. In late Merleau-Ponty, the primacy of perception is now often explained through a search of appearance that de-coordinates eye and mind in painting and poetry. That is how, more directly than philosophy, the arts are expressing the intimacy of feedback called perceiving-thinking-writing. The argument here concerns the concept of objectivity, because this unequivocal kind of report is one guise of the natural attitude. Objectivity is crying out for the reduction! In our address to drawing and painting, we usually live happily in the objectivist illusion that we have learned to accept: that things are as they are represented. "The two-dimensional perspective is clearly the only solution of the problem posed in these terms, and so the development of children's drawing is described as a progression toward perspective" (*PW* 148). But "two-dimensional perspective is not a form of realism. It is a construction" (*PW* 148). By this standard of a deformation that "shows [things] as God sees them" we discount children's expression (*PW* 148).

It is characteristic of Merleau-Ponty that he describes our rescue of the child's drawing as a "liberation from the constraints of perspective," which is gotten through a search of appearance conceived as freedom. The aim of the true, mature, professional painter, as in his mention of Claude Lorrain and Cézanne, will be to repossess the child's naïve vision on the other side of the usual objectivist illusion: "The aim is to leave on the paper a trace of our contact with this object and this spectacle, insofar as they made our gaze and virtually our touch, our ears, our feeling of risk or of destiny or of freedom vibrate" (*PW* 150). *Made our feeling of freedom vibrate*: phenomenology's technical term for this particular effect is *expression*, and the opposed term, *representation*, is open to historical unmasking and rhetorical scorn.[6]

---

[6] The sober synthesis by Lawrence Hass in *Merleau-Ponty's Philosophy* (2008) is at its most original in defining *expression* as something commentators have overlooked, whereas in fact expression takes us to the full extent of this philosophical method and, in defining it, we understand "his revitalized vision for philosophy itself"—as against, for example, Heidegger's "end of philosophy" or Wittgenstein's ladder to be thrown away. Hass quotes the philosopher as saying, "Expressing what *exists* is an endless task," and Hass adds this useful clarification: "But not a futile one. It is the ongoing work of renewing our connections to the world, of embracing our very being as flesh and nature, of remaining alive to our being with each other. At the same time, it is also about celebrating the creative, transformative powers of thought, language, and philosophy itself" (9).

(We shall see the carefully chosen verb "vibrate" again in references to sympathies of feeling and mention–foreshadowing the next chapter–that one non-obvious meaning comes from wave-particle indeterminacy in quantum physics).

The essay on the child's drawing, which ends the draft of *Prose of the World*, arranges three stages of consciousness, let us call them *expression 1* (child), *representation*, and *expression 2* (adult). In this implicit scheme, *representation* stands for the natural attitude of adults in the world and also for classical painting. *Expression* stands for the child's drawing—place that in theoretical sequence before representation. But *expression* also stands for the modern painter's search of appearance that is the epoché of the spectacle. Expression is thus the anti-natural, intentional-phenomenological attitude on either side of the natural attitude, and defining it may help to solve the puzzle started in Wallace Stevens's quotation where Stevens spoke of finding "a way of establishing that all things, *whether below or above appearance*, are one" (750; emphasis added). The trend of Merleau-Ponty's essay on the child, not as actualized by the philosopher but made explicit by us, is to affirm that zero-level expression in the child's drawing is what epoché-level expression in Cézanne must aspire to, by continuously keeping and negating representation.

A little girl known to the author made a drawing of an insect when she was three or four. On a thin unlined white page torn out at about 4x6 inches, she first wrote the words "I hate Bed time" in black magic marker, and below that she drew a chunky body that is plated by magic-marker triangles in red, yellow, blue, brown, gray, with a triangle head in green. The head has one large black eye, one small nose-hole, a straight quarter-inch line for a mouth, black bumps on the head to show hair and, from the back of the head, two one-inch antennae in red stretching up to cross the word "hate" in the legend above. There are also four comma-shaped feet in a line across the bottom, in black, tacked on so the insect seems to be standing-toppling on four musical notes. Plainly this girl knew letters, colors, and shapes, and the main features of an insect's body. She knew the pronoun for herself and the structure of a sentence, but she did not know capitalization, punctuation, or perspective.

Sixteen years later when she was in college, this girl stood at one end of a small kitchen to draw (on thick grainy watercolor paper) the other end of the room, back to the drapes covering the window and the far corner, with the left wall receding to the corner. The colored drawing has vertical+-lined yellow-white wallpaper, a fat upholstered chair with two front legs prominent and the back two curved down into cross-hatched darkness; the main statement here, centered on the 12x14-inch sheet, is the table with brown-mottled tablecloth and, on the cloth, a gray metal toaster and partly in front of that a brown betty porcelain teapot. There is a box-shaped wood-strip lamp hanging above with the draw-chain visible. We see the front two sides of the lamp; we see the bold, splayed wood legs of the table; we see linoleum at the bottom that's divided into squared off lines, with the vertical away-from-viewer lines narrowing at the back wall and broadening as they approach the viewer. Like her insect drawing, this work also has words inscribed: at the bottom, the nineteen-year-old has, in correct small cursive, posted her name, the name of the town, the street, and the date.

The point of our own try at descriptions, written in and about the prose of the world, is that between these two drawings the girl has learned perspective. She has also learned how to show the bulges of the chair by line and color, how to suggest texture by a mottling of colors, and how to claim depth of space and roundness on the toaster and teapot by the strategic placement of white that shows where light is hitting a surface, thus defining what is closest to the viewer. She has mastered the array of intuitive categories that represent the real in Western painting. Also, of course, she has become skilled as an inscriber of the system of natural appearance that masters her, along with all of the rest of us.

*

It is richly ironic, and also absolutely appropriate, that we need to convey visuality as such and in the painter's art by describing it all, including movements and lines and colors, in words.[7] Discussing drawing allows us to re-emphasize the primacy of perception in a thinker who more than any other celebrated the body—hauled into philosophy the embodied senses in relation to things and persons in the world. To invoke *Phenomenology of Perception* prepares us to leave it behind, since this book is concerned with the writings after 1945.

The purpose of the *Phenomenology* is, first in the Preface, to summarize the achievement of Husserl's foundational search of appearance, his resort to the reduction in the recognition of the natural attitude and, then, in the Introduction, to give a formal critique of the system of natural appearance, under the title "Classical Prejudices and the Return to Phenomena" (with headings on "Sensation," "Association," "Attention," and "The Phenomenal Field").

Part 2 is about "The Perceived World" (headings on "Sensing," "Space," "Up and Down," "Depth," "Movement," "Lived Space," "The Thing and the Natural World," and "Others and the Human World"). Merleau-Ponty has clearly responded to the major discoveries in Husserl on other persons as not only things and bodies outside the perceiving subject, but on others as co-constituting a social and historical world. Phenomenology in this version goes all the way from sense perception to cultural consciousness.

---

7 An article in *New York Review of Books* on the 2020 exhibition of works by Artemisia Gentileschi at London's National Gallery notes the powerful eroticism of her nude figures, like *Lucretia* (1620), with these words: "The sexual signals are chiefly transmitted by creamy impastos; refinement of line counts for little" (Bell). There is analogy between such work by art critics and the commentator on Merleau-Ponty who is obliged to read and cite mostly English translations. Even knowing how to read French, the original is hard to find and, anyway, it is standard practice to quote, for readers not in France, the easily found translations. As Merleau-Ponty himself says in *The Prose of the World*, "if we are to understand the sensible as quality, it must contain everything we think, although almost nothing in human perception is entirely sensible, since the sensible is indiscoverable" (106-0/). Still, with imaginative care, as in "creamy impastos," enough comes across despite the shift of communicative mode.

Part 3 takes about 100 pages to set perception into larger contexts of "Being-for-Itself and Being-in-the-World" (headings on "The Cogito," "Temporality," and "Freedom"). Especially here and especially in the concluding section on freedom, Merleau-Ponty brings almost to the surface an ethics of perceiving, in relation to culture and history, because the reader knows how to read his hints on what the French nation suffered throughout the years of occupation and war. The reader knows what is implied in the book's date of publication as 1945.

The contents of the *Phenomenology* are worth seeing again for the harvest of Husserl and for the massiveness of the critique of classical prejudices. More relevant to Merleau-Ponty's own originality is his comprehensive description of the many, many ways humans use sense-perception to access the structure and movement of things in time. Merleau-Ponty's knowledge of current sciences of physiology, psychology, language, and space and time is up-to-date, and he puts what he knows into practice in his daring insistence on the central role of the body for philosophy.

It is well to state in what deliberate way my making-explicit method of literary interference differs from the method of those trained as philosophers. Often I will imitate what those interpreters do and abstract the main lines of argument, and the wonderfully quotable phrases, from their contexts in paragraphs, chapters, free-standing essays, and whole books—that is a strong logical method for marching through topics. That method helps to speed along a commentator's narrative of one thinker's best thinking.

In addition and contrariwise, just as often I will follow the movement of ideas in essays and chapters, including the rhetoric of self-presentation and the perceptual images, that show the philosopher as the skillful presenter of his ideas across the curve of a plotted argument. This method will selectively slow down the story in order to read a major philosopher as a reader-friendly author. We literary readers assert our right of interference by such hunts for features of style, large and small. This is philosophy as writing which knows how to spring things on the reader and how to say things that arrest the reader. In Merleau-Ponty, this tool of style is nowhere more evident than in the late-career writings, where the author's thought is interfering with itself.

*

Shortly after the publication of *Phenomenology of Perception*, Merleau-Ponty began that book's afterlife with three publications that extend, while also quietly correcting, a few of its premises. 1) The first of these, dated December 1945, is "Cézanne's Doubt": the article shows that how the painter's true life, beyond the limits of outer biography, is the practice in pigment-on-canvas of the meaning of doubt in the Cartesian cogito and the Husserlian reduction. (I'll say more on this practice when I take Cézanne as my own example below.) The other two are not essays but rather extempore utterances: 2) One is an interview in two pages given to Maurice Fleurent at Café Flore, dated May 1946, and titled for publication "The Contemporary Philosophical Movement," and 3) the last is what appears to be a full-scale oral defense of his *Phenomenology* in the form of an address to the French Philosophical Association, titled "The Primacy of Perception and its Philosophical Consequences" and, in publication, dated December 1947. With its concluding fifteen pages of close question-and-answer, "The Primacy of Perception" must have been recorded and then transcribed.

Maurice Fleurent found, he said, "a big young man, simple and pleasant," who "shows proof . . . of a solid philosophical background" ("Primacy" 85). Fleurent asked about developments in philosophy in America and Germany, and about Sartre closer to home, and Merleau-Ponty replied in a few sentences on where he agreed and had reservations. Here the young man comments on Heidegger, re-stating in a nutshell his own position on how having a body involves us not merely in knowing the world but as the world: "as Heidegger says, I am the world. The role of philosophy is to make us rediscover this bond with the world that precedes thought itself" (86). Thus, if the mind is embodied, then there is no such thing as pure consciousness!

To read the third of these items is to find not a simple and pleasant young man, but rather a mature intellectual infighter, who is resourceful and responsive on the spot. (The event with prestigious colleagues resembles the French state doctoral oral exam as explained to me once by Michel de Certeau, describing his own experience, which he found exhilarating: eight hours of unrelenting grilling by the top people in the field, with a large number of seniors aiming critiques at a junior scholar, all of them on a dais in front of an invited public.) Merleau-Ponty's eloquent insistence on the primacy of perception was delivered to, and defended against, the very people who represented what he had slammed in his book as *the classical prejudices*.

The report of the session on primacy of perception begins with Merleau-Ponty's exposé on his recently published *Phenomenology*, in thirty-six solid paragraphs, where he is able to summarize the argument, point up possible areas of contention with an audience still working in a classical framework, and also make a few engaging concessions. The most vulnerable concession is where he admits that in his attempt to recover the consciousness of rationality, through and by means of the sensible, his *Phenomenology* "is still, in this respect, only a preliminary study, since it hardly speaks of culture or of history" ("Primacy" 101).[8] Here, as throughout the opening statement, the philosopher has understood that attacks, when they come, will be on the issue of the consciousness of rationality. He needs to make overwhelmingly clear that his particular take on perception is not abandoning rationality but is rather giving it a new role in relation. At just this point and paragraph comes Merleau-Ponty's strong incisive definition of the primacy of perception:

---

[8] Another edition of this same translation by James Edie was earlier published by Northwestern, in 1964, in a general collection under the title *The Primacy of Perception*; that book also has "Cézanne's Doubt" and "Eye and Mind," along with essays for instance on the child and on philosophy of history, and is plainly an early attempt to provide a general selection for readers of English. I am quoting from the Toadvine-Lawlor *Reader*, which updates and improves on the earlier selection.

> By these words . . . we mean that the experience of perception is our presence at the moment when things, truths, values are constituted for us: that perception is a nascent Logos; that it teaches us, outside all dogmatism, the true conditions of objectivity itself: that it summons us to the tasks of knowledge and action. It is not a question of reducing human knowledge to sensation, but of being present at the birth of this knowledge, to make it sensible as the sensible, to recover the consciousness of rationality. The experience of rationality is lost when we take it as self-evident [this the classical framework], but is, on the contrary, rediscovered when it is made to appear against the background of nonhuman nature. (101)

In the Q&A to follow, the assembled senior colleagues will speak of rationality under the name of the natural sciences, but Merleau-Ponty knows (what at one point they directly admit) that they are *using science as a code* to impugn perception as pre-propositional, preliminary to thought, and thus unphilosophical. Characteristic of his style, here, Merleau-Ponty formulates arguments in images that are persuasive because they are perception-based: *constituted, nascent logos, teaches, summons, present at the birth, recover.* Also, with his phrase *against the background* he brings into play the figure-ground, structural plan of Gestalt psychology, influential on phenomenology, and here extended from visual image to knowledge theory.

An effect of this thinker's way of working is that he often produces his most striking formulations in mid-paragraph, where they can get lost: that is true of the passage on perception as a nascent Logos and also of this recognition: "Left to itself, perception forgets itself, and is ignorant of its own accomplishments" (95). As I shall emphasize as preparation for the rest of our own essay, the "forgets itself" statement is most obviously true of the visible, but it is also true for language within phenomenology's own account of the reverse side of speaking and writing. Merleau-Ponty opens his statement on phenomenology's standard example of the invisible backs of the silhouette of the lamp or the cube: "Perception does not give me truths like geometry but presences. I grasp the unseen side as present. . . . The hidden side is present in its own way. It is in my vicinity" (90-91). I restore the true size, he says; I restore the true color. He is referring to the reduction of the natural attitude here, but he does not bring in those German terms for his French audience. There is "another modality," a "beyond," so the appearance of something "requires both this presence and this absence" (Primacy 93). This condition puts into the center of philosophy the question of the relation of perception to intellection, the very question that—open and full of promise—we have assigned ourselves in this book's opening paragraphs. It puts into philosophy the organic experience of the body, and it gives us Merleau-Ponty's largest claim, also made in passing, that philosophy is "the agency without which life would probably dissipate itself in ignorance of itself or in chaos" (96). Consider the implication of this claim framed as counter-arguing to his professional auditors in his formal statement's last paragraph: "There is thus no destruction of the absolute of rationality here, only of the absolute and the rationality separated from experience" (103). The value-term, as always, is *experience*.

Before I select highlights of the question period, insofar as these relate to my own concern for Eye and Mind, I would comment on the atmospherics. The French philosophers have organized their session to foreground, first, the hot-heads and the attack dogs (Bréhier, Lenoir, Bauer, Cesari), then to get second-last to the partly sympathetic heavy-hitter (Hyppolite), and then to close off with a foolish question from a lightweight (Parodi). At one point Émile Bréhier speaks to Merleau-Ponty as "you" and then, strangely, turns to the others and refers to him as "he." The questioners are very willing to come right to the edge of rudeness with phrases like "[y]ou don't have the right to incorporate Montaigne or Hume.... exaggerating... fatal contradiction" (Bréhier). One accuses him of sponsoring "realism" when, Merleau-Ponty says, he deliberately avoided using that misleading term. Merleau-Ponty is unfailingly polite and always directly responds to the questions asked and their larger contexts although, near the end of the session, he mentions that it would help if questioners had actually prepared by reading the book he had written. Clearly his seniors are promoting their own view of the rational as philosophy's obvious center of concern as they struggle to understand the primacy of perception; clearly, too, their ingenious resistance is forcing the presenter, the focus of their probing, to deliver explanations that are coherent, crisp, and original.

Well before this debate of all-against-one, Merleau-Ponty had anticipated in his book and also in his opening statement, that his questioners would be brilliant and subtle operators of traditional dualisms. It would be his task to prevent any easy settling into rationality, as against pre-propositional perception, or (in the visual and verbal arts) representation, as against original expression. When Bréhier says that to combat rationalists like Montaigne and Hume he "attribute[s] to them a notion of reason they do not hold," Merleau-Ponty replies, "Then I am in agreement with them" (105). When Parodi states that "the body is more essential for sensation than for perception," he slyly asks, as the final sentence of the whole session, "Can they be distinguished?" (118). As against Lupasco's contention that philosophical awareness is "possible only on the basis of science," his long reply condenses his basic argument in one sentence, both stubborn and conciliatory: "Philosophy has nothing to fear from a mature science, nor has science anything to fear from philosophy" (113). His late-1940s non-dualism, here, of perception and intellection is bringing him a stage closer to the core, late-career mode of thought that I am calling interference, for really, *can any of these be distinguished?* No.

When, in order to help the presenter and evoke something positive, Jean Hyppolite pretends to be worried that the book under discussion will introduce "a new problem and a new form of life," Merleau-Ponty replies: "I am in complete agreement with that" (116). Certain other in-passing statements should not be lost:
- "In this sense all consciousness is perceptual, even the consciousness of ourselves" (90).
- Perceptions: "not... truths... but presences" (90).
- Every perception "takes place within a certain horizon" (89).

- "The perceived thing is not an ideal unity in the possession of the intellect... it is rather a totality open to the horizon of an indefinite number or perspectival views which blend with one another according to a certain style, a style which defines the object in question" (92).
- On the cogito: "The very fact of doubting obturates [blocks] doubt" (98).
- "It was never my intention to posit the other except as an ethical subject" (106).
- "It is only when one has conceived the world of the natural sciences in all their rigor that one can see appear, by contrast, the human in his or her freedom" (112).
- Short circuiting the usual stimulus-response theory of normal science: When we apply the procedures of scientific thought to perception, we see "why perception is not a phenomenon of the order of physical causality": rather we observe a "response of the organism [that is, the body, or the embodied mind] which 'interprets' the stimuli.' The configuration that results isn't, then, produced by the stimuli but rather from the organism and from the behavior of the organism in the presence of those stimuli" (114-15).

Here in brief are themes he will develop in the '40s and '50s in essays, books, lecture notes, and working notes toward the overall project of the theory of truth. All these terms, which may seem disparate, actually define and support each other in a coherent program: the structural description of consciousness, presences within horizons, style that defines the object painted or written, the epoché of doubt, the other, creative freedom, and the organism or, by another name, the humAnimal body.

There are two other moments for rescue. 1) Where Merleau-Ponty, asked by Bréhier, "Do you posit the other [person] as absolute value?" remembers his war experience for two sentences: "Yes, insofar as a human can do so. But when I was in the army, I had to call for an artillery barrage or an air attack, and at that moment I was not recognizing an absolute value in the enemy soldiers" (111).[9] 2) Where responding to Roire on the topic of arranging a scale of value for types of experiences, Merleau-Ponty answers, yes, but whatever is "left at the bottom should not be suppressed." Then he goes on to say that every scale supposes a point of view, thus a hierarchy, and you get different hierarchies from different points of view, so why not consider that henceforth "[o]ur research must be concentric rather than hierarchized" (112). This latter move is typical in his 1950s writings: changing the metaphor for thinking as a way, practical and not merely rhetorical, for creatively reorganizing the discussion.

---

9 Speculating: given the birth-dates of the participants, the young presenter who spoke relevantly of his war experience may have been the only French person in the Session who was in active duty against the Germans; he kept his references to Husserl to a minimum in his statement because (excepting the presence of Jean Hyppolite, the eminent Hegelian) references to anything German might have been inconvenient in such a late-1940s setting.

(Learning from him, this is the rationale for our own Search of Appearance, and for Cognitive-Aesthetic Interference in the next chapter).

Eye and Mind in painting and writing

Perception as embodied—perception as an action—perception as a forgetting so it can become automatized—perception as inseparable from thinking and writing, linked in feedback loops: that is the professional philosopher's career-long concern. Merleau-Ponty knew from early on that he would be misunderstood as someone dismissive of rational thought, so he kept quietly insisting that the rational and the perceptual need each other when, in the human animal, our minds are inside our bodies. No priority, no hierarchy, but since philosophy in its classical frame has a bias toward minds, bodies need special emphasis, to bring them back into and, thus, redefine the relation.

Continuing themes for future work after the *Phenomenology*, already set going in that masterwork, are perception and its relation to the rational within the body; the natural attitude and the reduction; Husserl's contributions to the field; the visible, including distance and depth; the nature and role of language; attention; and freedom, beginning in the movements of the body and culminating in human politics, culture, and history.

From the late 1940s to 1961, new or new-emphasis themes emerge in this philosopher's writings. Of interest for the work of this study are the interference of cognition and perception as a structure of relation; the role of other persons in perceiving-thinking-writing; Marxism and the dialectic; expression as a value; painting and writing as modes of inscription; truth; moving from experience to existence, or the gradual replacement of phenomenology with ontology; and philosophy as a practice.

In my own synthesis, to follow, I select the sense of sight because the philosopher finds seeing as the most representative and productive of the senses. To show the continuing relevance of what he says about perceiving-thinking-writing, I will start by referring to three of his late-career utterances on the visible. Also, his commentators deserve a look, because they have written so helpfully on this phase of his thought. What the commentators in his tradition emphasize in him, and what I take from them, will highlight the arguments that keep him an active presence in 2024. We begin, then, by entering the larger structure and then pass through a short series of narrowing portals toward the Merleau-Pontian work of (his terms) interrogation, description, and disclosure.

Claude Lefort was Merleau-Ponty's student, later executor of his estate, and still later his editor. As commentator in *Sur une colonne absente* ("On An Absent Column"; separate essays gathered in 1978), Lefort asked, "Qu'est-ce que voir?" ("What is it, to see?") in the title of one of the articles that he wrote in tribute. In this essay's last paragraph, summarizing the phenomenology of seeing, Lefort banishes classical philosophy's framework of the priority of the rational. He conveys the center of phenomenology's new kind of thinking—that the rational must be relational:

> What is it, to see?—That question underlies every other question all the way through—not because we see before we see or think, but because we have always spoken of this seeing in the forgetting that we are speaking; because to question this seeing is to reawaken the questioning that it already carries and that stirs both our eye and our voice; to question it is to welcome the enigma of expression, to finally learn that there is no opening without a reopening, and that seeing and thinking come to terms only within the unending movement of desire. (154-55)[10]

The rational must not be relegated; it must learn to be relational. To be true to phenomenology's founding premises, we need to deny the idea that rationality begins it all, that rationality constitutes and institutes. In its place comes process: the always-already of seeing and thinking, together in relation, Also, since thought was there, language was also already there in perception: how otherwise could it be in the embodied mind? How otherwise could it exist in a being driven and glorified by the unceasing action of *desire*? Desire is not a term that you often find in this kind of discourse, where *intentionality* (or directedness of conscious experience at an object) is, after Husserl, the defining characteristic of consciousness. Here I think Lefort means desire not as instinct, but as intentionality taken with the force of humAnimal emotion to an exponential power.[11]

Desire is dialogic, a lance of the individual, driving toward the cultural, and toward the social: toward a future freedom. Lefort, along with Kelly Oliver, whom I will consider next, is one of the rare commentators able to describe the full arc of Merleau-Ponty's thinking in the '40s and '50s, from technical work on perception in theory and practice to a philosophy of freedom-in-contingency of humAnimals as social beings. In Lefort, whose biography shows him engaged with French left politics and with Marxist thought in as anguished and intelligent a way as Merleau-Ponty, the affinity is ideological in the most direct way. In Kelly Oliver, there is never a mention of Marx or Marxism, but she is able to connect a philosophy of seeing and vision through many richly described stages to an ethics of perception in child development, earth-attachment, and social-political being more generally. Read Oliver first for a comprehensive survey of framing concepts on vision and then for a committed and admiring display of how one French thinker relates scientific discoveries to a believable

---

10 My translation.
11 Go to the Castle Museum in Colchester, UK, to see inconspicuous in a glass case little amulets that were dug up in that Roman garrison town—two inches long, metal, in the form of cock and balls with a pair of wings attached at the back to help desire search the known world. A thousand years from then, when these were carried a thousand miles from Rome: that is power. That is instinct converted into art.

scheme of value. After that, read her for incisive contrasts with contemporaries like Sartre, Lacan, and Levinas, to reach back to Hegel and Husserl and forward to J. J. Gibson and ourselves now and, for a dramatic *élan vital*, for what to quote where.[12]

Oliver begins by describing an offensive stare, or evil eye—in the way the gaze is described by Sartre in his "accusing look of the other," by Lacan with his idea of the eye as voracious, and also by Freud in his conceptions of self-consciousness— noting that in all such cases, "vision creates a sense of lack or alienation" (132). This contrasts with Merleau-Ponty's "alternative notion of subjectivity based on ethical responsibility" (133). She quotes from *The Visible and the Invisible*, where, she says, Merleau-Ponty "rethinks subjectivity through the body," explaining in her words that, for him, "the body mediates between subject and object, self and other. The body is both subject and object" (133) because, in his words in a great passage, "a sort of dehiscence opens my body in two, and because between my body looked-at and my body looking, my body touched and my body touching, there is overlapping encroachment, so that we must say that the things pass into us as well as we into the things" (qtd. in Oliver 133). (That dehiscence or splitting, that "overlapping encroachment" is rather a value than a problem, and *dehiscence* and *encroachment* are two of many synonyms for the constructive interference we ourselves claim for the essential spring of his whole philosophy.)

In an ethics of vision, Oliver next reveals that our embodiment in *flesh*, using that Merleau-Pontian late-period technical term, is what "makes communication possible," because flesh is *reversible*. "By [this, he] means that we are both sensing and sensible, both subject and object. By virtue of our flesh, we can sense and be sensed by others and by ourselves" (134). I am close enough to the other that, as he says in *The Visible and the Invisible*, "I almost witness, in him and in myself, the awesome birth of vociferation" (Merleau-Ponty, *VI* 114); here, the distance that the sense of vision requires is not "alienating or threatening. . . . [but rather] a means of connection and communion" (Oliver 133-34). Unlike the theorists of simple recognition and malevolent lack, for Merleau-Ponty vision is part of a system of sensation involving all the other senses, for instance a vision-touch system, what he calls "a palpation with the look" (qtd. in Oliver 135). This more corporeal kind of vision also acts within a new kind of space, what Oliver calls "space filled with the flesh of the world" (135). Oliver summarizes the gestures of the posthumous Visible/Invisible book, where Merleau-Ponty "describes vision in terms of thickness, corpuscles, tissues, grains, waves, channels, circuits, currents, embryos, and pregnancy, the very corporeality out of which sensation, thought, and language are born" (135). After pages that draw out the philosopher's influences *from* Gestalt psychology and *upon* J. J. Gibson's later ideas of the perceptual system (affordances, orientation to gravity, the environment in which perception takes place), Oliver pursues wider circles of explanation of our

---

12 See Kelly Oliver, "Beyond Recognition: Merleau-Ponty and an Ethics of Vision" 131-51.

senses' relation to the surround. For instance, we respond to "different types of energy in our environment—mechanical, chemical, heat, photic" (139). Beyond the anxieties of Sartre and the other "recognition" thinkers is a "kinship between my body and the earth" (140) that Oliver takes as ethical, especially when we share social or psychic energy with others (141).

She arrives at *collective and dynamic energy* in the final pages of her essay, referring to Merleau-Ponty's work on child development. The energy is begun at birth when sensory, perceptual, and motor systems are joined in one body, but human beings thereafter come into what psychologists have called *collective attunement*. We develop a responsibility to respond to others and to the earth. Oliver, in her essay, attains to originality and eloquence, where she is able to find a network of passages in the philosopher that refer to the double meaning of *witness* as both passive observer and one who gives active testimony of the world (146-47). Clarifying and extending what Merleau-Ponty says about a novel by Simone de Beauvoir at the end of "Metaphysics and the Novel," she says dazzlingly, "Because I am visible, therefore I am finite, but because I am a witness, therefore I am infinite" (146). By the essay's end, Merleau-Pontian seeing is responsible for the earth and for others and is, thus, inherently political and ethical. Brava! Reading Oliver's study in a staid black-covered collection published by a University Press, one almost witnesses the awesome birth of vociferation.

Turning now to Merleau-Ponty himself, I will read separately and sequentially three late-career writings on the relations of the aesthetic and the cognitive. The first, from 1945, the essay "Cézanne's Doubt," puts the painter in the title, while the other two (from 1952 and 1961) touch on that painter as representative of the modern artist for sentences or paragraphs at a time. The second of these, the long chapter 3 in *The Prose of the World*, is a first run-through-account of André Malraux's writings on the history of painting.[13] The third is "Eye and Mind," the philosopher's last published essay, where he is still asking, What is it, to see?

Obviously, Merleau-Ponty devoted many hours of his life over many years to viewing paintings in galleries and to reading novels and poems, so it is surprising to note that there is little description of actual, named paintings or novels—at just those points where non-philosophers would expect to see close analysis. He is leaving that kind of thing

---

13 Note that this topic is also addressed in the essay not cited here, "Indirect Language and the Voices of Silence," originally published in *Signes* (Paris: Gallimard, 1960). I will cite the earlier version because it makes more explicit the role of Husserlian thought structures of natural attitude, appearance, and reduction, and because I wish to emphasize the emergence of the argument in a late-'40s-early-'50s moment in Merleau-Ponty's career. A comparison with the "Indirect Language and the Voices of Silence" piece in *Signs* shows that the line of points is the same, the phrasing and length are tightened in a minor way, but the 1960 account of Saussure more accurately phrases the nature of his structuralist linguistics, and the ending is different. Also, chapter 3 from *The Prose of the World* is more useful for my purpose, because in its title and ending it more directly shows that painting is taken up in order to get to the greater complexities of writing.

to critics within the relevant disciplines; he is after something else. Phenomenologists are not interrogating, describing, and disclosing the same things as the rest of us, apparently. They are concerned with pretext before text, consciousness before style, perceptual content above all or, rather, as we shall see, the productive interference-relation, or entanglement, of the aesthetic and the cognitive. (In later chapters of this book I shall be suggesting that the rest of us can learn, from the disclosure-vocabulary Merleau-Ponty invented, to do another level or kind of reading.)

"Cézanne's Doubt" (1945)

The painter had "moments of doubt about his vocation" (Merleau-Ponty, CD 69), had "fits of temper and depression" (CD 69), and for his whole life was a loner, troubled in his human contacts. As painter of landscape scenes, still lifes, and persons he also had such a high reverence for things seen that he struggled until the end of his career, revising his relation to nature. Merleau-Ponty tracks the biography by quick touches and remarks, having plainly seen the paintings in galleries, read the life story and the letters, and followed the painter's vexed relation to classical painting, Impressionism and, especially, his senior contemporary in landscape, Camille Pissarro. The relation of the life to the actual work of arriving at and framing the scene, line and color, watercolor or oil pigment, is the philosopher's continual concern. That concern is explicit, but implicit is the Cartesian-cogito meaning of the title-term "doubt" because what we begin to be interested in here is how in detail Cézanne accomplishes the Husserlian reduction.

As usual, the epoché is the opening, the beginning continuously returned to and always followed by wider circles of consciousness as applied to the technical detail of the art. Merleau-Ponty has a grand paragraph (starting "He quickly parted ways with the impressionists") on complementarities in the color spectrum, sunlit colors, vibration of colors, how painters depict atmosphere, "chromatic nuances across the object," and "giving color priority over the outline" (72). Cézanne wanted to paint a primordial world (73), but to do so he had to resist separating sensation and thought—had to insist, in the work with pigment, that "the lived perspective, that of our perception, is not a geometric or photographic one" (73). Natural vision! The object in the act of appearing! The swelling of the object! (74). Without referring to a single painting for pages, the philosopher manages to find language of description for the pre-text of the continuous reduction in one admired artist:

> We forget the viscous, equivocal appearances, and by means of them we go straight to the things they represent. The painter recaptures and converts into visible objects what would, without him, remain closed up in the separate life of each consciousness: the vibration of appearances which is the cradle of things. Only one emotion is possible for the painter—the feeling of strangeness— and only one lyricism—that of the continual rebirth of existence. (77)

Here the verbs of value will be *gaze* and *vibrate*, and the nouns will be *things* and *rebirth*. At the essay's end, the higher-level, resolving value will be *freedom*.

But, before the end, there are several long paragraphs that may seem a huge digression into the biography of Leonardo da Vinci, based on 1920s analytical studies by Valéry and Freud. These are brought in to clinch the larger point, started in the opening paragraphs, about the painter's empirical existence being a necessary study, but also irrelevant. For, as thinkers in the "circular movement" of our lives, just like da Vinci and Cézanne, we might get beyond the ambiguous mess of the life to the obsession of the art. With the French painter of many investigations of Montaigne Sainte Victoire, "he himself was never at the center of himself, . . . It is still in the world, upon a canvas, with colors, that he has to realize his freedom" (84). For this kind of thinking, self-splitting in the artist-thinker is the opening onto strangeness and lyricism that are the evidences of our freedom, but, since our lives and the appearances of things are intruding, we need continuously to accomplish our own rebirth. That is our freedom, but, as his last sentence says, "We never see ideas or freedom face to face" (84).

While Cézanne is still the focus, it further defines Merleau-Ponty's approach to mention a few more recent interpretations of the painter. Richard Verdi and Jessica Wiskus directly cite the philosopher as having come before them, and T. J. Clark seems vaguely aware of him. Unlike Merleau-Ponty, all three of them do what art critics do and devote paragraphs, or pages, to discuss named and dated paintings, and all three print illustrations of paintings they are inspecting. Verdi has written in a World of Art series for the general public, and he gives a biography of the painter with descriptions along the way of 182 paintings, all illustrated and 33 in color, and his accounts of the paintings, while brief, are exact and technical—also enthusiastic, as with this one on the still lifes of the 1870s: "Yet another advance over these early pictures is a sense of clear spatial intervals—or caesuras—in the composition, which endows the objects with a monumental dignity" (Verdi 83). Wiskus is a scholar of music who uses—explaining, extending—Merleau-Ponty to show how the terms he has generated help us understand the structures of paintings (Cézanne), literary works (Proust), and music (Debussy). In a University Press book for philosophers and humanists, for her the rhythm of thought is a structure of noncoincidence. Such music-like effects of gapping are the very intervals or caesuras Verdi identified, but here they are explored across all the arts and with the tentacular reach into consciousness afforded by French phenomenology. Her start is in sound, with musical rhythm as temporal, but rhythm also applies to painters and writers through effects of suspension: "reflection circles around noncoincidence and, thanks to temporal dislocation, projects backward into perception what I had already formulated" (5). Rhythm is what is not heard; the interval between sounds in Debussy; the gaps between steeples and walks and events in Proust; the light-and-air-filled spaces between Cézanne's eye and Montaigne Sainte Victoire. Wiskus has a bravado description of the painter's many mountain-paintings and watercolors, based on the phenomenological term "depth," the aspect of the hidden or the absent, and, as in Merleau-Ponty, these are all versions of the epoché as both beginning and continuation of new strange consciousness: "perceptual depth is . . . the experiential space that unfolds from . . . noncoincidence" (22). As we list the terms Wiskus has learnt from skillful study and burnished in her two chapters on painting—noncoincidence, depth, world, encroachment, expression, intertwining, style, institution—we may be grateful for her summary-quotation from what Merleau-Ponty has so well proclaimed as his project, "an ontological rehabilitation of the sensible" (qtd. in Wiskus 25). Also, remember what Wallace Stevens said in a line from one of his poems from the early 1950s about how our de-linking of eye and mind "makes the visible a little hard / To see" ("The Creations of Sound"). Here as everywhere: the reduction!

T. J. Clark, an art historian with a social conscience, is serious enough about the formal-technical side of painting to keep returning day after day to sit in front of the paintings of Claude, Poussin, Pissarro, Cézanne, and Gerhard Richter, to make close readings of every feature of every painting, including the laying on of paint and the effects of color in different kinds of gallery lighting. Merleau-Ponty did not do that and was much more skeptical about the role of museums, but Clark would agree on something the philosopher said, about how reproductions of paintings, losing the brush-strokes, approximating pigment by inks, never get the color right. They also agree that to write on Cézanne is to tell the story of how a modern painter defines his or her project over against, and beyond, the classical regime of representation. Clark does this by selecting the time in the mid-1870s when Cézanne went to live near, and paint outdoors with, Camille Pissarro. In his long article, he prints in color eight paintings, four landscapes by each, either of comparable scenes or of the exact same scenes. Like Cézanne, Clark inordinately loves the wonderful Pissarro; he finds, as Wiskus finds, the attribute of depth and (for instance, in *Paysage à Pontoise*) "the complete steadiness of its hold on a single plain state of the light" (16). Further and even better, Clark writes about eye and mind and technique: "the dullness of the scene, and the intensity of the dullness, inheres in oil paint's opacity, its smeared matt surface, which a reproduction is bound to tune up a little and render more 'lit from within.' There is no inner light in Pissarro, no trace of the numinous" (16). The lesson of Pissarro that brings Cézanne out of his early work into a new modern phase is "painting's disenchantment of its genre" and a new knowledge that "qualification— the holding in balance of strong contrariety and careful admission of the obvious— is strength" (16). The emblem of this anti-monumentality is what Clark quotes from what someone heard Cézanne saying later in life: "'Je vois, par taches.' I see in touches—patches—dabs—stains. Or I see by touches" (17). There is more in Clark on how the fellow painter separated himself from these lessons of Pissarro, especially in the handling of space and of "light in air," but enough is here to have shown Cézanne making a synaesthesia of seeing and touching like Merleau-Ponty. Clark concludes: "Modernity is loss of world. Cézanne is the painter who makes that cliché draw blood" (21). On this evidence, art history is just as much in constructive interference with phenomenology as literature.

"The Indirect Language," chapter 3 of *The Prose of the World* (written 1952; posthumous publication)

This chapter is the longest of a relatively neglected book in the canon. The author very likely held it back rather than abandon it, and then he mined it for the 1960 "Voices of Silence" essay devoted to Malraux and painting. This posthumous part-book is the only one that he declared to be a study of language and literature, so the materials on painting are there to provide a running contrast—they provide scant reference to named painters and works of art because he is doing perception-philosophy and not art history and because the purpose of his chapter is to find greater scope and meaning-making complexity in literary writing.

The Prose of the World, notably in this chapter, speaks to its moment when the intellectual scene was incorporating the structural linguistics of Ferdinand de Saussure and the psychological-historical arguments on painting and on museum-culture by André Malraux. To both of these towering figures he gives great credit, with special recognition to Malraux as author of the political novel *Man's Fate*. Since Merleau-Ponty has declared himself never to be solely on the attack, he is not here interested in refutation; the address to both of these major players is more like extension, or completion.

Clearly, though, if I may without preliminaries simply list the points on which he objects, the issues and the stakes are important for a developing phenomenology of perception. With Saussure, he accepts fully the new synchronic linguistics that begins by "defining signs…not as the representations of certain significations but as the means of differentiations in the verbal chain" (*PW* 31). However, he knows that this precision emerges from within the classical rationalism we have already seen him contesting in the natural sciences, and he positions himself to beat back any idea that human life is mere synchrony or that philosophy must now (to be in accord on language) eliminate the speaking subject as the responsible agent of perception and eliminate that agent's freedom-in-history. With Malraux, he accepts fully something he has himself argued in several published works, the large distinction between classical representation in the arts and what the moderns achieve by canceling or re-conceiving representation to achieve strangeness, new perceptions, and techniques as values. However, he will not accept Malraux's ideas about psychological individuality in modern painting as the signature style, and he thinks that the museum as an institution (which he calls "not entirely beneficent" [*PW* 72]) will flatten out and then archive the impulse to new perception in modern painting. In other contexts, Merleau-Ponty calls this societal agency, to render creative gestures routine and thus blandly familiar, *institution* or else *sedimentation*.

This torso of a book is one of two places where Merleau-Ponty states rather than assumes that language is subject to, indeed urgently requires, its own thoroughgoing epoché.[14] He spells it out in the first chapter of this book, where he is speaking of how humans share and select language from the common store: "Language is there, like an all-purpose tool" (*PW* 6), and thus "[c]ommunication is an appearance; it never brings us anything new" (7). We have put into other people only the words that we understand coming from them! As he says at the end of the second chapter, because of this tendency we need to shake up the apparatus of language or of narrative "to make it yield goodness knows what—precisely because what is said then has never before been said" (46). Accordingly, "we should consider speech before it has been pronounced, against the ground of the silence which precedes it, which never ceases to accompany it, and without which it would say nothing" (46). From this recommendation emerges the plan for the whole of the long third chapter with its argument that *we can use painting to perform the reduction upon writing*, thence perhaps to understand more fully the reverse side of language:

> We must perform a reduction upon language, without which it would still be hidden from our view—leading us back to what it signifies. . . . We should compare the art of language with other arts of expression which do not have recourse to language and try to see language as one of these mute arts. It is possible that the meaning of language has certain privileges over the meaning of painting, and that in the end we must move beyond this parallel. But it is only by trying to do so that we can see what makes the comparison with painting ultimately unworkable and thereby have the chance of discovering what is peculiar to language. (46)

The rescue of writing for creativity and meaning will come from working out a comparison with painting, the art that does not speak except with a language of silence. The terms of the comparison will, we predict, reveal something about language and writing that we have forgotten, lost, maybe even suppressed (as, for instance, the snobbish avoidance of the adjective)—namely, the perceptual content of speech and writing. Maybe we might learn how perceptions get into writing by understanding how they get into painting, the inscription that has conventions but certainly no code as infinite as the alphabet, nothing as intimate as speech-sounds, and no other-directed genres apostrophic or invocatory. The mute action of painting, visual action at a distance from the object, is here for the comparison. The painting is here to perform the epoché for writing, and both painting and writing are here to be philosophy's best instances of phenomenology of perception. The arts are better at delivery of the vividness of perception than the sciences or the humanities, because the arts are the most complete transforms of animal perception into living expression— into styles that continue creativity beyond the era when they were created.

---

14 The other place is Merleau-Ponty, *Recherches sur l'usage littéraire du langage* (2013). In these lectures, the philosopher finds a creative crisis in the careers of Paul Valéry (for poetry, with a hard look at the poet's writings on poetics) and Stendahl (for fiction), resulting in new phenomenological conceptions of language, of the speaking subject, and of truth-telling.

First, we notice the similarities and, immediately Merleau-Ponty, mid-paragraph, produces one of his stupendous sentences: "Like language, painting at first lives in the milieu of the exterior holy" (*PW* 48). In agreement with Malraux, the philosopher finds that this is art taking experience at the intensity of religion, through the modern mode of regard "detached from the sacred" and in accordance "with the modern awareness of expression" (49). Instead of the classical reference to representation—or nature or perspective—instead of the senses taken as natural, painting and writing will eschew objectivity: "There is no longer a search for the velvet of peaches, as in Chardin, but, as in Braque, for the velvet of the painting" (54). Soon Malraux gets faulted, however, for "his questionable theses on the individualism of modern painting" (56), and just as soon Merleau-Ponty finds that the art historian's ideas of *style* are a major contribution to a theory of creativity very like what a phenomenologist would offer. In the style of painting and writing, "we must give up every signification that is already institutionalized and return to the starting point of a nonsignifying world" (58). (These are all synonyms for saying we need to perform the reduction, and Malraux gets approval for almost saying it.)

Thereafter follow a number of pages where the philosopher sponsors and re-states for phenomenology two of Malraux's best ideas: first, that "perception already stylizes" (59), that is, thinking and inscribing inform sensing, so there is no natural or innocent sensing; second, what artistic vision does to the sensible seen, the visible object, is a "coherent deformation" (qtd. in *PW* 60). As to the first: "We must see [style] emerging at the point of contact between the painter and the world, in the hollow of the painter's perception, and as an exigency which arises from that perception" (59). As to the second, no "pre-established order of significations" (60)! "Pictorial expression assumes and transcends the patterning of the world which begins in perception," and style and signification exist as soon as there are figure and ground, top and bottom, dimensions, syntax, logic, a system of equivalences that fit the contingent circumstance, a unique technique (61). To conclude on the similarities, in a summary sentence Merleau-Ponty uses one of the linking locutions most typical of his mind, "just as": "The painter re-arranges the prosaic world and, so to speak, makes a holocaust of objects, just as poetry melts ordinary language" (63). For him, no namby-pamby deformations! A certain violence is required, of just the sort that makes paintings suffer when set up for comparison in museums, and makes novels turn into lists when they get put on the shelves of libraries. The philosopher, unlike the art historian, should value the creator, not the curator.

Tracking Merleau-Ponty through this baggy chapter we find that the link is slender between the pages about museums as institutions that exhibit history and the six pages that follow concerning the philosophy of history, Hegel, and the dialectic. What emerges from these pages is never stated directly, but it involves how the sister arts signify. Both painting and writing are expressive, and both achieve creativity through deformation of ideas and things that are readymade. But only writing has the semantic thickness, spontaneity, specific address to another person, and link of the

"The Indirect Language," chapter 3 of The Prose of the World (written 1952; posthumous publication) — 53

individual through to the universal. It would appear that all painters from Lascaux to the moderns are similar in relation to perception, and all writers, especially since the moment of modernity, are dissimilar.

The chapter moves from painting to writing. "A novel achieves expression the same way as a painting" (*PW* 88), namely, through delivery of theme; but the virtue of novels is not in the theme, but rather between the words, in the delivery of "new experiences, and . . . perspectives that can never be ours" (90). Yes, the painter is open to things and can never say what comes from him or her and what comes from things (67-68), so as long as the painter is painting, the painter is in the middle of life and world—of perception, of expression. From the painters of caves to Vermeer and Cézanne, "each . . . work opens up an horizon of inquiry" (82). So much for perception and history, two of the problems Malraux addresses more or less accurately.

But Malraux has, perhaps, not considered the third necessary assignment, which is language (87). First, we need to see that it is "legitimate to treat painting as a language" (87), because there is a "*perceptual* meaning which is captured in the visible configuration of the painting" (87, emphasis in original). This legitimation makes painting comparable, but it also shows by profound contrast how language as spoken, written, and read—that is, language "whose sounds and sentences are cleverly suited to ready-made significations"—reveals beneath itself (a struggle, a search that never ends) "an operant or speaking language, whose words have a silent life like the animals at the bottom of the ocean and come together or separate according to the needs of their lateral or indirect signification" (87). This recognition is the reveal of the chapter as a whole: "Painting is unable to speak" (100); "nothing equals the ductility of speech" (102), nor yet equals the permanence of speech, because Olympian statues and paintings "cannot resist time the way a manuscript does" (102). Furthermore, "[t]he writer can conceive of himself only in an established language, whereas every painter refashions his language" (100), and this confinement means that every writer "must remake *his* [or her] language within this [extant, anonymous] language" (110). The result of this line of thought is that the writer's assignment of creativity with structures of expression is more massive than the painter's and, further, more than with the painter, the writer's assignment tells us something essential about how the sensible must contain everything we think. Logically, then, because "almost nothing in human perception is entirely sensible, since the sensible is indiscoverable" (106-07), the sensible must also contain everything we write. We always knew, without good evidence or argument in the history of philosophy, that writing involved sensing and thinking, but it is a new idea that sensing involves thinking and writing. By insisting on this, we insist not only on the primacy of perception, but we also insist on the first-among-equals relation of feedback and interference, that we are calling perceiving-thinking-writing. Now, language and writing are part of the assignment. Once Merleau-Ponty touches on language, sure to be nearby are literary instances: Rimbaud, Mallarmé, Valéry, Saint-Exupéry, Balzac, Stendahl, Proust, de Beauvoir.

"Eye and Mind" (originally published both in *Art de France* and *Les Temps Modernes* in 1961)

For putting all his critical terms into play, for the reach into other fields including emergent computer science as well as painting and writing, for the remembrance and continuing relevance of previous philosophy, for the sense of history and the promise of creativity and freedom as values, and for tight organization and memorable phrasing, this is Merleau-Ponty's best essay. Unlike Husserl, who was the prolific producer of huge multivolume works, the French phenomenologist could move easily in the world of scholarly and political journals, indeed he edited *Les Temps Modernes* in the 1940s and 1950s, so by the time of the late-1940s he had mastered short-form speculative writing.[15] From several sources, we know that one of his main ways of getting ready to write was to produce working notes that contain bursts of thinking on a small range of topics, often returning to comment further on his and others' ideas, according to a principle of circularity: "everything that is said at each 'level' anticipates and will be taken up again," he wrote (*VI* 177-78).[16] By this plan we have in "Eye and Mind" seven scattered references to Cézanne's paintings that prepare for a dramatic late couple of pages on Rodin as sculptor and several opening paragraphs on contemporary natural science that resonate with mid-essay pages on Descartes and seventeenth-century optics, culminating in a last-section critique of American cyberneticians. In an upward spiral of redefinition, we have the crucial terms of the philosopher's frame of thought: classical science, suspension, history, paradox, body, seeing and visible, touching and touched, dimension, essence, imaginary, depth, encroachment, truth, space, light, being, system of equivalences, genesis, incompossible, dehiscence, speech, understanding, creative. To these terms he adds two new ones for the relation of eye and mind, the verb *gaze*, for the painter's and writer's intensity of address to the visible which performs the reduction and the adjective *secret* for what is searchable in appearance, silent behind speech, hollowed out behind things. Here, too, are "just as" and "co-," the locution and the prefix of mutuality.

There are five sections. Natural science, as standing in Merleau-Ponty for rationality as detached from the body and its senses, "has given up dwelling" in things " ("EM" 351). However, art and especially painting still lives in the "pool of brute sense" (352)—that is why painting is invulnerable to expression of or attacks by mere opinion. Art is the "secret science" (353) that natural science avoids but that philosophy can seek to understand (section 1). The painter's body, through its antennae and clairvoyance, becomes in creation the "intertwining of vision and movement"

---

15 As evidence, three collections: *Sense and Non-Sense* (first French edition 1948); *In Praise of Philosophy and Other Essays* (first French edition 1953); *Signs* (first French edition 1960).
16 From (and actually about) the working notes at the back of *The Visible and the Invisible*. The ultimate reason for circularity: "The end of a philosophy is an account of its beginning" (177).

(353) that produces new knowledge. The paradox that the body is simultaneously seeing and visible leads to other paradoxes. Through the body's gaze, painters, also the rest of us, use the eye as the "computer of the world" not to see things, but to see according to things, because of things. Painting in relation to knowing is like a birth, but it is one that keeps on birthing (section 2). Descartes in his *Optics* fails to solve the essential problem of vision, which is to understand action at a distance. Descartes did write about the visual art of engraving, but (though he was right on space and on perspective) he missed how we integrate understanding and body to get visualization (*voyance*). Vision-visualization is always "a conditioned thought"—conditioned by the body (section 3). The history of painting in the modern world engages a dimension of depth that is not on the radar of classical painting or Cartesian thought about optics. In Cézanne, this lack is (in a great odd phrase) a "deflagration [burning consumption] of being" (369), involving new uses of color, light, systems of equivalences beyond mere attempts at representation. The eye can move and can anticipate movement, and, tracking both the eye and what it sees, we search for the genesis of the visible in painting. This process involves "dehiscence [or self-splitting] of being" (375), so that we may show in things their "lining of invisibility" (375). Merleau-Ponty here uses an astronomical analogue: precession, an anticipation of the torquing of planets, gets us back to the idea of the presuppositionlessness of painting's silent science of reduction (section 4). No acquiring of new assignments, no progress in painting between cave-artists and Rodin-Cézanne-ourselves, not for literature or philosophy or even cybernetics. The basic assignment of getting beyond natural-attitude seeing to clairvoyance is the same across all eras and all human professions even if the rationalists will not admit it. The assignment is still the continually renewed birth of the creative gaze (section 5).

Two sentences represent this essay. The first looks back to my making-explicit of the meanings of both Husserl and Merleau-Ponty and to earlier points about painting and writing: "The effort of modern painting has been directed not so much toward choosing between line and color, or even between figurative depiction and the creation of signs, as it has been toward multiplying the system of equivalences, toward severing their adherence to the envelope of things" ("EM" 371). The second, from the essay's very end, looks ahead to my final chapter on ordinary creativity: "If no painting completes painting, if no work even is itself absolutely completed, each creation changes, alters, clarifies, deepens, confirms, exalts, re-creates, or creates in advance all the others" (378). Assuming that there is a mind separate from or living within the brain, the eye and the mind reside harmoniously but not without contention, miscues, and illusions in the same body. The eye is the mind's reach out into space, distance, movement, things, otherness, and other persons. The mind performs the reduction upon what the eye brings back, brings in, but the eye cannot look forth without transforming seeing into, and gazing into voyance, without being conditioned by thought. The mutuality is also an interference. This structure of humAnimal consciousness, within phenomenology as a science, is the topic of chapter 3.

*

There exists a more recent, very different French thinker on perception: Michel Serres. For Serres in his book *The Five Senses*, the dreaded rational enemy of perception is language: language as, for him, a second-hand, detached, routinizing collection of formal institutional structures that can only betray the immediacy and vividness of the senses.[17] The method of his book was to take hardly a side-glance at the whole history of philosophy (he neglects history, while Merleau-Ponty condemns/replaces it) and to substitute for citation and topical order a set of personal, seventy-page perception-packed reveries, individually keyed to each of the five senses, with a final set on synesthesia or blends. That approach is persuasive in the way it enacts embodied mind and loads every rift with perceptual ore, but it is not phenomenology. Also, Serres's weird, self-conscious philosophy of language is to condemn language even as he must use it to deliver the attacks that alternate with the rhapsodies.

By contrast, when Merleau-Ponty uses language everywhere to rehabilitate the body and perception, the body and perception already include language. That is what he meant when saying "that perception is a nascent *logos*" ("Primacy" 101).

Just as

From the writings here made more explicit, I conclude that Merleau-Ponty took up the pigment-language of painting so that he could get to the word-language of literature. Painting was already a mode of inscription, with the eye directing the implement in the hand and, to respond to painting in museum catalogues or articles in the *London Review of Books*, words and sentences transform the pigment into an entirely different mode of perception in the eye of the reader who is also a writer.

Merleau-Ponty took up writing so he could get back to philosophy because philosophy (not even excepting Plato recording or inventing what Socrates says) requires an author who tells his or her argument like a story, in propositions, which

---

17 Original edition: *Les cinq sens* (Paris, 1985). Serres also wrote *Eyes*, trans. Anne-Marie Feenberg-Dibon (Bloomsbury, 2015); first published in French by Le Pommier, with the title *Yeux* (2014). The book on eyes is a large-size picture book with beautiful reproductions of paintings and photographs of creatures with eyes and of networks of things eyes see, a world full of networks and connections between animate and inanimate things. Serres writes a series of three-paragraph essays to accompany the dense flurry of illustrations (The world looks at itself. Is it also looking at us?), but his best work is in many short descriptions of the illustrations themselves, detailed and also thoughtful. There is a short section on literary eyes but, even here, he provides nothing on language, and only the mention of an author's name.

are words and sentences. Husserl and Merleau-Ponty made something powerful and revelatory by writing thousands of sentences about the pre-propositional.

Just as Merleau-Ponty had earlier taken up perception so he could get to thinking and writing, he took up painting and literature so he could go from there back to philosophy, but a philosophy that is a phenomenology of perception.

"*Just as*" to start a sentence is one of Merleau-Ponty's frequent and favorite linkages, a signature of his style. His mind is restless to pull in connections, transformations and intertwinings, from disparate places and ideas. But, as with him, one who says "just as" will always need, nearby, to make an active turn to the coordinate word "but."

Chapter 3: *Ineinander*: Energies of Interference

Oneinanother

Late-career Merleau-Ponty, as he is getting ready to write parts of his trilogy on the origin of truth, or lecture to students, expends a great deal of time speaking to himself in working notes, and these jagged drafts were published after his death. While he is in his workroom, he many times recurs to his set of preoccupations, like depth, openness to the world, passivity of mind as against activity, the reduction, and so on. As he adds new possibilities for defining these concepts, he adds new problems: instances are the definition of truth, the movement from phenomenology to ontology, and the role of the other person in development of our perceptions and our thinking. He returns again and again to Husserl's discoveries and Husserl's vocabulary, and I think we learn about his own mind by what he is still learning from Husserl's. The terms he wants he takes over directly in German and, often in his notes, we find him italicizing and using *Ineinander*, literally "in one another," or *oneinanother*, where the preposition "in" makes a linking third.[1] Husserl's German term gives him something French and English cannot, a concept that exemplifies itself as a multiple within a single, a three-in-one unhyphenated compound word. This occurrence is a minor (but frequent) instance of a logic of relationship that the philosopher will, increasingly in his later writings, advance on several fronts as the vanguard of his thought. It also becomes the method of protecting his thought against any diminishment of complex union *into the one or the other*: in this case, into the no-no of cognition or of perception *taken by itself*.

Polemical thesis: Nothing in Merleau-Ponty is ever taken by itself.

A question to be resolved in chapter 3: What if *Ineinander* and related terms like *Füreinander* are coded signals, not of inclusion, or not only of it, but rather of tension-contention, of interference?

---

[1] I count four uses of *Ineinander* in the one hundred and ten pages of "Working Notes" in *The Visible and the Invisible* (written 1959-61, English translation 1964), and 11 uses of this term in the seventy-one pages of his lecture notes in *Husserl at the Limits of Phenomenology* (written 1959-61, English translation 2002). "Portmanteau" is another word that exemplifies its own concept and is the general term for this kind of item. Examples of two-in-one portmanteau words in use in this book include "humAnimal," "frenemy," "grammetrics," "dialectics," and, notably, "phenomenology." Plainly Merleau-Ponty needs and enjoys such locutions. Note that the uncompleted plan for three books on the origin of truth was, at the philosopher's death, to include the unfinished *The Prose of the World*, the draft chapters and working notes in *The Visible and the Invisible*, and one other book.

Defining *interference*: the most useful meaning is the technical-quantum meaning, where two states (wave and particle) are intertwined and are thus indeterminate and impossible to measure separately in any known experiment.

Another question: Can there be states of being that are separable in concept, unchangeable in action, yet inextricable in experience?

Defining *experience*: Temporal experience of speaking-subject consciousness, experience of experiment, experience of measurement, experience of writing and reading, experience of rereading. Each of these experiences cannot be disconnected when they actually occur, although they can be distinguished conceptually.

*

Ineinander, but what, or who, is the other? In his late notes on Husserl, it is most certainly, for Merleau-Ponty as he keeps learning from Husserl, a who before it is a what. For instance, he reveals his recognition of a "who" or an agent, in his reminder-to-self on intersubjectivity in Husserl's thought. He makes his comments in his course notes, writing of plurality of subjects—transcendental intersubjectivity, referring to the two viewpoints not as alternatives but as taken together. Writing of the cohesion of a *Füreinander* [for one another], Merleau-Ponty is resisting both addition and alternation, as descriptions of how we describe the relationships that matter to us (see *Husserl at the Limits* 47). Beyond these denials, what is of relevance here is the human otherness of the other, a major theme in the validation of perception in later Husserl and later Merleau-Ponty, and the insistence that a more capacious philosophy takes *the two viewpoints together*.

Thinking goes best with, in, and for the other, and (in addition to a person) that other can be a state, a concept, or a thing. Usually, in Merleau-Ponty, the *Ineinander* is constituted by the together-in-resistance of cognition and perception. This dynamic is shown in the larger structures of argument in nearly all of his non-autobiographical later works as well as in brief, sub-paragraph passages that are easily lost in books and essays. For larger structures of argument, think of reversible-oppositional titles like "Indirect Language and the Voices of Silence," "Eye and Mind," *The Visible and the Invisible*, "The Intertwining—The Chiasm." Constructive interference of *Ineinander* is evident in short runs of sentences, like these to follow. I find such surfacings of the essential mind of Merleau-Ponty everywhere, but never with the term I am using for *interference* as a structure of relation.[2]

---

[2] Selecting four of the clearest examples as evidence: 1) from the essay "Cézanne's Doubt" on not choosing between sensation and thought (73); 2) from chapter 3, "The Indirect Language," in *The Prose of the World* on how those who share an era in time share a problem-set, with entangled thoughts (94); 3) from "Eye and Mind" on how Cézanne's "Mont Sainte-Victoire" paintings blur categories of visible and invisible (359-60); and 4) from the chapter "The Intertwining—The Chiasm" in *The Visible and the Invisible* on reversibilities which are the ultimate truth: reversibilities of the seeing and the visible, and of speech and what it signifies (154, 155).

The philosopher could have used "interference" for such occasions, because he found this term in the classic discourse of quantum theory, a subject well known to him and also a topic of ten pages in the 1950s lectures on nature. But he did not use the term. I am using it in order to make the relationships more explicit, and because it calls attention to a structure of thought with a dramatic metaphor, one that is capable of shaking out implications from the elements within his phenomenology that are friendly to the subtle interference of literary reading,

I find more than twenty such passages, in work between 1945-1961, and I flag these because they show a habit of thinking typical of him and in the process of development. These moments in the writings occur in several different contexts—for instance, perceptual, painterly, linguistic, ethical, historical, political. What they have in common is playing off forces against one another, basically oppositions. However, up front it is essential to emphasize that these moments do not have in common any belief that one side wins out or one side is Derrida-like masked (through cultural connivance) in its priority. A stoppage of the ongoing contention, or to have victory of one force over another, is to have alternation, obvious progress, but these bad effects are only synonyms of secret stasis, the arrest of a process and a relation, the arrest of thought. Rather, like those wild thistles in the poem by Ted Hughes, the opposed states keep coming back to fight it out over the same patch of earth. Gestalt-like, they are figures on the ground of each other.

Why is this phenomenologist increasingly drawn to this kind of relationship within (not between) separate sectors such as concepts, things, words, persons, political parties, and eras? I suggest three reasons: 1) Increasingly in his extensive post-1945 reading in the natural sciences, psychology, and the history of philosophy, partly determined by teaching assignments, he is coming to believe that this kind of relationship is the primordial structure of the created universe and that this unfinalizable and constructive contention comprises the way humAnimals and things relate to each other on Earth and in time. 2) In this 1940s-50s moment, two assignments are advancing to the front of his work, as he seeks definitions that will advance his kind of thinking within the professional discipline: the dialectic and the ideas of quantum physics. 3) During this whole period he is still concerned to answer attacks from classical historians of philosophy who wish to impugn philosophies of perception and who wish to lever against phenomenology the knowledge-claims of the natural sciences.[3] That is, he knows this reproach concerning science, or what he sometimes calls scientism, is a guise for old-style Cartesian, French-flavored rationalism. He needs a compelling mode of thought, to lead the natural sciences to admit that perception and reason are compatible, part of each other inseparably

---

[3] See Joseph Rouse, "Merleau-Ponty's Existential Conception of Science,", where he concludes: "Rationality is not a problem to be solved. . . . The rationality of science, like all rationality, is contingent. It is to be continually achieved, rather than secured once and for all" (288).

and positively, with no hidden or admitted priority of essence. Such a philosophy of science, aporetic, is a competition of states that will refuse to choose between sensation and thought, each be moved by and entangled with the other, blur all our categories, and be two aspects of the reversibility that is the ultimate truth.

Structures of relation: The dialectic and (not *versus*) quantum superposition[4]

More than most philosophers, Merleau-Ponty thinks with and through metaphor, the figure that puts two in one, making connections between improbably related categories. In rhetoric, in literary thinking, and in actual intellectual work in almost all fields except maybe music, the metaphor is after all the prime trope of relation. The metaphor can be a punctual, exploding knot of complexity at turning points of the line, stanza, and paragraph, where meaning is conveyed through image and, as such, it seems to stand out against the propulsive forward movement of the sentences and their temporal-sequential stringing. But, as with the two types of thinking to be considered in this chapter, there can also be constitutive metaphors that direct the whole text or the whole plan of thought.

The metaphor-for-thinking most formative, and challenging, for Merleau-Ponty is The Dialectic. In philosophy in the West, this special focus is one of a small set of central problems, not only because of the proliferation of logical pathways it opens, but largely because of Marx's historicizing use of it to foresee the ruin of bourgeois capitalism and the revolution that will bring in the proletariat as a new ruling class. Merleau-Ponty reassesses both the logical and the political implications of this mode of thought in about twenty mostly separate pages of *Phenomenology of Perception*; in pages and paragraphs in many of his essays; his political studies *Humanism and Terror*, a late-1940s book mostly about political violence in a novel by Arthur Koestler;

---

[4] In this section, I shall rely more than usual on experts in several fields outside my own field of literature, other than Merleau-Ponty himself, whom I am taking as my helpers, so I wish to post their names here. Claude Lefort, "La politique et la pensée de la politique," chapter 3 of *Sur une colonne absente*; Fredric Jameson in *Valences of the Dialectic* (2014) and, also, brilliantly useful, Jameson's *The Hegel Variations: On the Phenomenology of Spirit* (2017); Michael Gardiner, "'A Very Understandable Horror of Dialectics': Bakthtin and Marxist Phenomenology" (2000); Karen Barad, *Meeting the Universe Halfway: Quantum Physics and the Entanglement of Matter and Meaning* (2007); Philip Ball, *Beyond Weird: Why Everything You Thought You Knew About Quantum Physics is Different* (2018). I have quoted in the Introduction, though not here, the excellent study by Charis Anastopoulos, *Particle or Wave* (2008).

In addition to Lefort's and Gardiner's superb chapters, I have found useful (on Merleau-Ponty's non-communist Marxist politics) the chapter by Lydia Goehr, "Understanding the Engaged Philosopher: On Politics, Philosophy, and Art" in *The Cambridge Companion to Merleau-Ponty* (2005).

as well as his mid-1950s *Adventures of the Dialectic,* on historical theories of Weber, Lukács, Trotsky, and others.

Elaborated metaphors of opposition are frequent in the history of philosophy, from Plato's developing, dialogic reveal of deeper and more complex positions as Socrates teaches his partners in debate to David Hume on reason and Immanuel Kant on Hume and Hegel on Kant, and Marx's transformation of the Hegelian dialectic. Each later figure gives a strong critique of the earlier ones. There is an implicit critique in Merleau-Ponty's title *Phenomenology of Perception* because Hegel earlier wrote *Phenomenology of Spirit* with many more openings to self-satisfied rationalism and soul-believing idealism than an up-to-date modern thinker of, and on, the embodied mind can accept.

Still, Merleau-Ponty stuck with Hegel and kept updating and modifying the dialectic for his whole life, probably in part because of the example of his senior contemporary, Jean Hyppolite, most influential of French Hegelians. Between Hegel and Merleau-Ponty comes Husserl, whose oppositional search of appearance, in the reduction, both accepts and revises The Dialectic in Hegel. This is another reason for us now, to keep exploring structures of opposition, with and beyond Hegel, in a writer who views reality as a grand reconciliation of forces and faculties. *Ineinander* is a reply to Hegel from within the German tradition, via Edmund Husserl and Jean Hyppolite to a French phenomenologist.

Standard expositions of the dialectic emphasize a method of philosophical argument that involves a contradictory process between two sides: a back-and-forth of debate leading a progression of positions. Hegel thought that reason in itself creates contradictions, and that the method that confronts the two sides must result in and from a speculative mode of thinking. For him there were three moments: the moment of Understanding, a phase of fixity when all is stable between the sides-to-be-defined; the dialectical moment of Confrontation, thus of instability, where what is fixed passes into its opposite—that is the process marked by the German verb *aufheben*, or self-sublation, which involves both sides both canceling and preserving themselves; the third moment is the Speculative Moment, where we grasp the unified result of this process of dissolution-transition. We may say with Hegel, "must result in," because there is a logical necessity in the process, an earlier state self-sublated into a later and more comprehensive-universal state.

Other places in Hegel have him speaking of the triadic example as Being-Nothing-Becoming, and later thinkers who took over the dialectic, including the cruder of the Marxist dialectical materialists, called it Thesis-Antithesis-Synthesis. As Jameson shows in *Valences of the Dalectic*, dialectics is, in the nineteenth century soon generalized from the Dialectic, and there is still today an ongoing serious attempt to raise dialectics to the level of a genuine science, along with a vast contradictory array of partial and biased interpretations. Because this seems to be the case, it is useful to anchor ourselves in Hegel's own faith that reason, through dialectics, means not only logic but everything in general, the principle (he said) of all natural and spiritual life, and that rationality is not only in our heads (as Kant said), but it is in both us and the world itself. That principle is the link through to Merleau-Ponty and a phenomenology of perception, because with him dialectical reason is already within things in the world.

Does everyone find what they themselves want in Hegel? Which Hegel is the believable Hegel for Merleau-Ponty? Jameson, early in *Valences*, notes that Hegel "uses words like 'dialectical,' 'truth,' 'rational,' 'reason' sparingly," in order to avoid the errors and illusions of that first moment in the process, namely, the Understanding. The inevitable errors are "the baleful effects of *Verstand*, of 'Understanding,' an external and spatial picture thinking (*Vorstellung*) it is tempting to identify with the more modern (although still no doubt distantly Hegelian) term 'reification.' *Verstand* is reified, reifying thinking; its domain is [the] real world of Being, of physical objects . . ." (Jameson 81-82). Because of trouble at the very start of the dialectic, namely, the challenges of *Verstand*, something Jameson says elsewhere seems pertinent: "not many people are capable of thinking dialectically all the time" (279). Jameson has in mind the select group of those who can do this all the time, including the Hegelian heroes of his book: Marx, Lenin, Georg Lukács, Jean-Paul Sartre, Jacques Derrida, Paul Ricoeur—this last, worth over a hundred pages, a major interpreter and continuator of Husserl, who became a phenomenological commentator on the novel.

Now add Merleau-Ponty, who was also capable of thinking dialectically all the time, and he, like Hegel-made-more-explicit (through Jameson), worried about reified thinking. This concern is Michael Gardiner's point: "there are two major strains in modern dialectical thought—the logical and objectivistic on the one hand, and the corporeal, intersubjective and 'dialogical' on the other—and . . . theorists like Merleau-Ponty have been concerned to deflect Marxist thinking away from the former towards the latter" (121). Gardiner's argument is that in this preference for the original dialogism of Plato, as a way of defining practices of opposition, Merleau-Ponty's thinking "parallels Bakhtin's own theoretical trajectory" (when Bakhtin criticized dialectics, he was against what it had become, dialectical materialism, in 1930s Russia). Bakhtin's trajectory involves a dialogism that is multi-voiced, endless, and unscripted, a clash of unmerged minds, quintessentially social because occurring between living-spoken (or virtual-written) voices of interlocutors. (In Bakhtin, there can be no utterance without a subject behind it, no voice without a person behind it, who speaks for a spatial and a class position.) Merleau-Ponty's trajectory resonates with other Western versions of the Marxist dialectic, concerned, Gardiner argues, "to return dialectics, and hence the Marxist tradition in its entirety, to its Socratic, dialogical roots, by placing the phenomenon of language at the centre of philosophical inquiry. . ." (128). Thus, the French philosopher is in agreement with the Russian theorist of communication that dialectics was born of dialogue—and that literature is the treasury and condensation of dialogue, product of personalities in conflict, irresolution, difference, misunderstanding, suspicion, implicit knowledge, unfinalizability, and, we shall see, constructive interference.[5]

Merleau-Ponty rejects bad dialectic and the old logic and supports a recognition of Being or what comes into being through good dialectic, as bound wholes. This kind of thinking, "hyperdialectic" in the philosopher's own neologism (*VI* 94), takes as its mission the search for arguments, terms, and images that will disallow the separation of thinking and perceiving. This kind of thinking by bound wholes—the idea that thinking and perceiving can never be separate but are really bound wholes that are an intertwined unit—derives from the brutal primordial fact of the embodied mind. The old logic in philosophy and the natural sciences has resisted, and still resists, this fact, so it will now be convinced to find another relation to perception than its rule by the rational mind.

Merleau-Ponty stayed with the dialectic and then supercharged it with the idea of hyperdialectic, because he was preoccupied with the mental and logical phenomena of contradiction. He had a professional need to develop figures of opposition, especially those that held the conflict in suspension. This need is evident in *Signes*, his collection of long representative essays published in Paris in 1960. To track, in it, the references to "The Dialectic" is to encounter a frame of mind, not a mere obsession. The English translation *Signs* in 1964 has in its Index thirty-four page references (including a few from the Translator's Preface) on such topics as "of the body and the world," "of carnal intersubjectivity and logical objectivity," "as the phenomenon of expression," and "of synchrony and diachrony." However, we ourselves would not be on the side of the good dialectic if we did not admit to a doubt that is not a critique: what if the philosopher stayed with the dialectic, exemplified it, and refined it, because it had limitations that needed to be sublated—that is, surpassed?

A few remarks that Merleau-Ponty made in passing showed him speculating about reading Husserl's mind, projecting what the German might have written had he lived and had further thoughts. Plainly, he knew that others would do this with him, and it is immensely sad that what he left unpublished at his death was both promising and enigmatic. But such projection beyond the evidence would be in the nature of an extension and a completion. That would be a normal activity in those (like him with Husserl and us with him) who came after the founder of a school and had their own body, era, formation, nation, and sector within the method in which to be creative. The projecting might turn out to be, also, a correcting, a deflecting, a making-explicit.

---

[5] Selected for range of sources, variety of topic between political and perceptual, and style of exposition, here are passages that capture Merleau-Ponty as he is thinking dialectically: 1) from chapter 3, "The Indirect Language," *The Prose of the World* (85-86); 2) from "Socrates," *In Praise of Philosophy and Other Essays* (38-39); 3) from the opening and closing pages of the Epilogue to *Adventures of the Dialectic* (204-05, 233); 4) from chapter 3, "Interrogation and Dialectic," *The Visible and the Invisible* (94).

What follows here is consciously going beyond the written evidence to be found in the small pandemic library to which I am restricted, because to my knowledge, while Merleau-Ponty knew quantum theory, he never took the final step into it, as a development beyond the dialectic to quantum superposition. No matter; going one step beyond, in order to further define his special turn within phenomenology of perception, matches his style. The reader will remember: my purpose is to make his ideas explicit, and this task must involve speculation, supposition, and also—maybe—avoidance, mistake, and misunderstanding.

Because we are going beyond the evidence, this effort can be more brief than the exposé on the dialectic. However, *since constructive interference includes everything we have said about the dialectic*, with no loss, the argument is for a more comprehensive kind of thinking. Bohr's explanation of quantum physics will encompass and subsume Hegel's logical-temporal *moments* of contention.

Once we are on the quantum far side of the back-and-forth method of philosophical argument, we can imagine what Merleau-Ponty would have found lacking in Hegel. 1) The dialectic requires a beginning move, the *Verstand*, so, in order to start, we must cut into the process and must assume something limited that will need to be brought up to more capacious Understanding, which, by the time that has happened, is no longer moment number one. 2) The dialectic requires two contending sides, and one of those will take over; thus, dialectics requires alternation of the original states or entities; there is in dialectics the lingering sense that, yes, dialectic is a process of enquiry, but nonetheless one of the states is flawed from the start, unequal, so is it a genuine contention? Merleau-Ponty himself noted this predicament in "Working Notes" to *The Visible and the Invisible*: "not only ... the two viewpoints as *alternates*[,] but the two viewpoints *together*" (3). The dialectic requires that the triadic process of enquiry result in something like progress [in moral standing, in social class, in economic system], so there may be in its interior essence a whiff of triumphalism; in Marx, it may have been a neutral necessary process, but in Marxists this attitude sometimes meant a too-hopeful way of doing history—see, for example, the struggles on the left in 1950s France over the meaning of revolution, of violence, and of the role of the CP (4). In the third Hegelian *moment* we have completion, which is a mediation, and to get to this position the contradictory states have been each simultaneously destroyed and conserved. (It is easy to imagine Merleau-Ponty approving the positive indeterminacy of this one feature of the dialectic.) Certainly, the third moment is the least well-defined feature in Hegel's explanations and raises questions such as: What is it like to be both destroyed and kept whole? What are the stages and results of such a process? Examples?

In Physics, quantum theory has its own internal debates, inconsistencies, counter-intuitive phenomena, and (to outsiders to the mystery) bizarre technical terms, but quantum theory avoids all the limitations of the dialectic. Except for the destroyed-conserved thesis just mentioned, the wave-particle duality offers an entirely different take on how two entities may be in a relation of contradictory contention. It does so from within the fortress of natural science, which Merleau-Ponty had had ranged against him from his questioners at his "The Primacy of Perception" session: science as standing for rational thought, science as his massive 1940s-50s reading project to make himself ready to face the issue with up-to-date information on how natural science describes and uses perception.

The lectures eventually published as *La Nature*, from 1956-1958 at Collège de France, show him processing work in several fields and languages, not only reading but judging, resisting, synthesizing, partly in order to place himself as an equal on the issues: "The concern of the philosopher is to see; that of the scientist is to find a foothold. His thinking is directed by the concern not of seeing, but of intervening. ... The philosopher must see behind the back of the physicist what the physicist himself does not see" (*Nature* 86-87). He is ready to admit that the new natural science is massively different in intent, sophistication, and thinking on perception, and in the relevant ten pages on classical and modern physics, he begins by stating that quantum mechanics "has shaken up our fundamental categories" (88). Immediately he asks, honestly, "What can one say, in a serious way, when one lacks technical competence?" (89). But following this question he has found much to say in pages dense with a range of citations, competent summary of all the names and numbers (for instance, Laplace, de Broglie, Einstein, Bohr, von Neumann, Heisenberg), and a philosopher's last-paragraph willingness to admit that modern physics "destroys certain prejudices ... [,] provokes philosophy, pushes it to think valid concepts in the situation that is its own" (100). Among the topics he covers are the failure of the wave-based theory of light, the particle-based theory of light, effects complementary but mutually exclusive, probabilist indeterminism, Heisenberg's relation of uncertainty, the effort toward a new logic with families of trajectories of photons, the measuring apparatus as prolongation of our senses, the role of the observer—and the topic closest to himself—how "the dualilty of the body and the field evokes the duality of the perceptual process" (97). For him, the movement from classical to modern physics is a provocation to philosophy, allowing, as he says at the last here, a retrieval of the perceived world, that anterior idealizations had made us forget.

Quantum physics describes the smallest things in the universe—subatomic entities upon which depend all we are and do. The universe is full, a plenum with no vast holes between the stars, no little vacancies at any level, micro to macro. The Theory of General Relativity, begun by Albert Einstein in 1905, approaches entities macroscopic; the Theory of Quantum Mechanics, born around 1900 and brought to best first expression in the 1920s, approaches entities microscopic.[6] The

---

[6] It is worth noting that Merleau-Ponty, who focused on wave-particle entities in his account in *Nature*, had one sharp-worded encounter with Einstein on entities macroscopic: see "Einstein and the Crisis of Reason" in *Signs*. In that short essay, following and developing Henri Bergson's critique, Merleau-Ponty speaks of Einstein as the extreme limit of classical science's assumption that the world

standard account says that quantum objects can be both waves and particles (wave-particle duality); that they can be in more than one place at once (superposition); that you cannot simultaneously know exactly two properties of a quantum object (Heisenberg's uncertainty principle); that quantum objects can affect one another instantly over huge distances (entanglement, which Erwin Schrödinger called *the* characteristic of quantum mechanics); and, that you cannot measure anything without disturbing it (so the human observer cannot be excluded from the theory). In his feisty book for informed beginners, helping us to get *Beyond Weird*, Philip Ball writes: "Yet quantum mechanics says none of these things. . . . All the claims above are nothing but *interpretations* laid on top of the theory" (Ball 11). But, of course, we who need language and metaphors traffic in the currency of interpretations and so must physicists and historians and philosophers of science who will explain themselves to others, like Schrödinger just quoted. Ball's whole book, Karen Barad's whole book, and this section of this chapter are what Ball in passing calls metaphors for the mathematics.

One leading consequence of the mathematical rules of quantum mechanics is quantum interference. This concept is often illustrated with the double-slit experiment that involves firing a coherent light source, such as a laser beam, into a plate pierced by two parallel slits, and the light passing through is observed on a screen behind the plate; and, then, light and dark bands appear on the screen, a result not expected in classical physics. The light is absorbed by the screen as discrete points, as individual particles rather than waves. Each detected particle passes through one slit, as would a classical particle, and not through both slits as would a wave. Philip Ball explains, "a quantum state, as defined by a wavefunction, encodes the expected outcomes of measurements of specific observable properties . . . This 'two (or more) states at once' is called a superposition" (62). He further notes that the e-slit experiment "exploits a characteristic phenomenon of waves called diffraction, which is a consequence of how waves interfere" (65-66). That is, when peaks and troughs are not in step: "For two interfering light waves, constructive interference will increase the brightness whereas destructive interference will produce darkness" (66). Leaping ahead to the end of Ball's opinionated summary, he says that what he has described "leaves us with a strange hybrid theory, peppered with types of behavior that do not seem to quite make sense: superposition, non-locality, contextuality. . . . Increasingly, it looks more logical to frame quantum mechanics as a set of rules about *information*"

---

is rational, with reference to the paradox of multiple times, each linked to the observer's standpoint. "The physicist wrongly attributes to Paul the image Peter forms of Paul's time. . . . [T]his lived time, Einstein said, had no jurisdiction beyond what each of us sees, and did not authorize extending our intuitive idea of simultaneity to the whole world" (*S* 188-89). It is a crisis of reason that the physicist will not accept the philosopher's time; phenomenology comes to correct the physicist's reason, in order to reinvigorate reason.

(308). Increasingly, such a frame seems friendly to an argument that must consider the relation between states more broadly defined, finding sophistications and crossovers between physics, philosophy, and literature. Interference, now on the way to becoming a metaphor, will be a multidisciplinary set of rules about perceiving, thinking, writing, and, especially, reading information.

In another phase of quantum thinking, interference is a prime expression of kinetic energy: measurement of momentum, tracking of trajectories—if possible. In the standard account, no matter how a quantum particle is prepared, it is impossible to get a precise prediction for measurement of its position and also for its momentum. That uncertainty principle, formulated for physics, might yet be a workable metaphor for the painterly and writerly arts, as indeed it has been in Gestalt psychology's Law of Prägnanz and figure-ground ambiguity, so well known to Merleau-Ponty. To make the transfer from one discipline to another, here, we need to define *kinetic energy* in terms mental and macro, as movement of mind and deflection of attention. What would reading be if it were reconceived in terms of energies of interference?

Ball has written a trustworthy guide to a difficult topic, packed with illustrations. His supreme virtue is clarity. Barad has written a synoptic study of a scientific topic that coordinates theoretical particle physics with ranges of curricula, including logic studies, fields in humanities and especially literature, feminist thought, and progressive politics. ("[I]f causality is reworked," she says, "then power needs to be rethought" [23].) More innovative than Ball, more willing to make big claims, her supreme virtue is daring inclusivity. Ball's study is personal through clever foreknowledge of what readers from outside natural sciences need to know, and how they take in information. Barad's study is personal in her large intention to bring science into a wider universe of thought by means of lengthy accurate explanations of quantum mechanics. She moves from that basis to get to a five-hundred-page linkup of matter and meaning, science and humanities, scholarship and politics.

The coordination and the linkup occur at a level high and believable. In *Meeting the Universe Halfway*, science meets non-science halfway and the book has been well received, both by commentators in science studies and on the other side of the curriculum. This work is unusual as a contribution to science studies, because of Barad's resources of reach to thinking outside physics, including several substantial references to Merleau-Ponty and the phenomenology of perception. As her book is a study that obsessively foregrounds the phenomenon of interference, it is also inevitably and brilliantly a study about perception and its discontents, as theories inform perception—and perception helps organize information into the building of theories. In contemporary writing, Barad is the thinker who has the most extensive and compelling elaboration of the figure of interference. Her first pages on "Entangled Beginnings" show an intent that we now adopt as ours in a more modest repurposing of the relation of interference:

I am not interested in drawing analogies between particles and people, the micro and the macro, the scientific and the social, nature and culture; rather, I am interested in understanding the epistemological and ontological issues that quantum physics forces us to confront, such as the conditions for the possibility of objectivity, the nature of measurement, the nature of nature and meaning making, and the relationship between discursive practices and the material world. (24)

The features of Barad's overall argument that can foreshadow and help our own are her opening scene on a literary work, Michael Frayn's play *Copenhagen*, which dramatizes the differing approaches to quantum subject matter of Bohr (he of complementarity) and Heisenberg (he of uncertainty). She considers why Heisenberg went to see Bohr in 1941; she is severely critical of the way the play presents their discussions on the theory of knowledge. Most important from my perspective, she considers the constitutive metaphor of interference, here specified as the optical phenomenon of *diffraction*, which describes the way waves combine when they overlap and spread out when they hit an obstruction. Hers, she says, is a diffractive methodological approach, one different from the other optics of sameness-making *reflection*, because "diffraction attends to patterns of difference" (29). Barad's literary, philosophical, and scientific purpose is fully delivered in her chapter 4, where she focuses on the value of Niels Bohr's epistemological framework in his philosophy-physics: like all major scientists, Bohr questions accepted ideas on the nature of how things are represented, but he "also concerns himself with the nature of words, including questions of the nature of meaning, practices for making meaning, the conditions for the possibility of intelligibility, and the co-constitution of an excluded domain, a domain of unintelligibility" (Barad 31-32). Now *diffraction* and *entanglement* have been preserved for a specific science and liberated for wider use.

Chapter 4, with Bohr and ideas of quantum entanglement as the focus, is where Barad best argues for her signature idea of "Agential Realism," a radical reworking of the traditional notion of causality. *Entanglement*—a technical term in quantum physics and in her extension into philosophy—refers to a state of matter where properties become so intertwined that description of the individual parts is no longer possible. The result, if we pursue the patterns of difference and of intertwining all the way, is that the world's radical aliveness comes to light, the nature of relationality is reworked, and other core philosophical concepts (such as space, time, structure, subjectivity) are reconceptualized (33).

And Merleau-Ponty? Barad's working concept, her own and not from physics, is "intra-acting," which means that a word or thought can be both cause and effect, and apparatuses of bodily production are mutually constituting of one another. Without calling it a diffractive methodological approach, that is exactly what Merleau-Ponty was arguing in the 1950s when, in "Working Notes" to *The Visible and the Invisible*, he spoke of openness to the world in perception and language, of "the *Ineinander* of the others in us and of us in them," and of how "the idea of chiasm and *Ineinander* . . . is the idea that every analysis that *disentangles* renders unintellgible. . . . It is a question of creating a new type of intelligibility . . . through the world and Being as they are"

(*VI* 180, 268). It is not ironic but inevitable that natural science, previously his friendly antagonist as the bearer of classical rationality and representation, could be the sophisticated carrier of a new type of intelligibility. Quantum physics, now sweeping up and including the dialectic as an earlier description of relationship, enters to give a new heuristic for thinking. A phenomenology of perception in the embodied mind, it would appear, is now able to do different kinds of work on difference, as a theory of constructive interference.

Verbal art as interference

For at least a century, because quantum mechanics has shaken up our fundamental categories, the emergent discourse has entailed the possibility of a new way of thinking and a non-dualist set of locutions. This set includes *oneandanother*, *oneagainstanother*, *oneinterchangeablewithanother*, and *oneseenasanother*. We can reverse those, too, and start with *another*, but the thing we cannot do (or inquiry stops) is add *onewithoutanother*.

Interference very likely had a long cultural run as a word for personal relationships starting to go wrong, and then quantum mechanics turned it into a metaphor to describe the action of light below the level of visibility, and that useful figure has been a major meaning for a century—despite difficulties of observation, the need for equations and apparatus, and substantive disputes between physicists concerning the behavior (a non-physics metaphor, so I should rather say *movement*) of photons.

Now is the time to bring back from the archives an article by Jan M. Meijer, who explicitly states that "the term interference is borrowed from physics, where it designates the meeting of waves and the results thereof" (319). In 1973 Meijer, then a Russianist at the University of Utrecht, published "Verbal Art As Interference Between a Cognitive and an Aesthetic Structure," as a chapter in a collection of essays called *Structure of Texts and Semiotics of Culture*. Immediately, he says his "main debt is perhaps to formalism," meaning not what Merleau-Ponty means but East-Bloc poetics including writings by Gustav Spet, Osip Brik, Roman Jakobson, Yurii Tynjanov, Jiri Levi, Jan Mukařovský, and Felix Vodička.[7] This reference means Meijer is concerned in a most detailed, technical way with devices in poetry and prose and with the way

---

7 Merleau-Ponty understands "formalism" in the standard Marxist way, as the error of treating concepts in theory and devices in literature as detached from the contradictions of a historical era. I find one short passage on the topic in *The Prose of the World*, where he says: "It is certainly correct to condemn formalism, but it is usually forgotten that formalism's error is not that it overestimates form but that it esteems form so little that it abstracts it from meaning.... The true opposite of formalism is a good theory of speech which distinguishes speech from any technique or device" (89). Meijer has a debt to formalism, but he would not be on show here if he and those like him did not have a sophisticated theory of speech.

devices perform the energies of perception in the work of verbal art. I intend to draw on his ideas of cognitive-aesthetic interference in a later, more literary chapter, but here I wish to re-emphasize that, for my purposes, his title-term "Aesthetic" directly refers to perception, and "perception" is the root-meaning of the word in the original Greek. This reference is the line through to Merleau-Ponty, because Meijer's definition of interference, out of the deep well of the era of structuralism and semiotics, shows how texts exhibit energies of attention, in the words themselves and also in the minds of readers. Interference of thinking and perceiving is what energizes writing and reading. Though he did not explicitly make this statement, Merleau-Ponty knew the meanings behind it. Jan M. Meijer after 50 years helps me to say it explicitly, and (in pages to come) with a sufficient set of Merleau-Pontian terms.

In a long essay, Meijer groups his points into numbered sections, short or long as needed. 1) Verbal art is distinguished by the character of its material, language, that "has a structure of its own" which must be reckoned with. 2) This linguistic structure will never be identical to the structure of the work, as the art-structure is rounded-off from its milieu: "the elements of the work of art enter into much closer and stronger relations" than an utterance in natural language (313-14). 3) A structuralist approach does not render a positive or a negative judgment of a literary work. 4) Cognition and beauty: "the basic cognitive structure does not really need the aesthetic structure" and "there is no one-way dependence upon the other"; since each can influence the other, we conclude that "the two structures interfere with each other" (315-16). Any alternative structure would contain less. Irregularities are not there for their own sake. The notion that poetic speech is abnormal speech "which certainly had a heuristic function in its day, seems to have outlived its usefulness now" (316). 5) There is a total structure that encompasses both the aesthetic and the cognitive structure; neither of these is the total structure; no element of the work of art "remains outside either of them," but this quality does not mean these two structures are equally represented in a fifty-fifty manner (but "0-100 and 100-0 are never reached)" (318). 6) "Once we start rhyming, we can go on and on. It is a structural principle that puts an end to the process" (318). 7) The term interference is "borrowed from physics" (318). Once we grasp a principle of aesthetic structure, like rhyme, we expect continuation, so as in the physics of waves, "structural principles are dynamic forces" (319). Another point of contact with physics is movement toward an end from which the waves rebound: "A most important condition for a work of art is that it have an end" toward which author and reader feel their way. Until the end, we get a "continuous stream of positive and negative signals" on the constraints of the developing structure (319).

That covers the first seven of thirty-one sections: they offer enough to justify a claim that structures of interference, cognitive and aesthetic, take a physics of energy into an account of energies of anticipation and resolution in works of verbal art. Meijer goes on, with the completion-tendency of his structural premises, to fill in some needed points: he offers something promising for how we might read poems and novels with his method. Works of art, he goes on to say, have hierarchical orders, but the hierarchies are not fixed: they differ from work to work. Structural principles that can go on indefinitely are always and only the aesthetic ones, so they need to be interfered with to stop. The reverse is not true: "Cognitive principles can operate without the interference of aesthetic principles" (322). The best strategy would be to replace the opposition *normal vs. abnormal speech* with an interference between a free cognitive structure and a cognitive structure in interference with an aesthetic structure. Interference of structural principles creates dynamism, from reader's expectations: "a tension that propels the work onward and takes the reader along." In a fully realized work of art, the aesthetic structure "tries to reduce the cognitive structure to matter, and vice versa " (327). Resilience in both structures makes this result impossible, so in the realized work, "neither structure is reduced to zero" (326). Finally, "The dynamism . . . is the most important aspect of interference. There is interference at each point, but up to the end there is always energy left to activate the next interference and counteract the inertia of the structural elements. Only at the end do we find that everything has its place" (333). From Meijer, one implication for the practice of quoting examples would be to quote only whole texts of poems, and with the novel, to relate whatever you do quote to the actual ending.

To connect back to Merleau-Ponty, we notice that in Meijer's same 1960s-70s moment Barbara Herrnstein Smith published *Poetic Closure* (1968), a book whose claims about endings are identical to Meijer's about the dynamism of expectations—as these meet the rounding-off of no-expectations, which is the poem's end. Herrnstein Smith's book owes a major debt not to formalism or physics, but to the figure-ground and Prägnanz premises of Gestalt psychology, one of the leading formative influences on Merleau-Ponty's phenomenology.

As a minor trial of method, here is a perfect jewel of a poem by Paul Verlaine, "Marine" ("Seascape," 1866):

> L'océan sonore
> Palpite sous l'oeil
> De la lune en deuil
> Et palpite encore,
>
> Tandis qu'un éclair
> Brutal et sinistre
> Fend le ciel de bistre
> D'un long zigzag clair,
>
> Et que chaque lame
> En bonds convulsif
> Le long des récifs
> Va, vient, luit et clame,

Et qu'un firmament,
Où l'ouragon erre,
Rugit le tonnerre
Formidablement.[8]

In Verlaine's collection of beautiful nasty poems, the one before this is titled "Nightmare" ("Cauchemar"), and that previous poem also refers to a hurricane ("ouragon"). That link might help the reader, here, to sense a certain threat. The tone, or speech-act emotional relation to the speaker and the reader, will be beyond conscious control, dramatic, a brain-storm inside a weather disturbance in a wide panorama, dark versus light, regular waves versus roiled waves, coming versus going, and silence shocked into roar. That experience might be the reader's encounter with a first grouping of interferences in perceptual content, but the reader will further note that some of these are alternations and not entangled interactions. What makes the oppositions meaningful as a set is the sequence of "while-while-while" coordinations that convey simultaneous action, even as they need to be revealed across sixteen lines in four ABBA-rhymed quatrains. The poem strives for simultaneity of sight and sound, even as it has to take time, painting in stripes of bistre and zigzag of light, with sound of thunder and changes of the image of the waves, and with movement from surface of water to over-arching sky.

It is a poem of description, in the genre of landscape writing. What is described is a world in chaos, like a roiled, god-cursed Turnerian seascape with waves whipped up in the foreground. But, plainly, that non-human weather-world is an outer sign of a disturbed inward state, so all the elaborate devices of imagery are internally divided: one larger effect of this poem's specific relation of interference. With no self-reference whatever, and with no vantage-point for human viewing, the reader does not know who is registering the visible and the audible seascape or who is speaking other than the world of things. The keynote is instability. What is mysterious in perspective, chaotic in point of view, is pushed further into dehiscence, that phenomenological state of interference, by the superior cohesion of the framing aesthetic structure of rhyme and meter. These devices, boldly obvious and intrusive but seemingly natural to the reader, interfere with sentencing and punctuation. They also interfere with, as

---

[8] *Poèmes saturniens* (Paris: Gallimard, 2010), 30. My thanks to Kenneth Martin for help with the following translation:

The ocean full of sound / Throbs under the eye / Of a moon in mourning / And throbs again, // While a lightning-flash / Brutal and malign / Rips across the black-brown sky / With a long zigzag of light, // And while each wave / With shuddering, leaps / Along various reefs / Comes and goes, gleams and screams, // As in the great sky / Where this hurricane roams/ Thunder roars / Fantastically.

well as prepare, the maximal closure of that five-syllable word that is equal to the last line and hits up against the one only period.

The poem is equal to, that is, entirely overlaps, the sentence that carries it. Verlaine has performed what may seem to be a trick, the poet's trick of knowing how to allocate the lobes of the line within the syntax of the sentence. "Marine" moves across a set of five-syllable lines that are grouped and separated, with each of the separate stanzas defined by rhyme-words that appear every five syllables, each of the two middle stanzas open at either end. Punctuation, or not, of commas either cuts or opens the lines at their ends. The sentence scissors the lines and the lines scissor the sentence. In this context the huge adverb that takes the whole last line is enough of a jolt to be a closural effect, as the rhyme slams home onto the period. A crazy-perception painting exists, fantastically, within a finely calibrated verbal machine. Verlaine's skill with this craft has kept his tiny seascape open for consideration 155 years after he performed it.

At every level, from tone and meaning to formal device, in every chink and turn of every line, "Marine" is an example of interference of verbal art as the interference of the cognitive and the aesthetic structures. The reader processes simultaneously the sentence and the line, *Ineinander*, not one without the other.[9]

Moving toward writing

Perceiving-thinking-writing is the triple in my title. Chapters 1-2 have concerned perceiving, and chapter 3 has thinking. The rest of this essay will head toward literature and writing, though of course my phenomenological assumption has been that first and last the triad is inseparable in experience, circulating in the embodied humAnimal self, and so circular in argument that any beginning is arbitrary.

This book on perception has proved to be the continuation of my earlier book on *The Scissors of Meter*. In *Scissors*, I first discovered and presented Jan M. Meijer, who now, accompanied by my little demonstration with the French poem, goes to insist once again that the energies of interference are the energies of attention in reading. To extend this recognition to phenomenology will be a theme and topic in what is to follow.

However, it is not enough to speculate that Merleau-Ponty's later writings are trending towards a core belief and leading idea about the usefulness, to

---

[9] I have set forth, with many examples, the principle of interference in poetry in *The Scissors of Meter: Grammetrics and Reading* (Ann Arbor, MI: The University of Michigan Press, 1995). In a more recent book, I have analyzed an array of twelve different kinds of texts to show how perception and expectation work together in interference: see chapter 5 of *Animal Perception and Literary Language* (New York: Palgrave Macmillan, 2019).

phenomenology, of the constitutive metaphor of a relation of interference. I want to show that whether or not my speculation is correct, he has invented and defined a set of philosophical terms that exhibit the relation of interference. Whatever these terms do for the cogency and defense of his own system (and I believe they do a very great deal), the terms are helpful to the rest of us in the after-time, in our approach to verbal art. This array of nine terms is one of his major contributions—one so far insufficiently noticed by commentators, though recently a few of these terms have been picked up and used with skill by capable readers.[10]

Modes of Attention:
- movement
- depth
- chiasm
- reversibility
- non-coincidence
- rhythm

Powers of Attention:
- interrogation
- description
- disclosure

For literary study the leading concept is *disclosure*, and what is disclosed is the complex value delivered by movement occurring in a body, which, when perceived, relates inner and outer. Disclosure is revelation, through movement in time and space of the unseen hidden in the seen, the silence that comes before and after articulate speech. Disclosure is the most prominent, effective expression of Merleau-Ponty's big-hearted rationality.

Taken together, these concepts are the distributed team of agents who perform the phenomenological attitude. Within each of them is the structure of interference that is the endless epoché of the natural attitude that is the search of appearance.

---

[10] Some of these terms (notably *depth, disclosure, non-coincidence*) have been redefined for reading and put to use by these persons, whose writings are listed in the Bibliography: Mauro Carbone, Andrew Inkpin, Kelly Oliver, Louise Westling, Jessica Wiskus.

Chapter 4: Recovering the Subject in the Act of Speaking—and Writing

On thinking from and of the body

Western (though not Eastern) philosophy has been unwilling to accept the original constructive interference, which is that the mind happens to be parked in a binocular bipedal front-facing body. Embodied brain—embodied mind—is so well lived-into, employed, understood, entangled, and intertwined that the fact of it is normal to assume, easy to forget. Once the brute fact is lost, it is tempting then to say that the brain that is a mind supervises the body, floats free of it, has reason and does science and goes to heaven without it. Always, since the Pre-Socratic Greeks there have been thinkers who adored, or at least admitted, the body; but, on this topic, the most significant recent shift occurred, a sort of break or breakthrough, with phenomenology—for Husserl and Merleau-Ponty embodied mind is the source of all else in their elaborated, coordinated system of thought.

Emphatically! For phenomenologists, embodied mind is the basis, warrant, and reason for everything they do in philosophy. For them, corporeality is already part of the Logos; the Logos is already part of corporeality.

Our question will now be: Why is perception a nascent Logos, and why take perception into cognition through sentence-structure? The answers begun in this chapter will be further pursued in the next.

The power of the Greek term Logos, as *speech/word/discourse/reason/law* and many other meanings, including *sentence*, is that it conveys a unity between language and thought before they get differentiated—also between literature and philosophy. Accordingly, to answer the question just asked, in this chapter I will bring perceptual content back into the center of literary study, and to do this I will use what I know of literature to collaborate with, interfere with, and perhaps even colonize philosophy. I will take further steps to make explicit Merleau-Ponty's contributions on perception, on the animal and human body as the agent of perceiving and thinking, and on language. Also, I will reveal links back to Herakleitos and Herder on language. Along the way, in reference to his later essays, I will continue my literary style-story of how Merleau-Ponty presents his thought. Now, what he himself thinks of style is part of the story.

Indeed, why cannot style be a great deal more of the story? Throughout, I will give reasons for using the English sentence as a primary unit. The argument will be that the sentence, as shown by my trial with Verlaine's "Marine," performs the cognitive side of Meijer's relation of cognitive-aesthetic interference in verbal art; the sentence is also *within itself* cognitive and aesthetic, so there is a hidden an internal relation of interference. Of course, it complicates things that the word for "sentence" in German, *Satz*, is also the word for the philosophical *proposition* and that in English "sentence" also means a judgment and a prison- term. It complicates things that sentences as units are variable and, for all practical purposes, infinite in structure and, thus, messy and unpredictable as forms. Also, Husserl and Merleau-Ponty do not often discuss sentences and, usually, for them the ideal unit is not a stretch of syntax but an experienced perception. (Still, as they know, one way or another before or after the experience there comes writing; it is entirely phenomenological and makes sense that English and French both put two meanings into the one word: "sense," *to perceive* and *to think*.) For Mikhail Bakhtin, the only believable unit of dialogic discourse is not the sentence but the utterance. Professional linguists do not like to talk about sentences, and Ferdinand de Saussure, who founded the modern discipline, has only three brief mentions of the sentence in his *Course in General Linguistics*.

Nonetheless, even though we ourselves are limited to giving non-technical description, we are advancing the claim that sentences as forms are intelligent, unpredictable, flexible, logical, speculative, emotive, creative, coercive, abrupt or lazy, personal and impersonal, laconic and pompous, sexual, stuffed with little listed things, quizzical and exclamatory, gorgeous, sesquipedialian, dignified, Thoreauvian, or Merleau-Pontian. They will go wherever we go, because they are ours, the possession of humans evolved from animals. They are ours, so why is it we still do not know how to follow where they go? Maybe we need to search that appearance, too.

On perceiving-thinking-writing, previous to phenomenology

Herakleitos said: "Man, who is an organic continuation of the Logos, thinks he can sever that continuity and exist apart from it" (22).[1] From Herakleitos we are fortunate to have the less than two hundred scattered sentences that manage to convey with and through the gaps an entire philosophy-physics-psychology-theology and even, as here, a satirical kind of mind. Herakleitos was one of the first to appreciate the full reach of Logos, a term untranslatable because it was richly overdetermined, indeed the summation of a culture's values. We start with Herakleitos because he insists, ironically, that humans err when they try to exist in their minds separated from their bodily selves or vice versa. Maurice Merleau-Ponty, who wrote "that perception is a nascent *logos*" ("Primacy" 101), uses the term untranslated, though in our alphabet. The weight of his philosophy shows him in the line from Herakleitos (whom he cites

---

[1] Translation by Guy Davenport. All we have of Herakleitos's book *On Nature* is the quotations from it by other ancient writers. That title must influence our reading of what we do have. Later I will speak of the relation of sentences and propositions in language and logic: here in Herakleitos, we already have strong evidence that bare detached contextless sentences, with no certain sequence, can become a full philosophy, coherent and magnificent.

more often than Aristotle), though the Greek is criticizing individuals for going off on trivial private searches while the French Phenomenologist is thinking about modern scientists who start their work by hiving off dignity-conferring reason from ordinary perception.[2] Both are animalists in the definition I have employed in this essay, because both accept the organic continuation of the Logos, or in the current phrasing, the embodied mind, and that continuation includes the links, both ways, between sensing and thinking. Both thinkers also address themselves to the way human beings inadvertently and also deliberately forget, obscure, deny, block, and badmouth the corporeality of perceiving-thinking-writing.

These thinkers, however, do not map exactly one on the other. While Merleau-Ponty would never imagine denying the Greek philosopher's premise that the senses unaided by reason are untrustworthy, he made it his life's work to add something Herakleitos (and many thinkers since) would never say: that reason unaided by the senses is impossible. For him in the tradition of his discipline, and for those in his line, a question emerges: how do we get from sense to reason, from reason to sense, from perception to writing, from a writer's coding of perception to a reader's decoding? How do we get from phenomenalism to phenomenology?

*

"The reverse side of language" is Merleau-Ponty's technical term from the "Working Notes" at the end of *The Visible and the Invisible*. The phrase is meant to convey that speaking-writing as bodily operations are exactly similar to things and persons in the world, whose unseen sides are imagined or projected—or the things or persons move, or we do, and we see round the back. Like perception itself, speaking and writing are also covering their tracks in the midst of experience: we do not *decide* to see or hear, and we do not *think* "now I will begin to talk" when we begin to talk. For this kind of philosophy, the reverse side of language is the silence that comes before and after the event of speaking or hearing or writing or reading.

So the reverse side of language is actually the layer of Being that gives us the senses through our skin and the openings in our animal bodies. Creatural-corporeal. In this sense, the reverse side of language is the Pleistocene as it evolves into and remains a resource in our embodied minds. The reverse side of language is *constituted by* the bodily perceptions, which stock and organize its storehouse, and which we repress helplessly or deliberately in order to act efficiently within our *Umwelt* or surround. We

---

2 Merleau-Ponty in his most relevant citation of Herakleitos refers to speech, topic of the present chapter: he explains that works of visual art in the form of the "bleached, broken" statues of Olympia promote "a fraudulent myth about Greece" ("Indirect Language" 279). The statues

> cannot resist time as a manuscript, even incomplete, torn, and almost illegible, does. Heraclitus's writing casts light for us as no broken statues can, because the meaning in it is deposited and concentrated in another way than theirs is in them, and because nothing equals the ductility of speech. In short, language speaks, and the voices of painting are the voices of silence. (279)

do this for survival, but also we repress our bodily perceptions to separate ourselves from our animal origins: we cheer ourselves up as top predator.[3]

Johann Gottfried Herder observed: "While still an animal, man already has language."[4] This first sentence of his "Essay on the Origin of Language" (1770), with *still* versus *already*, immediately involves him in the vicious circularity that while still an animal man had already taken the step that certified man's humanity as no longer animal. If Herder had known about the theory of evolution, or imagined the hybrid concept humAnimal, he would not have fallen into this trap of logic. So let us try revising this to say: "While still an animal in evolutionary terms, every day in 2024 the human being carries animalist perception all the way through to cognition, thence to language." But let's not stop there, because Herder in his charming confusion is trying to find a thought for what is impossible to know, the moment (not to be placed in space/time but probably millennia-long) in prehistory when language emerged among hominids and made a difference within the animal. It was brave and innovative to invoke the animal, and indeed this invoking was only possible in an era when materialist historicism had some presence in intellectual circles. Herder was thinking his way toward the hypothesis of evolution, with the concepts at his disposal. From our point of view, he got the logic wrong but the larger argument right, as we can show by reading the essay as a whole, but also by a minor rewriting of our provocative study-text: "While still an animal, man still has language." Since nobody knows about the origin of language, anybody can plausibly fantasize, and Herder told a good story involving screams of pain, imitations of animal cries, and ruling out a divine in favor of an animal origin, a step ahead for progressive anthropology in the Enlightenment.

Herder's internationalism, his ingenious though fanciful examples, and his stylistic flair helped the "Essay on the Origin of Language" win a competition and also

---

[3] *Constituted by* is another philosophical term of Husserl and Merleau-Ponty, referring to the way physical or mental events occur without intentional thought and get normalized by thought later on, through habit. Things, persons, events, relationships, contracts, scientific fields, and governments assume power over us through the act of constitution, and this dynamic is the way things, usually, render us passive. In later writings, Merleau-Ponty proposed to reduce the unconscious agency of constitution and to change the relationship by justifying a change of term—*institution* is stronger and preferable, because we use our freedom to choose to do it. He argues at length for this in *Institution and Passivity* (2010).

[4] For an admirable essay on the phenomenology of language from the 1970s, see Don Idhe, "Singing the World: Language and Perception" (1973). Only in the last generation have humans become intensely aware that some animals like bonobos, gray parrots, dolphins, and elephants have language-like capabilities, theory of mind, ability to grieve, and other skills that had been reserved, previously, to human beings. Our current knowledge of skills in non-human animals is exactly counter to what Herder wanted to show: how human language might have grown out of, or at least has suggestive analogues to, the vocal cries of non-human animals. Herder was anthropocentric, helplessly but also restlessly so.

the attention of the ages, including a mention by Merleau-Ponty (who likes what the "Essay" says about sense-perception) and pride of place as a "hinge figure" in Charles Taylor's study, *The Language Animal* (2016).⁵ Doing the history of the philosophy of language, Taylor wisely looks not behind to inscrutable origins but ahead to Herder's heirs (including Merleau-Ponty) when trying to describe a "more situated understanding of thinking" (16). Taylor finds this, specifically, in Herder's "grasp of holism" in meaning (17) and in Herder's statements about embodied mind as well as the "crux of [his] thesis, that language is constitutive of reflection" (*Besonnenheit*; 9). Though this correction is never stated directly, Taylor's title *The Language Animal* puts right the logic of the essay that starts his survey.

*

Ferdinand de Saussure, paraphrased: A linguistic system is a series of differences of sound combined with a series of differences of ideas; linguistics will have to recognize laws operating universally in language and in a strictly rational manner. As is known, Saussure's main contribution to structural linguistics was the two-tier theory of language as *langue*, the abstract and invisible layer, and *parole* or actual everyday speech. (*Langue* is definitely in the first tier and is the object of study for a modern discipline; *parole* is important as part of the social circuit of a living culture but is unreachable if we wish to recognize universal laws.) Immediately after stating that description, we hit one of Saussure's other influential dogmas, the arbitrariness of the sign because, in French, the focus of the rational discipline of linguistics (*langue*) has now become the term that also means "tongue," and what goes on unthinkingly every day in conversations between living people (*parole*) provides the term for "word" since French unlike English has no word for "speech." To an English speaker, the former term has an over-literal under-meaning but contrariwise it makes a metaphorical leap, and the latter term specifies a named unit of language, which ordinary face-to-face speaking blithely overrides in the experience. The result is category errors galore, but who cares, it is French, that is what they say and they know what it means and, by the way, *to mean* in French is *to want to say* (*vouloir dire*). The sign is the organizing concept for linguistic structure, language can be analyzed as a formal system of differential elements, and the problem of *what may be the referent* and the problem of what goes on in practical speech acts that exhibit *parole* are not of concern to linguistic science. Saussure defined his theory through oppositions, most prominently that of *sign* versus *signified*, that is, in language, the *word* versus *the thing the word stands for* in the world, as for instance *dog* versus *the real barking animal*. Other oppositions are language/speech, meaning/value, and synchronic/diachronic, and it might be a plausible thought-experiment to translate all of these

---

5 Merleau-Ponty discusses Herder briefly in *Phenomenology of Perception* 52, 244, 248.

into relations of interference—because difference, say between phonemes in tribe and tripe, is specific and arbitrary and endless.⁶

The later Merleau-Ponty, influenced by Saussure like all his leading contemporaries, most certainly worked both sides of these oppositions and made judgments, and also mistakes, about what they could give to a phenomenology of language.⁷ His book of essays, *Signs*, owes its title to Saussure and puts first the long essay on painting, "Indirect Language and the Voices of Silence," where he begins by summarizing the linguist from Geneva and ends by claiming more for the subject in the act of speaking and writing than Saussure could ever allow. This book has four other essays on the topic of signs, which put forth a full and eloquent phenomenology of language.

In the chapter on "Eye and Mind," I referred to Merleau-Ponty's draft of the "Indirect Language" essay on Malraux, painting, writing, museums, history, and the ideas of expression, coherent deformation, and perception that "already stylizes"— that is, from the middle chapter of *The Prose of the World*, the unpublished part-book started in 1952. The revised and published essay on Malraux and painting-writing sharpens the commentary on Saussure after an eight-year interval, and I wish to comment on this later version.⁸

"Indirect Language and the Voices of Silence" reveals how coherent and serious was his engagement with and his departure from the most advanced language theory in the 1950s. Immediately, in the first sentence, and for two immense paragraphs, Merleau-Ponty cites and summarizes Saussure on how "language is made of differences without terms; or more exactly, ... the terms of language are engendered only by the differences which appear among them" ("ILVS" 241). The diacritical sense of signs calls forth a question about how much a hearer would need to know of what a speaker meant: "one would have to know [the speaker's whole] language in order to learn it. But the objection is of the same kind as Zeno's paradoxes; and as they are overcome by the act of movement, it is overcome by the use of speech" (241). The

---

6 Around 1910 these ideas (no influential or causal relation implied!) were invented: Saussurian difference, Husserlian reduction that both abolishes and conserves, and wave-particle interference.
7 Andrew Inkpin has a fully sourced, detailed survey of Merleau-Ponty's relationship to Saussure's philosophy of language, admirable on the affinities, borrowings, reservations, and misunderstandings. Merleau-Ponty, he says, "assimilated Saussurean ideas into his general view of language as an expressive behavior of embodied agents... [and especially affords, with Saussure's help, an] account of the disclosive function of linguistic signs." (119). I disagree with Inkpin's argument that Merleau-Ponty "overestimates the importance of creative expression," because I believe the philosopher is using the arts for his own purpose: to show science, including linguistic science, that there exists a fuller, messier, perception-imbricated rationality. See Andrew Inkpin, *Disclosing the World: On the Phenomenology of Language* (2016).
8 For ease of access, and because the 1964 translation of *Signs* omits material on Saussure at the beginning of the essay, I am quoting "Indirect Language and the Voices of Silence" from *The Merleau-Ponty Reader* (2007).

child first speaks phonemes, then words, then phrases, then sentences, begins to learn oppositive principles, and then "the whole of spoken language surrounding the child snaps him up like a whirlwind, tempts him by its internal articulations, and brings him *almost* up to the moment when all the noise begins to mean something" (242). And this is all possible "because the sign is diacritical from the outset, because it is composed and organized in terms of itself": the sign "has an interior and ends up laying claim to a sense" (242). So here where the sign in human language has an interior, we find what we learned about the internal dehiscence of the subject in Husserl, and a structure similar to what we saw elsewhere in Merleau-Ponty, where "the relation of my body to itself . . . makes it the *vinculum* [or link] of the self and things" ("Shadow" 166) And all these relations of reciprocal determinism in language are possible because of the embodied mind, that original relation of interference. Merleau-Ponty has now found the relation of interference at the hidden heart of the utterance.

Soon in the essay, he will give names to this relation, first as *expression*, meaning a unit of language, but much more pertinently meaning the subject's interrogation-expansion of itself and our recovery of the subject in the act of painting, writing, speaking; and, then, by essay's end, *expression* gets excited development with the name of *speech*: "nothing equals the ductility of speech" ("ILVS" 279), the essence of language, involving articulate sounds that may be written down and written in such a way that words and sentences imitate speech acts, depositing and concentrating meaning and thus preserving it. Painting is itself a language, and yet the voices of painting are lesser, despite their fabulous abilities to make a coherent deformation of the visible because they are voices of silence. Sometimes Merleau-Ponty calls it a marvel, sometimes a ruse, but the speaking-writing subject can be creative with the received signs—entering the realm of freedom where whatever's rational, constituted, readymade, abstract, and falsely objective is either left behind or swept up into the act. "Indirect Language" ends with a hymn of a sentence on moving obliquely toward the spontaneous source of our freedom, but the effective ending is a quietly substantive revision of Saussure on language. It acknowledges the lateral relation of one sign to another, yes, but philosophy needs more, in the full dialogic social resources of what has been so far set to the side, and that is the *signifié*, that is, *parole*. Saussure had sponsored these concepts, but Merleau-Ponty will now champion them.

> [L]anguage goes beyond itself toward what it signifies. It is of no avail that (as Saussure explains) each word draws its sense from all the others, the fact remains that at the moment it occurs the task of expressing is no longer deferred and referred to other words—it is accomplished, and we understand something. Saussure may show that each act of expression becomes significant only as modulation of a general system of expression and only insofar as it is differentiated from other linguistic gestures. The marvel is that before Saussure we did not know anything about this, and that we forget it again each time we speak—as this very moment, as we speak of Saussure's ideas. This proves that each partial act of expression, as an act common to the whole of a given language, is not limited to expending an expressive power accumulated in the language, but

recreates both the power and the language by making us verify in the obviousness of the given and received sense the power that speaking subjects have of going beyond signs toward their sense. Signs do not simply evoke other signs for us and so on without end, and language is not like a prison we are locked into or a guide we must blindly follow; for at the crossroads of all these linguistic gestures, what they mean to say appears—to which we have been given such total access that it seems to us we no longer need the linguistic gestures to refer to it. ("ILVS" 279-80)

Phenomenology of language is a philosophy of the ductility of speech, and by this term Merleau-Ponty meant what the dictionary says: speech can be stretched, drawn, or hammered thin without breaking; it is not brittle; it is easily molded, plastic, pliant. It is a welcome trait and a potential disaster, marvel and ruse, that speech is easily led, tractable. As is often the case, his metaphors carry his meaning about meaning, but not like a prison or a guide-book's set of rules; rather more like a crossroads. Above all, speech means to say (*vouloir dire*) our creative, recreative power to impregnate sensible being with meaning.

I will say more later about speech as the contrary to whatever is operational, rule-bound, abstract-rational, readymade, constituted, or representational. Here, I would add, concerning Saussure, that Andrew Inkpin has shown in detail the encounter of phenomenology with structural linguistics, with thirteen pages on Saussure that give the final advantage to Merleau-Ponty.[9] He has also compared the Heidegger-Merleau-Ponty language theory to that of Ludwig Wittgenstein, finding that the "phenomenological and semantics approaches" complement each other in a way analogous to interference relations in subatomic physics. (His careful speculative paragraph on this complementarity [Inkpin 289-90] is the only previously published use of the interference-metaphor involving phenomenology that I have seen.) Taking many more factors into account than I have shown, and making allowances for the mistakes both approaches made fifty and more years ago, he is led to a judgment: "[I]n the current context of post-Fregean philosophy of language the semantics approach [Wittgenstein] is of far more limited philosophical importance than is usually assumed— . . . its theoretical ambitions should be reined in just as those of classical physics were in the twentieth century" (290). The semantics approach, here suspect, theorizes a rules-governed, determinate, language-game understanding of language. I find one reference to this positivism of language in Merleau-Ponty's late "Working Notes" on Husserl, where he says: "Husserl takes language seriously, gives it an ontological function, makes that a leaf of Being is carried to it, precisely because he is not enclosed (Wittgenstein) (the British) in the immanence of language, conceived as a thing" (*Husserl at the Limits* 43).[10] So, half a century before Inkpin

---

9 See Inkpin, *Disclosing the World*, especially 129-33 for a direct comparison of Saussure and Merleau-Ponty.
10 Quotations from this work are exact and show the uncorrected status of the "Working Notes."

but without working through the evidences, Merleau-Ponty had himself identified a complementary contrary position in Wittgenstein.

Perceptual content of the English sentence: The trial with Henry James

Soon, to attach this chapter to the *Ineinander*-interference thesis of the previous one, I will give brief definitions of nine terms I am taking from Merleau-Ponty. These terms should help our reading of literary texts—in fact, all kinds of texts. (The *Powers of Attention* are interrogation, description, and disclosure; the *Modes of Attention* are movement, depth, chiasm, reversibility, non-coincidence, and rhythm.) In the next chapter, I will give more lengthy and plausible definitions of these terms, and in the second-next I will analyze, with these very terms, three full poems and a long stretch of a Henry James novel. All nine concepts contain within themselves the principle of interference, so the practical-analytical part of this book will be a little demonstration of the book's leading idea, itself a making-explicit of an unthought in Merleau-Ponty. Here I am taking a tiny part of the same passage from the novel by Henry James, to read a few sentences without the aid of the interference-terms: to read, as the person on the spot and in lieu of my own reader, with a pretend-innocence, in an attempt to work with just what we may presume to have from our own knowledge of English language and literary plotting. Call it a reading for perceptual content in pre-phenomenological frameworks and rhetorics—except let us begin with one thing Merleau-Ponty would himself take from his years of study of Gestalt psychology: Gestalt's master-concept, figure-ground, which will be given form in a story that introduces an agent into a scene. This concept, and other minimal-perceptual gestures, go to show what writers and readers have always known about how perception-in-language handles imaginary space and time and also discloses the moral scheme of a text. This procedure goes to show how much we already know implicitly and tacitly.[11]

With exact spatial sense and careful sequence, Henry James immobilizes Lambert Strether on a raised deck behind a country inn facing the landing stage on a river. Strether is James's chosen character of fine consciousness in *The Ambassadors* (1903). The scene takes place during a weekend idyll, an escape from Paris, when he is alone. It is an impressionist painting in brilliant colors. All that moves is the river. A rowboat appears around the bend of the river, bringing new agents, man and woman, on the scene. They advance toward Strether, who sees the rowing man's back and, obscurely, the woman's face.

---

[11] This will be a reading of and with the natural attitude. In rereading the longer version of the very same scene, later in chapter 7, will come the interference-principle and epoché-analysis of the natural attitude. The main difference, aside from length, will be added help from the nine terms for Modes and Powers of Attention.

> It [the boat] had by this time none the less come much nearer—near enough for Strether to dream the lady in the stern had for some reason taken account of his being there to watch them. *She had remarked on it sharply, yet her companion hadn't turned round; it was in fact almost as if our friend had felt her bid him keep still.* She had taken in something as a result of which their course had wavered, and it continued to waver while they just stood off. This little effect was sudden and rapid, so rapid that Strether's sense of it was separate only for an instant from a sharp start of his own. (emphasis added)[12]

This scene occurs at the end of book 11 of twelve books, where the accidental encounter, entirely shown by several pages of description without dialogue, is the revelation that must end this story. I have set my chosen text for a closer look in italics, for emphasis, and surrounded it with other sentences for a minimal context.

Four sentences. Nine pronouns as substitutions for nouns that are already launched earlier. Two periphrases: "our friend" for Lambert Strether and "the lady," whom we will recognize with a shock is a favored character we already know. Three repeats-for-emphasis of terms of tonality or movement ("nearer—near," "sharply—sharp," "rapid—so rapid"). Six interruptive additions of specific details of how things are happening. Some stereotypical but oddly precise idioms: "our friend"—"just stood off"—"little effect"—"sharp start"—"keep still"—"for some reason." James has the habit of fitting little additional elements into sentences (as in "in fact" / "almost" / "as if") so that long clauses have the effect of seeming jammed with smaller optional chunks. Overall, the effect is of information being parceled out in deliberate tiny sequential bits: we have the watcher's name but neither the rower's nor the lady's, we see the rower's back, advancing nearer, but then "their course had wavered," perhaps on the lady's warning, then it "continued to waver while they just stood off"; then, Strether, after only an instant, got a "sense of it" and took "a sharp start." This little scene is typical in one small way: from first page to last the novel is packed with cognates of "sharp," which function as intensifiers of feeling, and here it is first the lady who "remarked on it sharply" and then Strether has "a sharp start of his own."

These sentences are organic engines of perception. Equally, and in the same space, they are organic engines of cognition. They contain agents in space and time, and they have many methods of conveying placements, ratios, and relationships. They have exquisite and infinitely various modes of linking back from their start, ahead from their end. Internally, punctuation helps as rudders for turning the reader's attention, pausing it, and breaking it. Beyond cap-start and period-end, we know what a sentence is, even though no two are alike. This recognition is because the letters, words, clauses, form-classes of grammar, and syntactical patterns, are familiar Lego blocks of mental construction: any combination of known elements may be constructed or construed, unless the combo breaks rules of making (such as a

---

[12] book 11, section 4 of *The Ambassadors* (1903), here quoted from the 1909 New York Edition, which is now in the public domain (*The Full Text Archive*).

failure of agreement in number or an illogical shift of verb-tense). Recognition of the pattern occurs also because we are continually checking the perceptual content of the sentence against what we have come to know of ourselves, of how time passes, of the physical surround, of the historical context of the sentence-topic, and so on.

Sentences are entirely arbitrary structures that we have stopped and isolated for convenience, so that the contents of our minds, when we take in the new, do not run together like Molly Bloom's famous stream of consciousness at the end of James Joyce's *Ulysses*. (As the greatest maker of sentences—we call that style!—Joyce is also one of the best at contravening sentences—also style!) Merleau-Ponty in all his works, a dazzling stylist himself, has written more than a few but not many sentences about sentences. For him, the percept was the essential unit. Nonetheless, as engines or animals of perception and cognition, sentences do the work of his nascent Logos.

Let us look again at the sentence:

She had remarked on it sharply, yet her companion hadn't turned round; it was in fact almost as if our friend had felt her bid him keep still.

The perception words are *remarked, sharply, turned round, felt her, keep still*; the cognition words are the pronouns for agents, physical proximities, the turn at *yet*, the extension/explanation at *it was in fact*, the careful qualification at *in fact almost as if*, and the complex unscrambling needed to identify the male agent "him" (not Strether, but the rower) in *her bid him*. There is in the reader a tremendous riffling through lexicons to check to see that *bid* is the perfect little present-tense verb for saying that she gave the rower an order.

No perception without cognition, no style without sentences to contain and carry it. Reversibly, the dense logic of the sentence requires this perceptual content as material with which to build its strong subtle frame. To confirm the continuity, *remarked* as a verb and *sharply* as an adverb are perception-terms that operate cognitively, starting in sensing and then moving to feeling and thinking once we know context, once we track back to etymology. What is going on is a double recognition, where those on the river recognize the bank-side viewer's identity a little before he recognizes them, and once this has occurred (helped by Strether's imagining the intention of the woman), both sides know that everything in the moral universe has shifted. Recognition is wordless, instant, a product of the space-time and feeling tone of the whole imagined scene, but we would not know to say that unless we read words, clauses, sentences. Going to story-forms beyond sentences, at the end of this book, I will quote considerably more of the surrounding scene to show how James sets into motion his impressionist painting, digs into it for brutal facts of moral intent, and shapes it toward an ending.

Admittedly, I have taken an arbitrary segment of a barely described larger text, and have read it as an outsider to linguistics and philosophy of language. Admittedly, Merleau-Ponty said nothing about verbal art at this level of close reading; his constant topic was language as a human (and also animal) competence, taking perception and cognition as reciprocal, so my performance in thinking about sentences on the model of perception is just a projection of his outlook and vocabulary. However accurate or useful the trial may be, at least it has established a working phenomenological method for a small segment of verbal art. Perhaps, too, the trial with the sentences has led us to suspect that there is a reversible relation between perception and reason.

Interference as a metaphor for structure of mind

Maurice Merleau-Ponty, well-trained in the history of philosophy, knew that oppositions are necessary to organized thought. He understood that the whole edifice of Hegel's system, profoundly influential both in Franco-German professional philosophy and in Karl Marx's work and his political-intellectual legacy, was built upon a metaphor of forces-in-struggle followed by temporary resolution. He read through Husserl's investigations in logic that preceded by decades the formulating of the reduction and was well aware of how the reduction had come from ideas of conflict and how it proposed a continual and endless beneficial conflict in the suspension of the natural attitude. He was also permanently convinced by early reading in Wertheimer and Gestalt psychology that figure-ground and other Gestalt principles were not just theses but were the actual structure of humAnimal consciousness in the act of perception. In his own late-career refinement of a dialectical philosophy of existence, based on a return to the life-world this side of the objective world, he found but never named a method in which he could be creative in proliferating his own arguments—also, part of the job he took on was to find other writers falling short or going beyond.

Literary scholars have long enjoyed mapping the mind of Samuel Taylor Coleridge as a field of resolved oppositions, and I myself have set out a double-column list of such Coleridgean intellectual conflicts in my 2019 book on animal perception and literary language. Of course, such conflicts are never finally resolved: the choice of how (and whether) to handle them defines the mind in question. When I call Merleau-Ponty's structure of mind in his later writings a structure of interference, I am specifying that the cognitive-perceptual interference is open, indeterminate, intertwined, entangled, and endless, like the subatomic interference of wave-photon from which I take the source of my metaphor. This particular interference has a wide reach of possible topics that are different from Coleridge's topics or those of any other thinker except Husserl, who is his direct mentor and continuing dialogic partner in philosophy.[13]

---

[13] Jacques Derrida's ideas of difference, différance, and aporia are all effects of opposition derived from Hegelian dialectic. Derrida typically and powerfully reads study texts of his admired or doubted writer to find where an opposition seems to be on the level, as, famously, speaking and writing, and then he is able to show that one side of the conflict is covertly privileged. That is to deconstruct the

When I now present the partial list of Merleau-Pontian topics-in-interference beginning with those most general, I wish to offer a warning: these are suggestions, little devices to think with and then pass beyond.

theoretical meaning	*configurational meaning*
constitution	*institution*
objectification	*phenomenology*
the natural sciences	*philosophy*
the dialectic	*interference*
philosophy	*literature*
the natural attitude	*the reduction*
representation	*expression*
things-in-themselves	*other persons*
renaissance perspective	*modern Gestalten*
classical	*modern*
painting as voices of silence	*language that speaks*
well-behaved world	*"a wild-flowering world and mind"*
readymade	*co-created*
cognition/sentence out of interference	*cognition/sentence in interference*

These are not the map of a typical humAnimal mind, but a beginning attempt to show how much is in any mind and how far any mind ranges to imagine relationships: to inner what is outer by means of perceiving-thinking-writing. As a supplement to this list, consider the following terms and phrases that exhibit in themselves a habit and a frame of mind: "compossible"; "every constructed notion of time presupposes our proto-history as carnal beings copresent to a single world"; "configurational"; "simultaneity of things"; "constitute constituting consciousness"; "each one of us pregnant with the others"; "this renewal of the world is also the mind's renewal"; "that jointing and framing of Being which is realized through man" ("Shadow" 180-81). As index of how frequent such writing occurs in this author, these occur in the final three paragraphs of the essay on later Husserl, "The Philosopher and His Shadow," in *Signs*. That tribute-essay concludes in a blaze of interference that is also concurrence.

*

"Perceiving-Thinking-Writing" is the triple in my book's title. Chapters 1-2 have concerned perceiving and chapter 3 thinking. The rest of this study will head toward

---

opposition, and the method can be deployed to expose troubled logics, rhetorics, or politics. The massive deconstruction of human and animal in many studies across his career was the work that set me writing my book on animal perception and carried me through over three hundred pages. Deconstruction is positive and endless. However, to put the terms of the opposition fully and honestly on the level is, for thought, merely corrective; while never stating this idea, deconstruction implies *Aufhebung* or surpassing. Interference is different because it implies continuous recalibration of forces on both sides of the opposition. Derrida: structure of texts; Merleau-Ponty: structure of mind.

literature and writing, though, of course, my phenomenological assumption has been that first and last the triad is inseparable in experience, moving around in the embodied humAnimal self, and so circular in argument that any beginning is arbitrary.

Meijer, accompanied by my little demonstration with the Verlaine poem, goes to suggest that the energies of interference are the energies of attention in reading. This focus on interference/attention will be a theme and topic in what is to follow.

Turning now to the Modes and Powers of Attention, I shall give a preliminary definition of the nine terms I have chosen as representative of the philosopher's thinking. I propose to extend these to literary reading, but first I need to show how they contain within themselves the relation of interference. When, with these nine terms, we recover the roots of our rationality by studying our own habits of attention, we are already within rationality. Working from the particular to the general in a Merleau-Pontian scheme, I find six Modes and three Powers of Attention, where very likely these powers control these modes. The working terms paraphrase their inventor Merleau-Ponty and will be more fully defined in later chapters.

As my telegraphic and preliminary phrasing will suggest, one way or another all nine terms exhibit the interference of cognitive and perceptual structures.

Modes of Attention

1) *Movement*

Interference with: stasis; nescience

Perception as a direction; motricity is an original intentionality; my mobility compensates for, surveys from above, the mobility of things.

2) *Depth*

Interference with: surface; appearance

Depth is pre-eminently the dimension of the hidden, and also the dimension of the simultaneous; it is the experience of the reversibility of dimensions; in depth, things envelop each other, while in breadth and height they are juxtaposed.

3) *Chiasm*

Interference with: the intertwining; a going-straight-ahead, hence an absolute; phrases in parallel with no inversions

A me-other exchange between the perceiving and the perceived; chiasm binds ensembles of obverse and reverse, unified in advance of their being differentiated.

4) *Reversibility*

Interference with: the usual; one-way-street; ahead, as in position, direction; order; agreement

The glove turned inside-out; an opening-out, not a closure; the seer exposes herself as visible and thus exposed to the other person, thrown into the world; as analogue, the reflexivity of literary language.

5) *Non-Coincidence*

Interference with: same period of time, same place in space; causal relation; accord or agreement; coincidence

This process is the shift from monocular to binocular perception; perceptual depth unfolds from experiential space behind this non-coincidence; overlapping or encroachment of my body looked-at and my body looking, my body touched and my body touching.

6) *Rhythm*

Interference with: meter as hyper-regularity; irregularity of beat, accent; stasis, lack of movement; lack of succession; lack of pattern

Change form or place, and you change rhythm; the meaning of a phrase is inseparable from its rhythm or melody; rhythm consisting precisely in what is not heard; the interval between articulated sounds; an ongoing, dynamic process that looks backward and forward; the interval between articulated sounds; "words turning back upon words to disclose what had remained silent between them" (Wiskus 10).

Powers of Attention

1) *Interrogation*

Interference with: the natural attitude; the readymade; the constituted real; ideology

Since world is a wild being, which none of its representations exhaust, philosophy begins as interrogation, or concern for the open-ended as value. Philosophy installs itself at the edge of being, at the joints, where the many entries of the world cross.

2) *Description*

Interference with: the natural attitude; propulsive narrative modes such as dialogue or plotting; the statemental, to the neglect of examples; imprecision

To begin its work, this kind of thinking involves not explaining or analyzing but inspecting and listing; what is described is the things themselves, by trying to return to the world prior to conscious knowledge of it. Perception by description opens the horizons within which all knowledge is established.

3) *Disclosure*

Interference with: the natural attitude; fake news; acceptance of what is constituted; lack of inquisitiveness; keeping-hidden, covering over; ideology

The focus will be on our basic awareness of things, not an intellectual end product. We uproot objective philosophy in order to draw the picture of wild being, through disclosure of unfamiliar perspectives: the invisible behind the visible. Disclosure follows interrogation and description, but once the search has started it will be informed by these powers.

Late essays/notes on recovering the subject in the act of speaking/writing

When he was thinking about Husserl, Merleau-Ponty would defer to the founder of his tradition and would praise his dead and distancing master for his "essential audacity" and for awakening "a wild-flowering world and mind." When, as always, he was thinking along with Husserl, he would first remind himself in his typical antithetical phrasing that "any commemoration is also a betrayal" and, then, would measure a certain gap between the two of them, phrasing it as the evocation of an "unthought-of element" ("Shadow" 159, 160), that is, what we have here called a making-explicit of something in the original system. "There must," he said, "be a middle-ground on which the philosopher we are speaking about and the philosopher who is speaking are present together" (159). So the result of moving in this middle-ground would not be a critique, not be a summarizing presentation, but rather a projection forward into a new circumstance, a transmission with certain elements of rethinking: "present together," or, in terms of speech, dialogic. In this middle-ground, always he had something to say on the phenomenology of language and, with Husserl as the generator of terms and spur to new ideas, often found his thought in the form of a dazzling phrase.

After commenting on his changes to Husserl's vocabularies on speaking and writing, I will remark on the language-related essays in *Signs* by way of preparing the turn (his and mine) toward literary writing. Already, I have touched on the "Indirect Language and the Voices of Silence" essay from *Signs*, so I am leaving out of the survey this piece and another, relevant but slender, from *In Praise of Philosophy*.[14] When Merleau-Ponty is thinking along with and also beyond Husserl on language, the following subject-areas usually come into play:

- Resistance to the bifurcation of nature and mind;
- The falseness that comes of trying to think of things simply as things, or *blosse Sachen* in Husserl's German;
- My body as a field of perceptive powers;
- Other human beings as compresent, and as the guarantors and dialogic partners of my own body, its perceptions, and its speech;
- Thus, from these thoughts, the role of empathy or *Einfülung*; and the necessity of living *Füreinander*, for one another in society;
- "Faces, gestures, spoken words to which our own respond without thoughts intervening" (*S* 181).

---

14 "Husserl at the Limits of Phenomenology," *In Praise of Philosophy and Other Essays*. The essay here cited is entirely separate from the book of the same name, which I will soon examine.

Language, on this showing, is obviously a subtopic in the continuing redefinition of phenomenology as a philosophy, and of phenomenology in its relations with non-phenomenology, which is another of the Husserl-Merleau-Ponty topics. But perhaps we may say that humAnimal language is the topic whose complexities are the greatest—for history, for structure, for childhood learning, for subject-expressing-itself, for subject-in-dialogue with others, for basics of logic and creativity, for encouraging and preserving thought, and so on. Perceiving-thinking-writing is the most serious of the assignments because it is the greatest of the enigmas.

"The Philosopher and His Shadow," in *Signs*. The commemoration begins with what is Husserl's greatest audacity, the phenomenological reduction, where Merleau-Ponty remarks that "it is not through chance or naïveté that Husserl assigns contradictory characteristics to reduction" ("Shadow" 161). The reduction goes beyond the natural attitude but preserves the whole world and also the natural sciences that study the world; however, later Husserl, in *Ideen II*, problematizes the distinction "between pure subject and pure things" making a "new turn" in thought—an interpretation of the natural attitude not as illusion but as a primordial faith, that gives us "not a representation of the world but the world itself" (163). There is the compresence of bodies, things, and other bodies, and the question becomes: how can we extend this compresence of bodies to minds? Merleau-Ponty in his last paragraph hints that one vehicle or vinculum for this extending of understanding would be language, but the essay has little to say about language.

"Course Notes" on Husserl's "The Origin of Geometry," from *Husserl at the Limits of Phenomenology*. The issue concerns how Geometry became instituted as a discipline, and one main answer would be: that it emerged through the human language of interrogation, description, and disclosure. Drawings of the figures would never be enough, so a non-geometrical explanation is necessary as supplement, eventually as development of a system. The seventy-one pages of "Course Notes" have commentary on language scattered throughout, following and expanding on the sequence of themes of the reading notes as one thinker tracks another through an essay. These passages on speech are separated from each other in the notes but show the writer returning again and again to the interwoven nature of speaking subject, world, other persons, through language. The metaphors of weaving, hinge, transport, circularity, and entanglement carry the meaning that language *has us* when man, world, and speech are interwoven.

- "But language is '*interwoven*' (*verflochten*) with our horizon of the world and of humanity. Language is borne by our relation to the world and to others, and language also bears and makes our relation to the world and to others. It is through language that our horizon is open and endless (*endlos*) . . . . The thought of geometry inherits this tradition of language. . . . Neither have we exhausted the powers of speech. . . . As a speaking and active subject I encroach upon the other who is listening, as the understanding and passive subject I allow the other to encroach upon me. Within myself, in the exercise of language, I experience activity each time as the other side of passivity.... Speech is not the product of my active thought, standing in a secondary relation to it. It is my practice, my operation, my '*Funktion*,' my destiny. Every spiritual production is a response and an appeal, a coproduction" (*HLP* 8-9).

- "Objective Being implies *speaking man*. Language is correlative to *the objective world. Men, world and* Sprache *are interwoven*" (22).
- "... ideality does not dominate linguistic understanding as a higher possibility. Ideality is *at the hinge* of the connection between me and others" (24).
- "... the preexistence of the true in relation to the utterance (and not only the survival of the true in relation to the utterance) is founded on the written and language" (25).
- "[considering the ideal sense not once it is made, in the propositions, but at its birth], it is clear that it exists in fact through the transportation of *Sprache*, or across *Sprache*. *Sprache* makes the sense descend into the real world and sets it up at the same time in ideal being.... The emergence of ideality is reintegrated to the arising of language" (34).
- "Circularity of Heraclitus, yes: to go in one direction is truly to go in the other. A thick identity exists there, which truly contains difference. True Husserlian thought: man, world, language are interwoven, *verflochten*" (41).
- "It is the thought of the intentionality which is proper to language, interrogation of language, the *epoché* of language, the suspension ... revealing only *the operation, a contrario*. We do not *see* the operation, since it operates. We see what would be missing without it; we circumscribe it as what makes speech be a 'speaking of'... and not the conscious having of the idealities implied in speech" (44).
- "We do not have language; it has us.... What is at issue is to recognize the operation in us which is us and which is not ours" (51).
- "*Denken* does not envelop speech; it is entangled with it" (52).
- "Language, not as ready-made, not as a linguistic system, as a given field of the nameable including everything including my psyche ..., but rather language as being in the process of being made" (55).

Merleau-Ponty has exceeded Husserl in explicitness, in theorizing the epoché of language, as perceiving and thinking, speaking and writing are interwoven. These human skills are also encroached upon both ways, circular in both directions, intersubjective, coproduced, intentional, entangled, in operation, and in process. There is a strong preference for terms of relation and integration, which by now we know are also, in late Merleau-Ponty, inspired by logics of interference.

These two pieces on Husserl both begin and end with the interference-logic called by Merleau-Ponty "an ontological rehabilitation of the sensible" ("Shadow" 167). That phrase, from "The Philosopher and His Shadow," embodies embodied mind, which in turn embodies the point of that whole essay—which is that Husserl must bear his shadow, which is what resists phenomenology within us. Our dehiscence is non-phenomenology as natural being, or in the essay's term a "brute or unnamed state" (171). Perception is already in thought, and thought is already in language, so, the essay says, "[i]t is never a matter of anything but co-perception," that is, perception capturing thought but also entangled with *Einfülung*, or empathy with persons and no less with things.[15] It is possible to think without language, without names, and that was the imagined state of the science of geometry before it had to be taught to students and willed down to the next generation. Soon enough though, "the animal of perceptions and movements" will engage "perception as the *vinculum* of brute being and a body" ("Shadow" 169), and we leave the fiction-state of no names and quietly forever enter irreversibly the sign-state of speaking and writing. It is from that sign-state that philosophy now speaks of presuppositions, the pre-predicative life of consciousness, and *blosse Sachen*, or things in themselves. The phenomenologist must yearn toward his or her shadow because that is the self-assignment of this particular kind of thinking, but they must also bear that shadow and live within the chosen logics of interference. You would just as soon cut off your shadow as your skin! Your head! And so we are back to the Saussurean pages of *Signs*.

Introduction to *Signs*. The Introduction has three sections: 1) Marxism and postwar politics; 2) author's kind of philosophy, with attention to theory of language; 3) memories of Paul Nizan in the pre-war period. Only the second of these sections concerns us here, but soon I will trace a line of connection between all three. Like his presentation before his inquisitors in "The Primacy of Perception," the second section shows (many years later and with updates on content) the philosopher's talent for summarizing a whole system of related ideas in brief and convincing form.

"Now as before, philosophy begins with a 'What is thinking?'"; today's thought "overlaps that" of yesterday "because today I see farther"; so "I am installed on a pyramid of time which has been me," and I conclude, "time and thought are mutually entangled" (*S* 14-15). The next step: "Along with time's secret linkages, I learn those of the perceived world, its incompatible and simultaneous 'faces'"; and next, I learn about other persons "at the moment they appear in the world's flesh." Things and persons have their hidden faces; seer and seen are "exactly interchangeable" with "mutually enfolding glances" (16-17). This story of perceptions in bodies is interrupted by speech, however, because "speech takes flight from where it rolls in the wave of speechless communication" (17); speech tears apart meanings. Is it to continue Saussure or to surpass him that Merleau-Ponty goes forward now, mid-paragraph, to say that "[t]o make of language a means or a code for thought is to break it [?] . . . [Doing so] we prohibit ourselves from understanding the depth to which words sound within us" (17). We have a need to speak, words rouse thoughts, and words teach us our own thoughts: "Thought and speech anticipate one another . . . [and]

---

15 Husserl's student Edith Stein wrote under his influence a treatise to pursue, as early as 1917, what Husserl had opened in volume 1 of *Ideas*. See Stein, *On the Problem of Empathy* (1964).

continually take each other's place" (17). Indeed, all thought, he says, comes from spoken words. Further, "[w]e might think of the historical world according to this model.... Everywhere are meanings, dimensions, and forms in excess of what each 'consciousness' could have produced.... We are in the field of history as we are in the field of language or existence" (20). Once again, at the end of a chain of thinking we arrive at the insoluble abomination of a relation of interference that must be borne, lived with, thought through: "In a sense, the highest point of philosophy is perhaps no more than rediscovering these truisms: thought thinks, speech speaks, the glance glances. But each time between the two identical words there is the whole spread one straddles in order to think, speak, and see" (21). The trend of this middle section of the Introduction is to arrive at the philosophy of history: this outcome matches well with his intent of showing the working of the dialectic in theory and practice in the first section and in one tormented Marxist life in Nizan, in the third section. Merleau-Ponty thus integrates at more than one level his philosophies of perception and of history.

"On the Phenomenology of Language" in *Signs*. This essay, on a topic in the center of all he wished to show and be, is unusually tightly organized in short sections with few illustrations and few expansive digressions. Husserl in his early works theorized a universal grammar that enabled the existence of an "object before thought" and so restricted language to "an accompaniment, substitute, memorandum, or secondary means of communication" (*S* 84). But, in more recent writings, Husserl arrived at positions more capacious, more phenomenological, with language as "an original way or intending certain objects, as thought's body" (84). What is new in the later works is a movement into synchronic speech, now using terms from Saussure: synchrony and diachrony and langue and parole enveloping each other, producing "logic in contingency ... incarnate logic." In the child's growth-into-language, "organized signs have their immanent meaning, which does not arise from the 'I think' but from the 'I am able to,'" thus linking the individual child to the infinite system that existed before the child's birth (88). The quasi-corporeality of the signifying: "Signification arouses speech as the world arouses my body—by a mute presence which awakens my intentions without deploying itself before them" (89). New terms come into the widening argument on speech: expression as individual intention, speaking subject, "a certain arrangement of already signifying instruments ... (morphological, syntactical, and lexical instruments, literary *genres*, types of narrative ..." (90), the dialogic as face-to-face and also at distance, in writing; and, also, the phrase from Malraux seen elsewhere, "coherent deformation" of available significations in works of painterly or verbal art.

Merleau-Ponty returns to Husserl's last writings at the essay's end: he offers the Husserlian reminder that the necessary presence of others in the world—corporeal like us and languaged like us—embeds us in language and culture. "In a sense, phenomenology is all or nothing" (94). The body's "I am able to," the speech that gives us the idea of ideal infinite communication and yet embeds us in contingency, fortunately prevents all "acosmic" and "pancosmic consciousness" (95). There is a mocking sentence on this need to use our living reason to refute psychologism, historicism, and dogmatic metaphysics. Contrariwise and turning to positive and ultimate values: "Truth is another name for sedimentation [remainders of the past in the present day], which is itself the presence of all presents in our own. . . . [N]o light that shines more brightly than the living present's light" (96). All the themes of the essay come together in one long sentence in the last paragraph: "Now it is at the heart of my present that I find the meaning of those presents which preceded it, and that I find the means of understanding others' presence at the same world; and it is in the actual practice of speaking that I learn to understand" (97). That is the philosopher's "I" speaking, claiming his pronoun so he will not offend with the phoniness of "we," but it is not the autobiographical "I"; rather, it is the speaker who hopes to represent the rest of us. It is a delicately moral effect of style, showing how style may exceed device.

On style

In this thinker, style is a theme rather than a topic, so it emerges as a subheading of discussions of painting and writing across several essays. It is never pursued or argued through separately. It is never taken up in a massive way as development or failure of a period style, as in Charles Rosen's magnificent, example-packed survey of the flourishing and exhaustion of *The Classical Style: Haydn, Mozart, Beethoven* (1971), where we love to find the effect on the attentions of ourselves as auditors of "a closed, symmetrical structure, the central position of the most extreme tension, and the insistence upon an extended and complete resolution" on the tonic (99). Style is never explored in the inner intentional slippages of metaphors down to the fussiest detail, as in William Empson's *Seven Types of Ambiguity: A Study of Its effects in English Verse* (1947), where the scores of brilliant individual readings of texts entirely survive his vulnerable, literary critic's admission in the Preface to the second edition: "I would use the term 'ambiguity' to mean anything I liked, and repeatedly told the reader that the distinctions between the Seven Types . . . would not be worth the attention of a profounder thinker" (viii). And style is never surveyed across languages and centuries within a single but voluminous genre, as in Jonathan Culler's *Theory of the Lyric* (2015), where Culler concludes a wonderful chapter on lyric structure with arguments resisting "the allure of the timeless," in favor of "the lyric time of enunciation, which is both that of a speaker/poet and that of the reader, who may speak these words also" (294). Instead, Merleau-Ponty focuses on how style may define a way of living in all of us, in our thoughts and perceptions, habits, attitudes, and responses to contingency. He focuses on the lives of painters and writers as their creative works often move athwart their everyday living and behaving.[16]

---

16 Two writers have accounted for these topics in Merleau-Ponty's writings already, from the vantage

His essay "Cézanne's Doubt" and the mini-treatise "Malraux and the Languages of Silence" have most of his passages on style, and both of these have his startling thesis that art in caves like Lascaux and Chauvet, painters like Cézanne and Renoir, sculptors like Rodin, and writers like Stendahl, Balzac, and Mallarmé show that the creators are experiencing the same adventure, with style as a "demand that has issued from that perception" ("ILVS" 255). In this context he adopts from Malraux and foregrounds the grand mantra of the Malraux essay and of this book, "perception already stylizes" (*PW* 59). This idea, that style is not a manner but a mode of formulation, is productive because it hauls with it the full demand of the phenomenological attitude. That attitude would be the search of appearance, resulting in the reduction, resulting in the life-assignment of continuous demand for interrogation, description, and disclosure. This process would yield an analytical attitude beyond formalism and yet would be detailed and scrupulous in technical accounting. It would involve, in the philosopher's words from several sources, various elements: "a new system of equivalences" (*PW* 63); "emblems of a certain relationship with being" ("ILVS" 91); "style is not the style of [a creator's] life, but he also draws his life toward expression" (*PW* 74); "put[ting his] stamp upon even the inhuman world revealed by optical instruments" (*PW* 77); "a tacit and implicit accumulation" (*S* 76); "the true contrary of formalism as a good theory of style, or of speech, which puts both above '' or 'device'" (*S* 77); "adventures of constitutive analysis"; and "encroachments, reboundings, and circularities" (*S* 177). All this, once understood, could lead to a plan of action for a critic as museum-goer, devourer of libraries and review-journals and arts programming, though probably not for the philosopher. We must leave the appropriate labor to workers in the disciplines; it is enough to propose the right reasons for looking at pictures and for reading poems and novels, along with sponsorship for the harvest of detail.

A most unusual place to find four pages on moralized style is the lecture "Man and Adversity," given by the philosopher in Geneva in 1951 and published in *Signs* just at the end of part 2 before the straight-on political part 3. In the essay's last sentence, he speaks of the discussions of that era being "so convulsive because it is resisting a truth . . . right at hand" (243) and a sentence from the opening explains the facts: "We men who have lived as our problem the development of communism and the War, and who have read Gide and Valéry and Proust and Husserl and Heidegger and Freud are the same" (225). Mid-essay the topic is "this half-century's investigations . . . of a strange relationship between consciousness and its language, as between consciousness and its body" (232). Directly following this statement, Merleau-Ponty

---

points of art history (Gilmore) and philosophy of language (Inkpin). Rather than repeat their findings, which pull citations from several sources, I recommend the following discussions: Jonathan Gilmore, "Between Philosophy and Art," *The Cambridge Companion to Merleau-Ponty* (2005); Andrew Inkpin, "The Art and Science of Indirect Sense," chapter 5 of *Disclosing the World: On the Phenomenology of Language* (2016).

does not name his antagonist, who is likely to be Wittgenstein, and he may even mis-characterize him in a too-brief summary: "Ordinary language thinks that it can establish, as the correlate of each word or sign, a thing or signification which can exist and be conceived of without any sign. But literature has long taken exception to ordinary language" (232). He refers to the way Rimbaud and Mallarmé worked to free language from the control of obvious facts "and trusted it to invent and win new relationships of meaning" (232). Coming up to "our day," after the occupation and war and the struggles against communism and within Marxism, Merleau-Ponty claims that language "is the writer himself... no longer the servant of significations but the act of signifying itself.... no other way to comprehend language than to dwell in it and use it" (232). That is style, moralized and personalized, taken away from direct communicative purpose and deprived of direct political meaning—rescued for something lesser but more honest, namely, the writers themselves as professionals of language.

Oddly, this section begins with an attack on philosophers of ordinary language, who are taken as holding an absurd correlationist theory of language. That point would be much less easy to make if a better version of Wittgenstein were available to Merleau-Ponty: if, for fanciful example, he had been able to read Toril Moi's recent-to-us book *Revolution of the Ordinary: Literary Studies After Wittgenstein, Austin, and Cavell* (2017). Moi shows a much more believable language theory in the ordinary-language thinkers, one engaged with speech and with use and, also, a literary language capable of being engaged with politics and positions and still be literary, while skeptical of all theory whether in identity politics or in deconstructive or other analytics. Still, Merleau-Ponty might reply to her with some show of a point: her clever and sustained defense of ordinary language, as a powerful mode of approach to the reading of texts, seems to have no place for poetic devices, narrative modes of deceptive speaking and plotting, or style in any definition.

Mid-essay, the next topic, related to the convulsive adversity of the mid-twentieth century, is the playing-out and slow disappearing of surrealism. That creative movement, along with certain favored figures like Paul Valéry, who might have seemed more traditional, shared a view of language that pushed beyond a signifying literature to *semantic thickness*. This movement is "*style* in the strong sense of the term," whereby "poetic language does not die out in the face of what it communicates to us. [Style is where] in poetic language meaning calls again for the very words which have served to communicate it, and no others" (Merleau-Ponty, *S* 234). An earlier novelist is the example:

> That is, a new and very personal ordering of the words, forms, and elements of the narrative; a new order of correspondence between signs; an imperceptible yet characteristically Stendahlian warping of the whole language system—a system which has been constituted by years of usage and of life, which (having become Stendahl himself) finally allows him to improvise, and which should not be called a system of thought (since Stendahl was so little aware of it) but rather a system of speaking. (234-35)

Merleau-Ponty concludes that language is "that singular apparatus which, like our body, gives us more than we put into it" (235). In fact, style is the body, behaving in language in excess of what may be signified, and as such, style is a system of perceiving-thinking-writing.

Yes, the terms are themselves encroachings, reboundings, and circularities. That is one feature of Merleau-Pontian style, giving permission for the rest of us (now and then) to turn a name into an adjective.

His account of style is incomplete. (Nonetheless, it is far more extensive, and more worthy of consideration, than what we find in Moi.) What may be the Merleau-Pontian unthought?

We require a definition of style capacious enough to include exact determination of a poem's meter and the deliberate violations of it that give personality to poetic language.

We require a definition of style that describes energies of attention in the reader—especially in tracking what leads up to and away from sentences—and what the mind does with subject-verb-object and all the optional form-classes of grammar that surround (or obliterate) the classic SVO structure.

At the other end of the scale, we require a way to describe historical period styles like the rift between the Classical and Romantic epistemé between 1790-1830.

Also, we wish to describe, as a larger effect of style, Merleau-Ponty's habit of assessing the dark data of contingency and, yet, ending several of his late essays in the form of guarded references to spontaneity and freedom.

Chapter 5: Energies of Attention: Syntax in Depth

From perceiving and thinking to writing—and back

If, accepting Meijer's proposal as our own, perceiving and thinking are in a relation of interference, then thinking and writing are in interference-relations with each other and with perception. This subsequent relationship has to follow. It is a chain of mutual causation snaking around on itself: in the words of the philosopher, it consists of encroachments, reboundings, and circularities. While we are extending the chain, let us go further and add emotion and memory, and, indeed, other and all of the humAnimal faculties. Let us go for the largest claim and say consciousness is interference, or, rather, consciousness is in interference with itself. Let us also claim that changing the constitutive metaphor from the Dialectic to Cognitive-Perceptive Interference opens out new territories for intellectual work. Now we can ask the question: What happens if that tactic becomes our metaphor when we attend to attention in the making and stringing of sentences in our embodied minds? To add another metaphor of mutuality, a trope that is included in interference but invisible in it, *what might happen* is that performing these acts of daring we cross the bridge all the way to the other side from thinking to writing, from philosophy to literature. Cross the bridge—then go back. We can take it further yet: What is under that bridge? The flow of energy that is conscious intention. Why is that energy pent and directed and focused? Because that energy is intention as attention, which gains life through movement, gains force within constraints.

The skills of attention and the forms of energy that connect us to the world and other people

Through the last ten years of his life, Merleau-Ponty kept returning to the natural sciences as the representative, in his era, of the limits of rationalism. He saw the collapse of classical psychology and classical physics, failures of whole fields— psychology, by Husserl's achievement, replaced by phenomenology, and physics thrown into the modern world by quantum theories, at macro and micro levels. He wrote about Renaissance perspective in painting, which, at the beginning was a grand discovery but, with the coming of modern practices, placed an intolerable limit upon creative response to space. Linguistics leaped from the study of national languages and empirical data collection to synchrony vs. diachrony, langue vs. parole, the rule of arbitrary differentials. The earlier achievements were not entirely lost in some sectors, but were rather surpassed, surrounded, in Thomas Kuhnian replacements of ruling paradigms. The philosopher, like Husserl before him, tracked these changes and kept up a furious pace of reading of new work in several fields, because his phenomenology held the promise of bringing classical, representational, and objectivist natural and psychological science into an acceptance of the codetermination of perceiving with thinking. The corollary is the role of the humAnimal body, and the single-self point of view, in the production of knowledge. Merleau-Ponty is a cognitivist, and proudly, with hard thinking and a careful summary of what antagonists say as well as a heavy outlining of sequenced arguments, but he is a cognitivist only if perceiving-thinking-writing are put on the level once and for all. It is a life-project, and since he is not going to sacrifice *perceiving*, natural science will have to advance it to equality in the interminable feedback loop of attention.

Since the time of Merleau-Ponty's death sixty years ago, university departments of psychology have become more historical-theoretical, and new departments of cognitive science have emerged that are more measurement-based and empirical. He would have found cause for joy in the work of my colleague at UC San Diego in psychology, V. S. Ramachandran, whose most memorable triumph in a storied career is the curing of intense, painful clenching feelings in patients who had had one arm amputated. The pain was definitely in the missing or phantom limb: some muscle-memory of clenching of fingers. Ramachandran got a long narrow mirror for $5.00 at a hardware store and set it in front of his patients so that they could look at themselves in reverse, with a visible intact arm in the place of the phantom limb. He, then, gave them instructions: "Look at yourself in the mirror for about twenty minutes a day for the next month, and waggle your arm and fingers." The result was that sufferers tricked themselves into believing that the lost arm was still there and could be painlessly unclenched. Ramachandran's comment is that he is the first man in history who has amputated a number of phantom limbs.[1]

Consciousness is a topic shared between psychology and cognitive science. It is more likely to be studied and credited with validity in psychology, but on the whole it is an unusually contentious topic where little is settled as a standard teachable paradigm. Consciousness is not synonymous with "mind," and mind itself is the issue between most persons in psychology and another of my colleagues, Patricia Churchland in philosophy, who in *Neurophilosophy* (1986) wishes to substitute for mind the firing of synapses in the brain. Functionalists like Churchland are the antagonists of all phenomenologists of the embodied mind because the functionalists eschew first-person testimony and keep asking just where consciousness resides, just how it shows itself. Any survey of consciousness will have to spend most of the time describing third-person views, involving neuroscientific experiments and psychological theories. But most assuredly the first-person accounts are part of the field of consciousness studies, and these accounts have central importance for our work within the subtopic of attention. Here I am relying on the overview by Susan

---

[1] See V. S. Ramachandran and S. Blakeslee, *Phantoms in the Brain* (London: Fourth Estate, 1998). Merleau-Ponty writes on the phantom limb in *Phenomenology of Perception* 84.

Blackmore (*Consciousness: An Introduction*, 2004), who reasonably concludes that, for most of us, an integrated science of mental life will need to strike a balance between studying first- and third-person accounts.

Of Blackmore's twenty-seven chapters, she devotes one to attention. There she mentions, only to reject it with force, the old metaphor Merleau-Ponty also doubted, of the searchlight of attention calling up objects during a scan of a dark attic. She remarks early on that in one of the reigning assumptions of the CogSci field, from David Chalmers in the 1990s, the focus of attention is an example of the "easy" problems, compared to the "hard" problem of how physical processes in the brain give rise to subjective experience. What she identifies is a modern version of the mind-body problem. Descartes solved that issue by splitting the one from the other in philosophy's most spectacular and influential dualism, but few scholarly dualists exist anymore here or elsewhere. (In daily life, scholars and all the rest of us are dualists from the minute we wake up in the morning, as Buddhist thinkers rightly keep reminding us.) Churchland denies that there is a problem at all and that paying attention is ever easy. Is attention involuntary or voluntary, a resultant of force or a force, an effect or a cause? Just when does the experience of attention occur? The debates on these and other issues in consciousness studies continue to be argued out with ingenious evidence, and we need not try to resolve the issues. Blackmore and others report on the issues, taking sides here and there, but like her we need do no more than state a preference, try a mediation, follow what we need, as in these promising passages:

- "Focalization, concentration of consciousness are of its essence" (William James qtd. in Blackmore 51).
- "[W]hat should be let through to the deeper stages of processing. . . . [C]learly the brain does have a limited capacity for parallel processing. . . . . So somehow the many parallel processes [such as speech] have to be brought together, or selected, to ensure that a sensible serial output occurs" (Blackmore 52).
- "In other words, being attended to is equivalent to getting into short-term memory" (53).
- Attention is "the sentry at the gate of consciousness." (Zeman qtd. in Blackmore 53).
- The half-second delay in consciousness: "Libet's controversial suggestion was that sensory experiences are subjectivity referred back in time once neuronal adequacy has been achieved. . . . The question then concerns how subjective referral works. To what point in time is the experience referred and how?" (Blackmore 59).
- Husserl, Francisco Varela, and the origin of nowness: "As [William] James and others have described it, there is a three-fold structure in which the present experience, or 'now,' is bounded by the immediate past and future. Husserl introduced the idea of *retention*, which intends the just-past, and *protention* of the immediate future. Based on his work in neuroscience and in particular

on self-organizing systems, Varela attempts to relate the structure discovered phenomenologically to the underlying self-organizing neural assemblies" (378).

So some of the field's main working assumptions are *focus* as a visual far-near metaphor of how the mind/brain selects from the *Umwelt* or surround; *simultaneity of parallel processings* of different types of information; but also *successive attention to moving objects in time*, which is the time of expectation involving before and after, retention and protention; processing events in *short-term memory*; the need, yet the difficulty, of specifying *the evanescent now* of the moment of conscious attention.

Focus and concentration may well be the essence of attention, as William James says; they are the first thing one thinks of on the topic, and they seem to bring forward a simultaneous-spatial frame. Equally important, however, is the observer's time of expectation—indispensable if the objects of our attention are sentences and the stringing of sentences.[2] And sentences are our immediate but overlooked objects of attention whether we are reading Verlaine, Valéry, or Proust; Husserl, Heidegger, or Merleau-Ponty; or the back of the cereal box at breakfast.

When she titles her book *Consciousness* and covers a wide range of theories and experiments, Blackmore is unusual as a writer in this field. She is ready to discuss the brain under the influence of drugs, in detail, and willing to foreground Francisco Varela (1946-2001), a neglected theorist for whom a first-person account of attention is essential. Varela, with two others, wrote *The Embodied Mind* (1991), going entirely against the conventions of 1990s psychology by finding the lines of connection between the phenomenology of Merleau-Ponty and the meditation theory of Buddhism. (Merleau-Ponty is the hero of that book.) Blackmore prints Varela's own categorization of the major theories of consciousness, in the form of a diagram (380), where Consciousness is in the crossing-center of horizontal and vertical axes, with phenomenology (Varela himself as well as Lakoff and Johnson) in the whole left-half space at the end of one axis, and functionalism (Dennett, Churchland), reductionism, and mysterianism (McGinn, Nagel) at the ends of the other three lines. Blackmore gives careful summaries and full citations to the third-person accounts that dominate the field overall, but it is evident that, for her, the first-person accounts have more explanatory power. This preference comes out into the open in her last three chapters, on "The View from Within," "Meditation and Mindfulness," and Buddhism and consciousness ("Waking Up"). Her last page is about how Zen affirms the more perplexity, the better—how there could be a "way the direct experience of nonduality might be integrated into a neuroscience that only knows, intellectually, that dualism must be false" (414). In matters mental, knowing intellectually is never enough.

---

2 "Perception and Expectation in Literature" is the title of the final chapter in my study of *Animal Perception and Literary Language* (2019); there I analyze twelve texts in different genres and languages, reading to register my own and any reader's protention and retention.

In Blackmore's practitioner's version of Buddhism and consciousness, the doctrine cannot be spoken of directly because the whole point is not to have propositions that can be believed; rather, it is to have truths to be acted upon. The inquiry of Buddhism will, as is known, reveal the emptiness and impermanence of all phenomena, the illusory nature of self, and the origins and ending of suffering (402). The purpose is transformation of the self: dropping our illusions, having compassion for our own and others' suffering. All our Western ideas about the nature of the world assume that the things we perceive are unconditioned, independent, but the Buddha taught that these arising experiences are interdependent, impermanent, and not inherently divided into separate things (412). Everything is conditioned, relative, and subject to the law of cause and effect. Once these truths are actively considered, the skill of attending will itself be differently understood from our usual emphases on focalization and concentration.

Attention defined experientially: that task is where Gay Watson enters the story, because she has written an entire book about attention (2017) that explores Taoist and Buddhist teachings—with a nine-page interview of Blackmore and passing references to Merleau-Ponty. Watson had earlier written *A Philosophy of Emptiness* (2014), with a serious scholarly account of a particular emptiness that does not denote "mere absence or non-existence" but rather carries another side: "interdependence, a celebration of plurality, change and contingency" (*Attention* 11). "What I discovered was that such an understanding required a turning away from our Western, and mostly unconscious, fixation on presence and substance" (11). This understanding led to her next book, which is an exposition of the topic outside the theories of psychology and cognitive science, where she interviews a score of Buddhist-friendly thinkers in brain science, psychiatry, education, and the arts of literature, music, and dance, including a hunter who turns out to be a watcher of how prey and predator have matching antagonistic modes of attending. She introduces the topic with theoretical brio in the denial of theory in favor of experience, and she plans each interview and sequences the whole set in order to argue that neuroscience will never provide a whole picture of our experience as "embodied creatures, embedded in culture" (15). Like Varela, Watson rhymes phenomenology with Buddhist thought.

In this essay you are following, the *praxis* of perception-thinking-writing is now more overtly heading toward the end-point of reading, which is the co-creativity of those who understand. Here are statements on *praxis*, selected from Watson's *Attention* for guidance toward ethical aspiration and close analysis, within the meditation called reading. (Reading is performed by the eyes on language steeped in perceptual content, and thus reading is inevitably an embodied practice.)

- "While traces of understanding of contingency, the indeterminacy of existence and emptiness are evident in the work of many contemporary philosophers from Nietzegger, to Heidegger, Wittgenstein, Derrida and Merleau-Ponty, a concern with embodied practice is pretty much absent from all except the last" (Watson, *Attention* 23).

- "So in attention we have presence, receptivity, service, care, openness, curiosity and cultivation. Training the mind to attend to all of these—to the process of attention itself—we find our interface with world" (28).
- Watson interviews Blackmore on differences between brain in task orientation and brain in default mode—Blackmore speaking: "[scholars] now talk about four ... aspects of the self—the body schema ... ; the sense of agency; the first person perspective; and the sense of ownership of the body. Now that's all before you get anywhere near a narrative self or self image or social self. . . . , but *those* are in that default network, at least in the temporal-parietal junction and its connections with various other areas. . . . [D]ealing with these different aspects of self really helps to make it easier to . . . allow the self to not be one thing, not a permanently existing thing" (91).
- Watson interviews Ian McGilchrist, author of *The Master and His Emissary* (2009), on the structure of the brain—McGilchrist speaking: "The right hemisphere [is] the one that is able to understand a stretch, or depth or extent of time, as indeed it is the one able to understand a stretch, or depth or extent of space, whereas the left hemisphere seems to focus on a series of points in sequence in space or time, which is quite different and basically, therefore, doesn't have the experience of space or time. Perception is very much more dependent than the left. . . . [W]hat I believe perception to be . . . is a creative act; so that when we perceive there is no such thing as taking in data, we always take it in as something; we are always creating something out of it. And what we create matters, and the right hemisphere is much better at that" (77-78).
- Robert MacFarland, a writer on language and land in *The Wild Places* (2007) and in *Landmarks* (2015): "Language is fundamental to the possibility of re-wonderment. . . . [Writing about language and land includes] tact as due attention, as in tenderness of encounter, as rightful tactility" (qtd. in Watson 147-48).
- Alice Oswald, English poet, author of *Memorium*, subtitled *An Excavation of the Iliad* (2012): "To me the interesting part is the paradox that you are somehow there and not there. . . . You have to eliminate yourself and yet remain attentive. I am interested in the technicality of that and particularly how rhythm can achieve that [in oral traditions, in Homer's hexameter meter with its 'wobbling effect on the mind']. . . . So you're made anonymous by that mechanical effect but you're kept there and alert by an overbalancing effect. . . . [P]oetry, and the oral tradition in particular, maintains that paradox and keeps something vacillating between absence and presence" (qtd. in Watson 173-74).

Attention, it would seem, is an ethos as well as a technical skill. For Watson and her respondents, attention is a shifting away from self-control to an ethic of care; a trust in the co-arising of phenomena; a step out of the ordinary; a trust in the felt embodiment of experience and in the core quality of sentience; a finding of truth in uncertainty; a discovery of agency. When they are speaking of attention-in-language, she and her experts agree that this is the writer's and reader's ability to sustain, and even to exploit, interference, indirection, and paradox.[3]

What is implied for literary reading is a willingness to attend equally, and with apt co-ordination, to the broad range and the gritty detail and everything in between. Of course, we have always known this requirement, through the many changes of emphasis in the history of criticism. Perhaps we are now, in 2024, emerging from a broad-range phase and re-entering a moment of greater emphasis on detail: veering back somewhat from syntax in large, as identity issues, to syntax in little with more emphasis on perceptual content—and on form and style.

Against any challenge that this shift is surrender to formalism or to Buddhism, there is a last thinker to advance: Simone Weil's beautiful essay on the joyful relationship between attention and grace. "Reflections on the Right Use of School Studies with a View to the Love of God," written in 1942, concerns the proper aim of

---

[3] What do phenomenology and Buddhism share on what might be the role of humAnimal consciousness? An outsider to these mysteries, a non-practitioner but aspiring on both sides, can only begin to imagine. Plainly, though, these commitments have enough in common that the imperfect gesture toward Buddhist thought, already started, should be taken beyond what Varela covers and up to our own limits. (Merleau-Ponty himself has written on Eastern thought for one-sixth of an essay in *Signs* ["Everywhere and Nowhere," 126-58], but, with other aims than ours, has little to build upon.) 1) Phenomenology and Buddhism share a core commitment to a belief in the embodied mind. 2) They share a common distrust of appearance, along with acceptance that the physical world exists and appearance is necessary because things in the world are necessary. Appearance is where one starts but paradoxically it is always returning and always with us. In phenomenology appearance has another name: the natural attitude. In Buddhism another name is "dependent arising." 3) They share a desire to search appearance for what is behind it: in phenomenology this is called the reduction, and in Buddhism this is called the premise of emptiness. 4) They share a trust in the body in form of orientation to gravity and postural schemas, which in Buddhism takes the form of sitting in meditation. In both, the practice is to track physical and mental movements, thinking about thinking and paying attention to attention. 5) They share a concern that the common lot of humans is suffering: for Merleau-Ponty's phenomenology it is a dedication to social progress through left politics, as in his writings on WWII, adversity, violence under Marxism and Fascism, and also the mental agonies of single persons like Cézanne as painter and like characters in Stendahl. In Buddhism's opening declaration of the Four Noble Truths, the four truths are all about our ignorance, distraction, and illusion in the state of *Samsara*, our usual state of suffering. 6) Search of Appearance is continual, and the reduction is therefore continual as we confront the illusive visual with the revelations of the invisible. Yet, always, phenomenology gets beyond or through appearance and conducts the hard practice of sense-making, through practices of interrogation, description, and disclosure (among other forms of revelation that are the daily work of phenomenology as a life philosophy). The Buddhist equivalent is post-meditation, what occurs after the sitting practice, where Modes of Attention and concern are brought back to the social world of persons in communities. 7) Buddhist *rigpa* (or naked reality) and phenomenology's *life-world*, pre-conceptual, pre-propositional, pre-predicative, are the aimed-at states of the philosophical system; *rigpa* and life-world are always aspirational because these may never be reached. So neither philosophy of consciousness may ever rest in finality: always searching, always open to new experience.

school studies: to learn to increase one's power of attention, so that in later life one can turn one's whole attention to God. Classroom exercises, she says, are necessary, but bearing down on our papers with the "frowning application" of ambition and effort is not the right way to work. Weil proposes attention as a "negative effort" of thinking of something or someone external to oneself, like a class assignment or a fellow student, and then willingness to wait, allowing a message to arrive. "Attention consists of suspending our thought, leaving it detached, empty, and ready to be penetrated by the object" (111). This kind of attending opens up a void, into which rush the energies and beauties of the world. This kind of attending sets us up for the most rare and difficult thing, for the time which inevitably comes when we need to give our attention to a sufferer and ask, "What are you going through?" Weil's view of grace, coming from a Jewish woman who kept herself outside the Catholic church but nearby, arcs over to touch Buddhist thought in surrender of self, in the idea of negative effort, and in the commitment first and last to the suffering of others. Weil's attention is a practice that we need not call prayer or meditation. It is brave and sensible, developmental, nondenominational, ordinary-everyday, languaged, dialogic, moving between persons. It now prepares for all that comes next in this book.

*

Merleau-Ponty's own contributions to a true theory of attention are to be found in a short section near the beginning of *Phenomenology of Perception*, and, in separate explanations about energy, drawn together from several other texts that are written later. The passages on energy are set into sequence by Kelly Oliver in the essay I have earlier praised, on the ethics of vision: I shall rely on her brilliant synthesis, but will push beyond her points, in order to claim that when the philosopher is writing about energy, he is also writing about attention.

In the Introduction to *Phenomenology of Perception* (section 3, "'Attention' and 'Judgment'"), Merleau-Ponty is continuing and concluding his attack on classical prejudices, in order to clear the ground for what he, led by Husserl, has to offer. His own positive terms begin immediately next in a section on "The Phenomenal Field" and then in the rest of his long treatise. Here he is using the skill or faculty of attention in order to discuss empiricism and its opposite, intellectualism [fact vs. abstraction], both of which "take the objective world as their object for analysis . . . , both . . . incapable of expressing the particular manner in which perceptual consciousness constitutes its object" (28). The difficulty with what classical thought calls the objective world is one we have seen before: that objective world "comes first neither in time nor according to its sense" (28), and both empiricism and intellectualism delay and downgrade the prior and constitutive role of perception. With empiricism, attention is "a general and unconditioned power" like a spotlight illuminating pre-existing objects, and, thus, creating nothing. Intellectualism, on the other hand, begins from the fecundity of attention: every new appearance of the object "subordinates the previous one and expresses everything the previous one meant" (29). Either way, philosophy gets "caught up accounting for the illusions of appearances," those unavoidable-but-deceptive assignments for the epoché of phenomenology. "Consciousness is too poor in the first case and too rich in the second for any phenomenon to be able to *solicit* it" (30). The remedies for this wretched, prejudiced classical state of affairs: a close watch on the constitution of the object; contingency that is tracked into its transformation, into configuration; thus a more active subject. Merleau-Ponty concludes the attention-part of section 3 of the Introduction with a blunt command for a change within the discipline itself, so attention might be once and for all rightly theorized: "Consciousness must be brought face to face with its unreflective life in things and must awaken to its own, forgotten, history—this is the true role of philosophical reflection and this is how a true theory of attention is established" (34).

Before he concludes, though, he offers definitions of attention that relate this skill to topics elsewhere in the *Phenomenology* and in his later works: on freedom, horizon, and creation. These four passages, taken together with my covering comment, will guide an approach to energies of attention in the act of reading. They are the theory of a practice.

- "Attention, then, does not exist as a general and formal activity. There is in each case a particular freedom to gain and a particular mental space to keep in order. The object of attention itself must still be brought to light. Here it is literally a question of creation" (32).
- On how children learn about colors. "The first perception of colors . . . is thus a change in the structure of consciousness, the institution of a new dimension of experience, and the deployment of an *a priori*. Attention, then, must be conceived on the model of these originary acts, since a second-order attention that limited itself to recalling an already acquired knowledge would refer us back to the acquisition itself. To pay attention is not merely to further clarify some preexisting givens; rather it is to realize in them a new articulation by taking them as *figures*. They are only pre-formed as *horizons*, they truly constitute new regions in the total world" (32).
- "Attention, then, is neither an association of ideas nor the return to itself of a thought that is already the master of its objects; rather, attention is the active constitution of a new object that develops and thematizes what was until then only offered as an indeterminate horizon. At the same time that it sets attention to work, the object is continuously recaptured by attention, and re-established as subordinate to it" (33).
- "The act of attention is . . . at least rooted in the life of consciousness, and we can finally understand that it emerges from its indifferent freedom to give itself a present object. This passage from the indeterminate to the determinate, this continuous taking up again of its own history in the unity of a new sense is thought itself" (33).

The act of attention is thought itself, he says. I would make it more explicit by stating what is now obvious from his phenomenological attitude: attention is the skill which helps perceiving-thinking-writing to step down from general to particular, from horizon to thing and person, from uncertain to determinate being. Attention is the person's perception's interface with the world. It is an action that "emerges," is "continuous," is "thought itself" as in-motion and also the register of motion. Attention is thought in the firing of synapses—yes, you are forever correct, Patricia Churchland—but attention is also energy of a speaking subject exercising his or her own freedom, defining scope, creating out of contingent being—braving the new.

If attention is thought itself, is not the reverse true, too? For Oliver, at the start of her essay "Beyond Recognition," thought is perception; mid-essay thought is, in the Merleau-Ponty vision-touch system, energy both physical and social; at the end of the essay thought is moral witness—ethical obligation to other human beings. Having tried a summary of her synoptic account of perception earlier, and speaking of the sense of sight when we were concerned with painting, briefly this is what she co-ordinates on the topic of energy from several Merleau-Pontian sources. Thought-as-energy in what follows should be taken, speculatively, for one philosopher's reversible claim about thought-as-attention. In this round-robin of coordinated terms, attentive thinking can be an expression of the full force of the psyche's energy. That works for me, but at the least we can plausibly say that the energy-thesis is a fuller context in body and in world because of thinking attention.

In Oliver's argument, she is describing Merleau-Ponty's vision-touch system, and she is broadening out to claim that the senses "translate each other and work together to form perception" (136). As she describes the French philosopher's basic claim, he outlines a complex network beyond vision-touch to a postural schema, wherein "the senses form a totality" in the person's orientation to gravity. For Merleau-Ponty, she says, the person maintains equilibrium through her inner ear's relation to gravity, through a tactual system where skin meets environment and where vision is movement across space. "There are no gaps," Oliver says, "between us and the world since we touch it with our eyes, working as they do in coordination with all of sensation. . . . Movements of the body attend to the information available in energy" (137). Oliver's single reference to attention is here, in the context of these thoughts on the body's adjustments to environment and setting, with front-facing body and eyes on the front of our heads: exploring information (from airspace, sound, mechanical contact, chemical contact, and light) is a mode of attention. She concludes: "Energy, then, is the medium through which we perceive the world" (138). Energy surrounds, sustains, and connects us to the world and to other people; our bodies have a kinship with Earth's sustaining energies.

As a last instance of physical-mechanical energies, the very distance between us and other humans and animals also facilitates relationships between us. "Just as heat energy, chemical energy, mechanical energy and photic energy sustain life, [so too does] social energy, and psychic or affective energy, also surround us, connect us, and move through us to sustain us" (141). In *The Visible and the Invisible*, and in his writings on child development, Merleau-Ponty has "radical if fleeting passages that suggest that the transitivity between people can be more than a mere projection of one's own feelings or attitudes onto another, but rather a migration of feeling or affect itself" (Oliver 142). "We are profoundly dependent upon the environment and other people for the energy that sustains us," concludes Oliver (143). We are used to the double meaning of vision in this thinker, but Oliver adds the double meaning of "witness," something of which Merleau-Ponty was fully aware: *témoigner* as both passive and active and as both external-visual and internal-ethical. There is a juridical witness to something seen with your own eyes and an ethical witness to something you believe through faith. Such witnessing, according to Oliver's last and best revelation in the philosopher, is what enables communication but also communion: dialogic interaction with other people. "We could say that the inner witness operates as a negotiating voice between subject positions and subjectivity" (147). By this time we have passed beyond energies of attention, but those energies have carried us to deeper human concerns. Energies of attention have brought phenomenology to the verge of literature; now, we find that those energies are already within writing and necessary to the pleasurable decoding of writing in reading.

Energies of attention: Syntax in sentences and sequences of sentences

Expressed as a humAnimal life-cycle and in nouns and adjectives, here is the arc of progress of a phenomenological thought: *wild, primordial, spontaneous, free, contingent, passive, active, circular, encroaching, intersubjective, pre-supposition, pre-predication, natural attitude, constitution, proposition, reduction/epoché, horizon, interrogation, description, disclosure, institution, sedimentation*. My suppositional sequence is a construct, a collage, a philological fantasy based on reading Merleau-Ponty. Language was needed to imagine it, order it, and input it by means of a keyboard. Language was unstated but required as the anchorage of every term in the list, including *wild*, which is nothing like what is being signified by arbitrary letters in a certain language. And what is the anchorage of *anchorage*? To go in that direction is entirely unproductive. They are just words in a list that help to define one current of thought. The Logos may seem marmoreal, a statue of a ten-foot naked ancient spear-thrower in the museum in Athens, but the better image, for signifier vs. signified, is of having to keep skating on thin ice so as not to break through and plunge down to nescience. That is because the hiddenness of Logos is being or existing or happening as it comes to be. In such matters Merleau-Ponty showed a path of exit when he said, "the life of language reproduces perceptual structures at another level. . . . . There is a Logos of the natural esthetic world, on which the Logos relies" (*Nature* 212).

What may be this Logos of the natural world of perception, on which the written-down Logos relies? Is the spoken or written word itself in language what he elsewhere (in *Signs*) calls "the *vinculum* of the self and things," "the *vinculum* of brute being and a body"? ("Shadow" 169). Logos may be a word, but it may also be a proposition, and we know that in German the term for *proposition—Satz—*is the very same word Germans use for *sentence*. Did Hegel and Husserl, when constructing their systems of logic, that young-philosopher project, recognize the identity of propositions and sentences as they built their impregnable fortresses? Husserl did make this claim in a lecture of 1896: "The first and principal foundation of all logic is the objective, that is, non-psychological theory of dependency relationships between sentences" (qtd. in Moran 22). Husserl becomes more interesting to us and more useful when later on, after 1905, he identifies the natural attitude, exceeds it in the epoché, and speaks of mutual dependency relationships between humAnimal perceptions and things and persons in the world. Merleau-Ponty, following on, would speak of how the living use of language contains matrices of ideas—wild ideas like those listed earlier in italics.

Logos can also mean "sentence," which the household dictionary defines by showing that it is from the Latin *sententia*, disclosing already something philosophical because this is "*sentiens*, prp. of *sentire*, to feel, [or] sense" (*English World Dictionary*). So thinking covertly contains feeling and perceiving! The sentence is a "unit of connected speech or writing, usually containing a subject and a predicate, that in speaking begins following a silence and concludes with any of various final pitches followed by a terminal juncture" (*Webster's New World Dictionary of the American Language* 1297). Sentences can be used for stating, asking, commanding, or exclaiming something—exactly what J. L. Austin referred to when he called statements illocutionary, that is, sentences perform actions like declaring a political stance or saying "I do" and thereby being married.[4] The relatively free range of the sentence seems to have a more open possibility than proposition, as derived from Latin *pro + ponere*, defined as a proposal, but in precision of Logic means "[a]n expression in which the predicate affirms or denies something about the subject" (*Webster's* 1140), and in rhetoric it means "[a] subject to be discussed, statement to be upheld" (1140). "Syntax," which comes from the Greek *syn* (together), plus *tassein* (to arrange), thus to join together, refers to an "orderly or systematic arrangement ... of words as elements in a sentence to show their relation to one another": "groups, phrases, clauses, and sentences" (1444-45). A workaday dictionary is by no means definitive in these

---

4 Webster's includes under "sentence" a reference to twentieth-century generative grammar: "A noun phrase followed by a verb phrase, to which a degree of grammaticalness may be assigned." Very 1980s! It does matter what you define as a rule, and grammaticalness no longer seems subject to measurement by degrees. There must be rules, but rules are subject to redefinition and also to strategic violation. Literature's rules of syntax may differ from those of linguistics or philosophy. Passages here are quoted come from *Webster's New World Dictionary of the American Language*, 2nd ed. (Simon and Schuster).

matters, but, by this reckoning, the stringing of sentences in paragraphs and beyond is also syntax. The term *syntax* is phasing into a metaphor for larger organization for when we follow structures within and beyond the single sentence. How this happens I wish to explore.

Formal logic is an *a priori* normative science. In Bernard Bolzano, Gottlob Frege, and Edmund Husserl at the end of the nineteenth century, logic was based on the rule of consequences and the relation of deduction—the demand for ideal meanings with their corresponding ideal states of affairs. The logicians' antagonists were psychologisms and historicisms, which made inductions from experience expressed only as probabilities: against that, the Germans' formal laws of logic are exact, universal, and ideal. To secure the system, logical meanings have objective validity. Logicians start very purely with a view to non-contradiction and with propositions as ideal unities: subject and predicate exist in an interchangeable alignment of meanings: there is no unbalance, no ambiguity. Only when that is settled can the system consider judgments in terms of truth or falsity.

In his history of Edmund Husserl's intellectual development through accurate descriptions of all stages of thought, Dermot Moran writes: "Logic in its highest form, for Husserl, is the a priori study of all possible forms of theory, and includes a pure science of propositions, understood as the meanings of senses of judgements or linguistic statements or sentences. Husserl never abandons this strong sense of logic" (101). If this is true, then Husserl to the end of his days would accept the kind of sentence and with it the kind of ethos that Gottlob Frege sponsored, in the form *John is happy*. If this is true, then Husserl would follow the Bolzano-Frege hyper-emphasis on logic's rule of reason, the law of non-contradiction, which says we cannot posit a proposition and its negation as both true at the same time. This law is several times explained by Moran, who does say that as a form of thought it makes no reference to what is actually, subjectively thinkable. So what this law of non-contradiction excludes is, by a back-door horror of contamination, included within it as a form of thought. Merleau-Ponty had not Husserl's experience of training or interest in formal logic, and for his own purposes imagined the very Husserl he himself needed, but his considered view in his most penetrating published essay on the master has him concluding, "Originally a project to gain intellectual possession of the world, constitution becomes increasingly, as Husserl's thought matures, the means of unveiling a back side of things that we have not constituted. . . . Willy-nilly, against his plans and according to his essential audacity, Husserl awakens a wild-flowering world and mind" ("Shadow" 180-81).[5] Taught by Husserl, arriving at such a radical view of Husserl's development beyond formal mathematical models of logic, Merleau-Ponty at some level recognizes that the extravagant continuous action of quantum interference is the drastic blatant explosion of the law of non-contradiction.

---

5 So Husserl's philosophical follower disagrees with Husserl's scholarly interpreter.

I want to keep the meaning of *proposition* within the meaning of *sentence*, while also asserting the possibility of adventure. Frege's main premises involve non-mathematical but restricted predicates like *John is happy*, along with a predicate calculus that sets the true against the false, and the abolition of primitive connectives like *and, or, if* in favor of negations and conditionals. Frege's calculus is framed to starve both sides of the very opposition, truth/falsity, that it founds itself upon. At the level of *John is happy* or *Mark Twain is Samuel Clemens*, neither truth nor falsity sustains interest for long.[6] Absolutely, sentences are or can be propositions, but we need not lose the predicative even as we move into something more messy because it is based in perception, emotion, and memory.

What the law of non-contradiction excludes is included within it as a form of thought—included but never admitted. It has taken more than a century for this literary intervention, but I'll now propose to revise the law of non-contradiction to accommodate a new quantum circumstance and call it the *law of interference*, which says that contradiction and non-contradiction are so locked in struggle, so entangled, that we cannot determine the winner, much less which is which. This indetermination, keeping the theories at play, is the essential audacity that Merleau-Ponty saw nascent in Husserl and himself exhibited, while never naming.

If I am correct in this minor audacity, the promulgation of this new law is a making-explicit of the core premise of phenomenology, which is to put the agencies of perceiving-thinking-writing absolutely on the level. It is a new but entirely predictable unthought of Merleau-Ponty.

Given the indisputable fact of embodied mind, *it is reasonable and logical to think* that there is an irredeemable difference at the heart of humAnimal existence. *Therefore*, the law of interference permits us comfortably to think two or more thoughts at once. Read it and weep, Gottlob Frege!

*

Earlier, following the summary of Meier on verbal art as cognitive-perceptual interference, I analyzed Verlaine's "Marine" by counter-posing sentences against lines, with sentences acting out the cognitive side of the struggle. From here forward in this chapter, I wish to add a new possibility that takes us closer to stylistic analysis and, in particular, analysis of works where rhyme and meter are absent and the aesthetic side of the struggle is less obvious and, thus, harder to identify. *The sentence can interfere within itself, so that the cognitive-perceptual interference is internal; the sentence can interfere with previous and subsequent sentences, so that the interference*

---

6 In *Disclosing the World*, Inkpin has two pages on Frege (254-55) as representative of the semantic approach, ruling linguistics since Saussure and his followers and, now, under challenge by Merleau-Ponty through Inkpin. Inkpin firmly concludes, "the predominance of the semantic approach cannot count against the relevance of phenomenological facts to a philosophically satisfactory conception of language" (255).

is between sentences as units. The name for this kind of effect used to be *prose,* and that is the name Merleau-Ponty used for his 1952 title for his draft of *The Prose of the World,* but since this effect is the dominant in works that are obviously poems, the better term will be *the art-sentence*—used for prose-poems but also for all works narrative and discursive that lack meter and rhyme. It is in the spirit of cooperative interference that we extend term "art-sentence" to describe the ground-level writing in philosophical essays.

Ancient writing that survives is inscribed on animal skins or flat stones, and it sometimes presents as continuous runs of separate words with no indication of internal divisions or breaks between sentences—even between words. It is as if there were no sentences, but a sort of sentence-sense exists nonetheless; if it could be written thus, unquestionably it could be deciphered thus. Probably not even with difficulty. Over millennia markers within and between sentences made the decoding process of reading more easy, and punctuation brought speed and disambiguation to the read-back of reading. The comma could isolate phrases and clauses and make them more movable within the seeming-infinite open structure; the semicolon could permit linkage of meaning backward and forward and productive extension of the thinking—crude parataxis or subtle hypotaxis to add shades of meaning and put breathing-breaks within the read-out. The marvelous dash-structure permits instant explanations internally or, at the end, the attachment of a tag that turns everything in a new direction. There was also thought beating back against itself in the parenthesis. (Samuel Taylor Coleridge, a philosophical literary man, loved the parenthesis for its recoil of thought, perpendicular to the rest of the sentence but also internal to the sentence.) The strongest resource of all is the period: the aimed-at end-mark of closure or anti-closure.[7] The period prepares for the next sentence's unrolling of meaning through words divided by internal relations of form-class, and by punctuation, so the period is already part of a beginning, unless it is the last period.

Though some languages do not have subject-verb-object, or do not have those in that order, and some do not have pronouns or little linking words like *of* or *and,* they get the job done for their native speakers. We know not how that works, but in English we are acutely aware that, in the normal SVO order, the subject moves across the verb to the object to provide a *vinculum* to the surround, physical or mental. That is positively phenomenological. The sentence is divided internally by these and other structures, all of them optional and none of them obligatory. Inside the frame and between the capital-letter first letter and the final period or line of suspension dots, any form-class of grammar can appear almost anywhere, but it is helpful (for decoding) that usually the sequence is more or less formulaic. In all of language, the sentence is the prime example of in-between-ness. It is usually more or less

---

[7] Russian short story master Isaac Babel said of the period: "No iron spike can pierce a human heart as icily as a period in the right place."

orderly and usually hovering somewhere near the seven-item span of words, that psychologists have found is the optimum number for untrained minds to remember. Inside its own internal interference of subject and verb, active and passive, transitive and intransitive, it manages to be in between the laconic and the overwhelming, neither too long nor too abruptly short. The aleatory internal complexity and the ease of external hookup afford the sentence immense freedom of choice in the economy of expressive style.

One form of in-between-ness is the way the sentence hovers in the gap between outer speech and inner speech. Russian psychologist Lev Vygotsky in the 1930s gave one of the best accounts of inner speech: developmentally our speech is entirely the result of coaching (at the right age and no later) from other humans. Sounds emerge before words. Babbling emerges before speech. Names and exclamations emerge before sentences. Once outer speech is installed after infancy, as we blunder into our own personal selves, inner speech grows in control and complexity. Our inner speech is literally but inaudibly ourselves as persons, and all ideas are personal though related to the cultural surround. Is thinking word-bound? Are there sentences in inner speech, or is it mostly images or broken-off phrases? Much remains to be studied. Other Russians working on inner speech are Mikhail Bakhtin, who sees writing in literature in relation to an inner speech striated by the social, and a small set of psychologists who did experiments in the 1960-1980s period, working in awareness of Vygotsky and Bakhtin. Bakhtin's account is part of his communication theory as a whole, which maintains that our dialogic nature puts speech on the border between ourselves and others, utterance responding to utterance, inner speech gestating the more formal utterances we try when we speak to others. The corollary is crucial: if we start speaking without dialogue with ourselves or others, that form of utterance is monologic, heading toward self-centered, isolated, demagogic, or crazy behavior. Unlike dialogism, monologism is readymade, fake-objective, and official in the sense of *impersonal*. Here are Caryl Emerson's conclusions in her study of Vygotsky and Bakhtin, an essay not recent but forever eloquent:

> These, then, are the ways an awareness of the gap between inner and outer might function in both life and literature: as an index of individual consciousness; as a measure of our escape from fixed plots and roles; as a prerequisite for discourse itself. . . . The eternal and inevitable inadequacy of all names permits new meanings and new messages to be created. This permission . . . is Bakhtin's novelistic gap . . . . And it is the lack, the absence at the center, that keeps the outer word and our inner speech in permanent dialogue, out of that danger Bakhtin saw of collapse into single consciousness, which would be non-existence. (35-36)

Emerson concludes that inside that gap, it is "always worthwhile to try naming it again" (36), and one of the names is the English Sentence.

Reading Merleau-Ponty's few references to Wittgenstein and ordinary language philosophy, it would appear that he finds insufficient a practical usage-concerned theory of language. We do not know how obvious the issues in the 1950s were or how much or just what the French philosopher read of the German philosopher working at Cambridge University. Not much was readily available between the *Tractatus*, published decades before, and the arrival of *Philosophical Investigations*, written in German and published in 1953, with a second edition in 1958. Early Wittgenstein had some dubious arguments concerning sentences as propositions: in the 1920s Frank Ramsey wondered, "what about the sentences that make up the *Tractatus* itself" (Setiya 37), if, in that work, sentences not obviously propositions are just nonsense? The form of thought was the form of the proposition so if the proposition had slippage there was a logical contradiction. We have met this quandary before in the law of non-contradiction, and apparently Wittgenstein addressed it in a novel but (as he knew) weak way "by contending that the surface form of sentences deceives us" (38).

Later Wittgenstein was both more cautious and more capacious on language, and he is the leading figure in Moi's persuasive evangelizing book on literary studies after Wittgenstein and others, *Revolution of the Ordinary* (2017). In her best short summary of the case she has to make:

> Ordinary language is not a normative notion. It is simply "what we say." And "we" here means every speaker of the language, not just a select high-status group. It is, simply, language that *works*, language that helps us to draw useful distinctions, carry out tasks, engage fruitfully with others— . . . language as the medium in which we live our lives. . . . Ordinary language, in short, comprises the full resources of human language, all its powers to draw distinctions. (161)

This assertion comes as part of Moi's argument that literature is not an abnormal language, separate from our everyday speech acts, not some domain of learning or privilege. Against the allegation made by Stanley Fish that Wittgenstein and Austin are positivists who think that only propositions convey knowledge, she marshals Austin's distinction between constative and performative utterances to show that cognitive utterances are always also emotive utterances.[8] "For Austin, there can be no such thing as a purely descriptive, literal, or objective language. For Wittgenstein, *use* always requires judgment, and reveals both how I see the world and what my own investments and values are" (Moi 161). On this question of a false distinction between propositions and sentences, then, there need be no appreciable difference between ordinary language philosophy, and phenomenology. Mid-paragraph, in his essay on "Indirect Language and the Voices of Silence," Merleau-Ponty finds a way to signal this accord on the ordinary or given language, and also to point a new direction for the study of the sentence. He is talking about how the given language that "penetrates [the writer] through and through and from the beginning sketches a

---

8 Pursuing and extending J. L. Austin's ideas about the strong performative nature of language, Enikő Bollobás has an admirable study of key figures in nineteenth- and twentieth-century American writing, with chapters on race and gender in classic texts: *They Aren't, Until I Call Them: Performing the Subject in American Literature* (Frankfurt am Main: Peter Lang, 2010).

diagram of his most secret thoughts, does not stand before him as an enemy" (*S* 79). Seemingly out of nowhere but actually a complete expression of the interference at the core of phenomenology, comes this totally amazing zinger: "If you wish, [the man who writes] destroys ordinary language, but by realizing it" (*S* 79). This process is the agency of the art-sentence.

Except for a few places where Moi argues that sentences are not equal to propositions—that the excess beyond propositions is what makes sentences ordinary, judgmental, emotive, interesting—she has written a whole book in sentences without mentioning sentences. By contrast, Jan Mieszkowski has written a book wherein no sentence is not about sentences. It is hard to imagine a more complete account of the topic than his *Crises of the Sentence* (2019). Mieszkowski's home-base is German literature and philosophy, and he ranges across disciplines and languages to address issues neglected in linguistics because they are considered too humanistic and in literature because they are too scientific. Until now the sentence has been so occluded within the natural attitude, so lost in the middle-space between academic fields and between other lengths of language, that it is hidden, minimized, or assimilated to something it is not. And yet, as he says on the first page of his Introduction, the sentence is everywhere on the job, "forever signifying, referring, and performing" (1). The author has strong opinions based in a comprehensive survey of the scholarly archive but, also, rooted in reading of original creative works in literature and philosophy. For example: "Everything we believe about events and praxis, and hence about history, politics, and even the priority of being over becoming, is shaped by [a] blind allegiance to subject-predicate thinking" (3); "there is a tendency to treat enjambment as one more rhetorical maneuver . . . rather than as an indication of how poetry can alter our conception of discourse" (5); "it is in the sentence that the tension between writerly freedom and linguistic necessity is most acutely played out" (7-8) ; "The English word 'sentence' . . . came to designate a finished thought, verdict, or judgment. . . . Today the situation is quite different" (12). He has harsh words for the influence of Saussure, Voloshinov, Jakobson, Barthes, Benveniste: Structuralism avoided the sentence or relegated it to statemental utility. It is, he says, impossible to read literary works according to the generative grammar of Noam Chomsky, because of Chomsky's "insistence on a stark opposition between the syntactic and semantic"; for Chomsky, "meaning always rests on an *a posteriori* interpretation of a structure, unlike the Saussurians, who at least had a more dynamic relation between morphology, syntax, and structure" (29).

In the book's chapters, Mieszkowski covers standalone sentences, the poetic line as pitting sentences against meter and rhyme in the effect of enjambment, the different ways sentences advance toward their endings, and, last, the politics of the democratic sentence. In the book's Conclusion, he makes it clear that the crisis of the sentence is in part a persistent doubt whether there is such a thing as a sentence at all. He raises, throughout, a question about whether style is ever simply a private affair. He finds ample reason to worry that the sentence is in alignment with the liberal subject and, thus, socially limited. On the positive side, the book's two final pages defend "the sentence's status as a hinge between individual autonomy and collective control" and articulate the way sentences are powerful precisely "because they are by nature sites of ongoing reflection and analysis and are thus permanently marked by an air of the provisional" (240-41). Mieszkowski's achievements in the book include his ability to bring the sentence into full literary and philosophical visibility through his informed linguistic sense of the varied internal structures of the sentence, his recognition of the crucial role of punctuation in dividing and determining meaning, and his commitment to a political reading of sentences inside larger textual frames. From my point of view, this writer's second chapter, on the relation of the sentence to the line in Walt Whitman and Emily Dickinson, noting Whitman's prolixity compared to her density, is an example of how to do textual analysis while keeping all the lines open to personal styles and historical contexts. It is a display of how the energy in writing comes from the differences, in this case the draping of the syntax over the end of the line in enjambment: "The most explicit clash between syntax and versification is enjambment, which sees a sentence continue from one line to the next with no clear pause or juncture to mark the transition or break" (87). The line cuts the sentence, but the sentence divides the line and, in reading, this meter and this grammar are processed simultaneously. In all of literature, that is the clearest irrefutable unfolding of the energies of interference.

Mieszkowski's *tour de force* is his seventeen-page, heavily footnoted reading of Gertrude Stein's project of internal demolition, and political feminizing, of the patriarchal sentence. His study-texts are *Tender Buttons*, *How to Write*, and *The Making of Americans*, where Stein is uncertain what a sentence may be or whether there are sentences—she having declared that as a girl her major passion was the diagramming of sentences.[9] He writes, "Anything that smacks of a code or a stable one-to-one relationship between a word and a unit of sense strikes Stein as banal, leading her to dismiss nouns and adjectives as categorically boring" (201). Verbs,

---

[9] Stein broke the back of the patriarchal predicative sentence, but it was for others to explore and remake what was now permitted. As an example of Stein's achievement and her limitation, here are lines chosen at random from *Stanzas in Meditation*, from the opening of part 2, stanza 4:

> All who have hoped to think of them or wonder
> Or maybe they will like what they have had
> More than they should if they went away freshly
> And were very modest about not knowing why it was
> That they were not denied their pleasure then
> For which they may be more than not inclined
> Which makes it plainly that in one way it made no difference . . . (23)

And so on.

though, he quotes from Stein, "are on the move, and adverbs move with them" (qtd. in Mieszkowski 201). Within the sentence, and between sentences as emotionless and paragraphs as emotional, the predicative structure is itself at issue. By a long chain of mediations, that structure is also the structure of capitalist economics: Mieszkowski connects Stein's version of the democratic sentence to Marxist literary theory in Fredric Jameson and to the work of the Language poets from the 1970s to the present day.[10] In Mieszkowski, Jameson, and Language writers like Ron Silliman and Lyn Hejinian, the sentence exceeds the proposition and becomes the nexus of creativity.

By profound aversion to the confessional poets of the 1960s—Robert Lowell, Anne Sexton, and Sylvia Plath—the San Francisco Language Poets surfaced in the 1970s, with the intent to abandon on principle anything like direct self-reference, along with those intricate constraining trammels, rhyme and meter. They were trained in structuralism, in generative grammar, and in Ferruccio Rossi-Landi's Marxist theories of language, and they spoke to each other in gatherings to refine an aesthetic and wrote books with titles like *Total Syntax* (by Barrett Watten), *The New Sentence* (by Ron Silliman), *The Language of Inquiry*, and *The Cold of Poetry* (both by Lyn Hejinian). They identified each other as a loose kind of school shortly after the 1967 publication of a collection by leading philosophers titled *The Linguistic Turn*, edited by Richard Rorty. There was no coordination between the poets and these Rorty-ites, who aimed to demonstrate that all philosophical issues can be solved or dissolved by attending stringently to issues of language. But the writers and philosophers were riding the same oncoming wave of the new linguistic theory from the continent and from Chomsky. Probably, the writers were aware of those who theorized the linguistic turn, but it is certain that the philosophers were not reading the mimeographed newsletters and the ten classy issues (1982-1998) of *Poetics Journal* in limited circulation.[11] Now, in 2024, the linguistic turn has long ago fizzled out, while the Language writers continue to publish impressively and to find new ways to excavate their original premises.

---

10 Mieszkowski quotes Jameson from *Marxism and Form*: "I remain faithful to the notion that any concrete description of a literary or philosophical phenomenon—if it is to be really complete—has an ultimate obligation to come to terms with the shape of the individual sentences themselves, to give an account of their origin and formation" (qtd. in Mieszkowski 43). That comes from a book of 1971, and in an essay on "Time and the Sea" in Joseph Conrad, Jameson is still being faithful to sentences as units: "[W]hat Conrad does with plot betrays the fundamental contradiction in modernism between plot and sentence . . . [between] the raw material of the story and its realization in sentences or in dramatic acts." It is worth noting that our most lyrical hymn to the preposition, as a form-class of grammar, occurs in Jameson's book on Hegel, Marx, Lukács, and Ricoeur, *Valences of the Dialectic*.
11 *Poetics Journal* was edited by Barrett Watten and Lyn Hejinian. Issue 10 (June 1998, Berkeley, CA) has as its first essay Pierre Alferi's "Seeking A Sentence," where he states: "The literary object is the sentence" (3); "Every sentence is musical" (3); academicism in poetry is "betrayed by a snoring syntax" and by line, rhyme, meter (4); "each sentence becomes its own unit of measure" (5); and "[t]he more the sentence pulls on the thread of reference, the more the rhythm distances itself from that of habitual perception, and the more things appear in their contingency" (8).

The idea was to find a lyrical possibility within entirely different sets of constraints and measures. The speaking subject was to be prevented from fact-stating or fact-bemoaning autobiography, but otherwise kept, rerouted, and diversified, so that there is a vast collection of sentences but very few of them having an owned personal pronoun in the subject position. If this kind of writing happened to include oblique self-reference, it might be something about the physical act of writing, or about features of language, or the alphabet, or typewriters or paper; it would not be about the writer but her or his task, her or his medium. If there would be a narrative content, it might be a hoax narrative. Lyricism would be gained by means of the return of refrains in short bursts of phrase, as in Hejinian's *My Life*, where her life turns out to be her memories and thoughts and feelings, where the returning phrase, printed as prose, will be "[a] *pause, a rose, something on paper.*" (That starts out iambic, changes meter half-way, and uses a soft kind of rhyme, so the refrain's more like traditional poetry than the rest of the sentences in long paragraphs that make up the main text.) If there is a hint of meter or rhyme, it comes as an instance and not as overall design, but there is no reluctance to put in hints, no reluctance to be outlandish, or gorgeous, or abrupt in the structures of sentences. Occasionally, there will occur rebarbative lists, proudly joking nonsense, sentences of similar length and structure set in a row, and straight-talk swear-words passed off as ordinary vocabulary. Stein, whom Language writers will perhaps claim as their mother, gave permission for creative manipulation of sentences and for some kinds of delightful meandering, but she also produced sentences flattened out, droning, repetitive-redundant, lacking forward motion or internal complexity. Language poets for the most part have a wider range of syntactic structures and vocabularies, so to make tighter art-sentences than Stein, partly as a way of not being Stein.

Without autobiography, without the this-happened-poem and the I-noticed-this-poem, without family history as the narrative, the Language writer has to find other ways of ordering the utterance in the large. Rather, on the analogy of serial music, at times these writers use external arbitrary formats to proceed through to an ending. This plan makes for a difference in the larger rhythm of the work as staging for the rhythm of the single sentence. Silliman has a two-hundred-page poem in mid-length sentences divided into groupings based on the Fibonacci principle, so that the opening is a short burst and the closing group takes up the whole second half of the book. That has to change the reading habits of the person following it and has to affect how we take in the single sentences that are about daily life, riding the bus, things seen, random bits of inner speech. The reader feels it could end anywhere. That is the point—the drone of ongoingness, along with the mini-shocks of interruption.

Hejinian's book *Tribunal* (2019) contains three long poems, all three in 52 sections for the number of weeks in the year or for something to do with the Mayan calendar.[12] In the first and third poem, each section has five sentences indented for separation, and the second poem, "Time of Tyranny," has long unmetered lines in sets of fourteen—clearly a mocking allusion to the length of the traditional sonnet. The arbitrariness of the frame is a little justified by the symbolism of the numbers, but the rationale will be that within these limits will occur wild thinking in ever-changing, self-interrupting sentencing. Through her informed and frequent references to *phenomenon, appearance,* and *description,* it seems pretty evident that the author knows the kind of philosophy that values, as Merleau-Ponty values, "the animal of perceptions and movements" (*S* 169). *Tribunal* is dense with perceptual content of two sorts: first, it includes pervasive references to things and persons in the natural surround, what Merleau-Ponty would call "the perceived object, with its viscous signification" (*PW* 106); and second, it provides immersive swimming in language-as-writer's-medium, language-as-reader's-experience-of-continuous-mini-shocks. As in *My Life,* but on a larger scale and with more counters to move around, there is a rhyming of theme and not of single words, with the body as a primary theme: tit, cock, cunt, ankle, genitals, tongue, spit, fart, shit. The human-in-itself is a theme in the first poem, "A Human of Mars," where other themes that emerge, without pattern but often, are death, the color red for Mars, the words "pause" and "rose" as ironic memories of the famous refrain line of *My Life,* time, and punctuation marks like the comma called as comma. In the second poem, "Time of Tyranny," the recurring theme references are to names of mountains and rivers around the world, and the terms include "tyrant" and "tyranny," fog, trees, dogs, death, cowboys, fear, arbitrariness, skepticism. In addition to this unpatterned emergence of themes, both these poems contain certain registers of language, including university-speak in long Latin-root words, and nonsense-writing of various sorts, including the illogical linkage of topics in a single sentence and the use of impossible words that together have delicious, speakable sounds. Instead of confessional poetry's "here I am," we have language writing's "who am I?" Also here: frequent interruption! Lots of suspension dots and exclamation points! Heavy deixis! Heavy apostrophe![13]

---

[12] For valuable commentary on Hejinian's intentions with structure of thought and sentencing, see Marjorie Perloff, *Unoriginal Genius: Poetry by Other Means in the New Century* (2010), Jacob Edmond, *A Common Strangeness: Contemporary Poetry, Cross-Cultural Encounter, Comparative Literature* (2012), and Craig Dworkin, *Radium of the Word: A Poetics of Materiality* (2020).

[13] First and most capacious of recent commentators on apostrophe as lyric address is Jonathan Culler in *Theory of the Lyric* (2015) 211-43. He finds the function of invocation, of indirect and direct address, to be central to the lyric. It may occur also in scholarly prose: the reader will have caught our own direct address in this chapter to a logician dead for a century and to a neurophilosopher who works in San Diego.

These signature devices are in service of the evocation of uncanniness in "A Human of Mars" and in service of oblique condemnation of a certain kind of illiberal politics in "Time of Tyranny." The book as a whole is a tribunal in the sense of arraigning the Donald Trump presidency without naming exactly what is being transacted, but with a secure sense of the joyous appreciation of values to set against our own anger and confusion down in the fields and cities. In words from the book, those are the values of "delight in appearance" (17), being "together," "the concept of sparkling as well as that of burbling and firing," "not willing to exchange . . . phenomenology for ontology" being "ungovernable" (16). "Attention: anarchy! And its assistant: poetry!" (48). And, best of all, the book includes "a mockery which tyranny cannot thaw, torture cannot make unkind" (52). The reader or auditor of these poems has an advantage over the critical interpreter, because these effects ideally require us to absorb the whole utterance; they are distributed and do not cluster or lend themselves to quotation. We limit ourselves to one passage as example. The following numbered segment of "A Human of Mars" shows some of the features mentioned and corrects, with forty years' hindsight, the lilting and memorable refrain-pause from *My Life*:

> 44
> A planet comes whole, home to a system, but can it carry details that disobey the system?
> A stream of elements, of turbulence, of petulance, of elephants,
> An elephant can't float like a cloud over a savannah, but—there!—we have pictured one doing so: have we defied the system?
> Indifference loses us, and all that advances chases after the sun.
> From the spheres comes music, and with it a lyric: "Now a pause,
> now a rose, and now a small coffin, Bitch!" (26)

As a rule, if nearby words have similar sounds, the first word has instantly generated the second one, derailing a possible logical sense and dashing off in another direction along the line of the sound, as in "whole-home," and also the "-ence" sounds of the second sentence, which arrives crazily at "elephants" and then produces the third sentence along that new line of sense. But the third line interruptively turns on a "but," a double-dash enclosing an exclamation (pure deixis), and a philosophical question on whether an evoked image has tricked the mind of writer and reader. The fourth sentence is like the end of that prose poem "Cities" by Rimbaud, where the whole scene is scrubbed by calling it a savage charade. That shift is the setup for wicked self-mocking in the last lyric phrase, where the earlier refrain from long ago, about an American girl's perceptual-cognitive-writerly life, is kept and demolished by "now" and by an epithet in apostrophe, with the force of exclamation: "!"

Coming again upon the word "phrase," which is the normal French term for "sentence," we may be reminded of another French writer, Roland Barthes, Merleau-Ponty's younger contemporary who was even more seriously an acolyte of Saussure, who said that "pense-phrase," thinker of sentences, is the other name for writer. To validate that name by reference to Hejinian's own trope of apostrophe in that "Bitch!"

addressed to her mortal self outside the text, we may think the Merleau-Pontian thought that here is a tiny instance of carrying details that disobey the linguistic system—and of destroying ordinary language by realizing it. Apostrophe is the icon of interference because it beckons some thing outside of language from within language.

Chapter 6: Modes and Powers of Attention: Nine Terms from Merleau-Ponty

The question of "how to read" with phenomenology's capacious categories calls for a reminder that Merleau-Ponty's overall aim was to recover the roots of rationality. It means taking perception all the way over to cognition and writing and back again. It does not mean abandoning rational thought, but rather preventing rational thought from isolating itself in its majesty.

In phenomenology, the reduction or epoché is the start-that-continues, following into further phases that interrogate, describe, and disclose the particulars of relation between our bodies and their surround in the things and persons of the world. The *praxis* of this way of doing philosophy is one of descent to the soil, not of vaulting to heights, and so it must lower the level of generality—for example, to the kind of items on the list that Merleau-Ponty set out in the "Working Notes" to *The Visible and the Invisible*: "dimensions, articulation, level, hinges, pivots, configurations" (224). These are all ratios of relation for differential specifying of perception in its performance. Because these are rational ratios, there is no lack of cognitive caution.

It's a matter of the reason we use for reading, whether we're reading the *Umwelt* or Edmund Husserl or Cézanne or Henry James. Note that Merleau-Ponty specifically sets out "dimensions" and several other preferred diacritical notions as replacements for four others—"concept, idea, mind, representation." These perception-terms are bringing with them a new regime of reading.

To begin reading in this style of thought, we need faith in the mind as embodied, a willingness to engage in first-person discourse, an abiding interest in how the perceptual field reveals itself to the human senses, and an abundant and mobile sense of how to describe examples. I have chosen nine of Merleau-Ponty's terms that offer further definition of the Modes and Powers of Attention, to take his approach to the process of reading.[1] In the next chapter I try out the terms on three poems and a long stretch of a novel.[2]

---

[1] The following paragraphs on terms contain summaries and paraphrases and making-explicit interpretations drawn from several sources, always with a lookout for a philosopher's help when we do literary and other reading. The reader who wishes to go to long passages by Merleau-Ponty himself should consult *The Visible and the Invisible*, which puts the term *interrogation* into its subtitle and which begins with three chapters focused on *interrogation*; this posthumous volume also has a chapter on "The Chiasm" and several additional pages on *chiasm* and on *depth* (214-15, 219-20, 263-64, 267-68). *Husserl at the Limits of Phenomenology* also has more than a few short but valuable definitions of *chiasm*. Wiskus has definitions and example-readings for *rhythm*, *depth*, and *non-coincidence*. Inkpin's book is devoted to phenomenological *disclosure* in general and specifically in theory of language. Also useful here is a book whose editor knew that a glossary of Merleau-Ponty's signature terms would extend his influence, and which has admirable essays on "Eye and Mind," on "The Intertwining—The Chiasm," and on movement or motricity; with a glossary entry on *Ineinander* by Wiskus: see *Understanding Merleau-Ponty, Understanding Modernism*, edited by Ariane Mildenberg (2019).

[2] Speed-reading a large pile of marked copies of books by Merleau-Ponty and others in order to write the explanations which follow, I have more notations than needed for seven of the nine terms.

Is there a detachable phenomenological method as such? No. For reading literary texts with Merleau-Ponty, it will be more a matter of an attitude toward experience, taking perceptions as variable units, than a matter of teachable system. In other words, phenomenological literary criticism is almost always not settled law but case law.

Modes of Attention

Movement

Movement is the first of the Modes because movement is at the heart of Merleau-Ponty's philosophy of perception. (Husserl had not said much about this topic, so it is the later writer's original emphasis.) Existence, being-in-the-world, is here conceived as change: perception as true mobility, the capacity for orienting ourselves in the sensible world, with the body and the body schema and the body's sense perceptions as registers of change. Movement means—corporeality and corporeality needs movement, in the relation between me and my body and me and the world. The philosopher thinks of the openness of the body as perceptual faith, and at some level this *pivot*, this relation, already contains meaning. That has to be so if perceptions are inscribed in shapes and qualities from the *Umwelt* of things and persons, that reveal their being to us. (A later phenomenological thinker, James J. Gibson, called these gestures, to us from the world, *affordances*.)[3] The analytical notions of "dimensions, articulation, level, hinges, pivots, and configurations" (*VI* 224) are themselves inquiries into movements, into traces of time in space. This has implications for writing and reading, as we think about the movement of *articulation* within the image-content of texts and in the very process of reading as exercise of perceptual skills. Intellectual movement is in this way of thinking a passage from the sensible world where we're fated to live our lives to the world of expression where we write and read our books.

However, the paragraphs on *non-coincidence* and *rhythm* have their origins in the book by Wiskus. These two terms are included because they are Merleau-Pontian in spirit and useful for our inspection of painting, music, and literature (she gives two chapters to each of these). Inclusion of these two terms is in accord with Merleau-Ponty's wish and my own to make-explicit the unthought of earlier thinkers. Late Merleau-Ponty wrote of late Husserl: "Circle: we presuppose his final thoughts and they presuppose this method" (*HLP* 115).

3 See Gibson, *The Ecological Approach to Visual Perception* (1986).

Depth

My body is a thing among other things, but in a richer and more dynamic way. I see something, say a black phoebe in the garden and know that the tuxedo-wearing flycatcher exists in the round even though I see one side; I know that I also have depth and that visibility closes in behind me, too. Introducing the French philosopher's notes on Husserl's essay concerning "The Origin of Geometry," Leonard Lawlor says that Merleau-Ponty prioritizes the soil: "orienting his entire philosophy toward the depth, in the ground, the visible, and not, as he says, in the heights, in the ideas, in the invisible" (*HLP* xvii). Painters and writers who work with a pre-established order of signification like Renaissance perspective, with its single and specified point of view, have renounced ambiguity, have made the perceived world disappear. The philosopher understands how this was a discovery of moment in the Renaissance, but perspective is now easy, automatic, sedimented. By contrast, the modern painters' multiple local views preserve the ambiguity of spontaneous vision—the true creative vision in this later era, where the perceived world has not disappeared, but we are aware that it is the surface over a profound depth. There's depth in language, too. This is in the philosopher's words and the title of my chapter, a "syntax in depth" (*IPP* 93), where the writer's system of significations and equivalences has an internal *articulation* which, Merleau-Ponty says *In Praise of Philosophy*, "reproduces the contours of experience . . . [in a] mode of composition . . . which breaks the mold of everyday language and refashions it" (93). Like the Husserlian reduction, which must remain incomplete, the Merleau-Pontian depth is never wholly constitutable in language. This is not a flaw, not an error, but does mean that such a philosophy never descends down to the deepest unreachable depth, so never rests, never ends.

Chiasm

Merleau-Ponty called the human being the animal of movements and perceptions. The agents and the actions in that phrase all fit together and require each other—require also a life-world or *Umwelt* in which to sport themselves. This would be philosophy from beneath, from the soil and from the thought which is before thought. Non-philosophy recruits philosophy and philosophy needs non-philosophy's openness to the exterior through movements registered by perceptions. To a far greater degree than before in professional philosophy, or in Merleau-Ponty's own thought before 1959-1961, now philosophy searches non-philosophy and the latter encroaches upon new writing. Other names for this project are the Intertwining, or the Chiasm. The inquiry into the *Ineinander*, or oneinanother, expanded into Chiasm in the last two years of the philosopher's writing life in the notes about Husserl on geometry as well as in draft chapters and the "Working Notes" to *The Visible and the Invisible*.

The *Oxford English Dictionary* has four related words, chiasm-chiasma-chiasmus-chiastic: 1) where the order of clauses is reversed; 2) where there's an intercrossing of two lines or sticks, like the letter X; 3) where there is a diagonal arrangement (especially in clauses of a sentence) in a grammatical figure by which the order of words in one of the parallel clauses is inverted in the other; 4) and where items are arranged diagonally. The idea behind the Chiasm that made it attractive is *intercrossing* or *reversal*, and we might submit that this is yet another synonym for our suggested metaphor of *interference*. The figure of *chiasmus* is a trope for the indeterminate interference of separate linguistic entities that are also types of thought, or, as Merleau-Ponty might say, *also* components of the dialectic. That these terms are closely related, all but interchangeable where to bring in one is to call up others, is not a slippage of logic, but rather a sign that phenomenology is identifying all its allies.

Entities that are being crossed, intertwined, interfered with come from all possible domains of humAnimal life. Many more domains could be shown than those that follow. The sample set I've chosen can be written out in a list where *and* could just as well be *versus*: the visible and the invisible, transcendental and empirical, ontological and ontic, theory and practice, philosophy and non-philosophy. It's a matter of *dimensions* and *levels* because such ground-up, *sauvage* or wild thinking is beginning its work in conscious defiance of ideas and abstractions. Late Merleau-Ponty, moving into this new set of proposals through emphasis on the terms that carry them, is increasingly trying to give an account of the genesis of philosophy itself.

Dialogue is also chiasm; the philosopher in *The Prose of the World* says that my perception of the other person, as thing and as speaking subject, "slips into my perception from behind" (136-37). Self-other, speech-writing, speaking-thinking, and countless other crossings have apparently no absolute difference between the two domains. Accordingly, there is no absolutely pure philosophical speech "since philosophy," Merleau-Ponty says, "like all literature can convey its meaning, signifying of things and of world, with words" (*VI* 266). Like all literature! He is in his later thought not only counterposing painting and writing as coherent deformations of the sensible, not only increasingly using literary examples from Stendahl, Proust, Mallarmé, Rimbaud, Valéry, and others to illustrate *configurations* in perception: he is also arguing that the tasks of the disciplines cannot be separated, have equality in searching appearance and assessing depth. In both kinds of inquiry transparent expression isn't reachable since both are restricted to words-in-sentences. Since sentences are and are not propositions, they are not entirely trustworthy for truth, but they are all we have. Neither philosophy nor literature can *articulate* ambiguity, simultaneity, chiasm, or reversibility as such. Interrogation, description, and disclosure are teachable skills but all three are limited to giving results in speech and writing.

And how to make the invisible visible in writing? We shall see.

Merleau-Ponty on occasion discusses the weakness of philosophy, the limping which is also its virtue. Philosophy itself is chiasmatic. When he writes a book of essays *In Praise of Philosophy*, he makes explicit how "the most resolute philosopher always wishes the contrary—to realize, but to destroy; to suppress, but also to conserve" (58-59). There is a difference in us between "that which understands, and that which chooses" (60). This chiasmatic thinking, limping but strong, enables him in these pages to comment powerfully on protagonists in ancient Greek tragedies and on the fate of Julien Sorel in Stendahl. The tragic hovering between the religious and the secular, between fate and free will does not come from malign outward events, or from fall from a height, or from the fact of a death, but from a recognition within the character, "since [the character has her or his] own contrary within itself" (58). He shows the birth of moral meaning in a literary personage. He puts chiasmic interference within the play's hierarchy of emotions and within the system of genres.

Reversibility

The first reversibility is that of the humAnimal body as both subject and object, and both of these simultaneously within the same skin. Paraphrasing, perception has a reversible meaning if we can see what sees, touch what touches, speak about what speaks. The second reversibility is that of myself and the other person, a reciprocity which is founded upon a primary reversibility between myself and the other—intercorporeal being. That's a reciprocal intersubjectivity of the sort late Merleau-Ponty recognized and saluted in late Husserl. It's not a fusion of self and other, but rather what he called a syncresis, an overlapping or coming together of distinct selves when we consort, when we converse. It's an ancient sociality older than me and beyond me that includes me, and Merleau-Ponty's account of self-other in living experience so impressed Lawrence Hass, in his book of commentary, that he said: this is once and for all a compelling solution to the traditional problem of other minds (see Hass 102-12). The philosopher found a beautiful phrase for it in relation to my voice as it recognizes another voice, hearing in her or him "the awesome birth of vociferation" (*VI* 144).

Speech is actually a *pivotal* case when we inquire into the topic with the philosopher's terms. In the dualism of traditional philosophical thought, the staple is *spoken speech*, readymade, already constituted, and also top-down with those well-known abstractions of concept, idea, mind, and representation. Spoken speech has its value in the realm of science and rationality which Merleau-Ponty would never downgrade but which he does not want as the only or starting premises of phenomenology. Spoken speech has its own value and indeed necessary status. However, spoken speech has habitual routines and logics of alternation—not of chiasm or interference—that make it impossible for humAnimals to see the point of *speaking speech*, or the utterance of spontaneity, of ambiguity, of what we've above called superposition. To get to the phenomenological attitude by means of search of appearance in existing spoken speech, the thinker must break out of routine habits, dissolve dualisms, and imagine the power of a contrary kind of utterance. That is where reversibility comes in: not as the overthrow of spoken speech, not as an alternation of the opposite point of view and the usual, not as substitution, but as an interdependence of equals. Reversibility as logic and as politics goes beyond the trap of alternation of oppositions, which kept Hegel and Marx fixated on the dialectic. Reversibility is encroachment of each toward and into the other, with non-absorptive relations between negative and positive, active and passive, readymade and spontaneous, spoken and speaking. Reversibility, no surprise, is a relation of interference, and it can never be complete.

Reversibility is based on the ultimate truth the late Merleau-Ponty theorized as Flesh, where the limits blur between ourselves and things and persons in the world. Flesh imagines an entirely new relation in the last writings: a metaphor of an intersubjectivity circular and reciprocal: the final *articulation and level and dimension and configuration* of the human in this system because it is the intertwining of being and meaning.

Non-coincidence

I take the negation of a term as a prized value. Coincidence is locked with its negation, and so it is built-in, necessary to the construct in language and in fact. Coincidence is often in ordinary speech called lucky or unlucky, because the event in question is happened-upon: unmotivated and unintentional, and we know how much thinkers of Husserl's era valued, perhaps over-valued, intentional acts. It must follow that non-coincidental events are motivated and intentional. Merleau-Ponty on speaking: "What we have to say is only the excess of what we live over what has already been said" (*PW* 112). And on the happy writer writing: "He must remake his language within this language, which provides him only with an external signaling of things" (110). So non-coincidence can be outside *excess* or inside *within*, as long as anonymous official language is taken beyond itself into expressive language.

In a short essay on Henri Bergson, Merleau-Ponty defines the structure of this concept of *beyond* as not an addition or a compounding or a merging-into, rather the acquisition of a new idea of how relationships occur. Bergson famously theorized coincidence as experiencing himself as transcended by being, but Bergson also conveyed another more capacious reading that commentators have missed because they don't yet know the phenomenological attitude. Perception grounds everything: everything is "there before us and yet [everything] touches us from within" (*IPP* 16). The best of Bergson is "the exchange between past and present, matter and spirit, silence and speech, the world and us" (29-30). Once we accept that the task is to search appearance to attain "this secondary, laborious, rediscovered naïveté" (18), we understand that "what we believed to be coincidence is coexistence" (17). From this we deduce that the world of phenomenology is like the world of literature, a hidden perfusion of intentionality.

Late Merleau-Ponty keeps returning to a self-assigned task of the definition of truth. The speaking woman or man and the happy writer do not obsess about whether speaking and writing are possible, because too much of that anxiety means social isolation and the blank page. They do not, the philosopher says, "contemplate the sorrow of language, which is the necessity of not saying everything if one is to say something." (*PW* 145). Speaking-writing to perform the truth, however, does require some serious and unhappy confrontation with the sorrow of language: "[W]e are dealing with a transcendence, and not a static identity, and here, as in language, truth is not an adequation, but anticipation, repetition, and slippage of meaning" (129). To work within the constraints of slippage of meaning, the writer, like the interpreter of writing, requires skill in use of the ratios of *dimension, articulation, level, configuration*. As with all else in this kind of thinking, the use of intellectual skills traces back to the core premise of the perceiving body open to experience: "For speech is the vehicle of movement toward truth, as the body is the vehicle of our being in the world" (129). *Movement toward truth* is continually closing the gap of non-coincidence but never getting there. What powers the *vehicle* of the being that speaks? It's the energy of giving and taking produced by cognitive-perceptual interference.

Rhythm

In statements like (paraphrasing) there is no signification without a movement— or like "speech endlessly renews the mediation of the same and the other" (*PW* 145)—Merleau-Ponty suggested more than he said about the *dimension* of rhythm. Nonetheless, there is sufficient reason to consider this as a Merleau-Pontian term to think with, in discussing *configurations* of language in poems and stories. Recently the term has been foregrounded by Jessica Wiskus, the scholar of music and philosophy, who extends the use of *rhythm* from her two chapters on Debussy to her two chapters each on Cézanne and Proust. (She has also quoted and used, for interpretive purposes, all the appropriate passages on *depth* and *non-coincidence*.)

To point a path for literary reading with the aid of rhythm as a mode of attention, here are my summaries of three passages (the philosopher and two others), showing rhythm in convergent contexts. 1) Merleau-Ponty argues that sensation is intentional because of a "certain existential rhythm" of being open or shut to an external being or thing: we can "slip into" an outside form of existence (*PP* 221). 2) Michel Collot in an essay states that in literature, as in music, "the meaning of a phrase is inseparable from its rhythm and melody"; the signified is "tightly bound" with the logic of what's being said and the structure of what's being said (35; translation mine). 3) Wiskus has a musician's point about rhythm-as-noncoincidence, namely, as "the interval *between* articulated sounds"; rhythm in music, as in literature, "promises an ongoing, dynamic process that looks both forward and retrospectively" (9-10); rhythm, for Wiskus, uses what had remained silent between words. These additional points help to justify my selection of rhythm as one of the key terms.

Also pertinent is the career-long eloquent and ingenious use of rhythm to demolish structuralism with its idea of the sign, by Henri Meschonnic, whose eight-hundred-page *Critique du rhythme* (1982) is an unknown masterpiece of argument in poetics. The point of this as of his other books in historical anthropology of language is that we live as embodied subjects in writing; that the poem holds both affect and concept in a single mouthful of words; and that rhythm, unlike mostly-metronomic meter, is the legible expression of ourselves as subjects.[4] In Meschonnic, the argument does not trend toward the relegation of meter, rather toward its placement as an acquired skill in both the writer and the reader. Rhythm by contradistinction is a fully felt, known-on-the-pulses enactment of embodied being.

Powers of Attention

Interrogation

There can only be the first reduction of the natural attitude, which must arrive and get performed like a thunderbolt of recognition. That initiating and only reduction is prolonged indefinitely by rational processes. We've called those processes the Modes and Powers of Attention, using language never employed by the founding phenomenologists. We've imagined that the reduction engages these nine operations to prolong its work into the future, into lived experience, and these operations (and others not included here) work all together simultaneously and continuously. We've imagined that the Powers distribute and direct the Modes, because their agencies are more general, more supervisory. Merleau-Ponty invented and used these nine terms, but we are inventing the story of how they might accomplish, in detail, an ongoing phenomenology of perception. Only after selecting these nine terms and testing how

---

4 Henri Meschonnic, *Critique du rhythme: Anthropologie historique du langage* (Verdier, 1982). Meschonnic on rare occasions mocks phenomenology, naming no names, but he is with them when he writes that "words are not there for us to designate things. They're there to situate us among things." This occurs in his "A Rhythm Party Manifesto," collected in Henri Meschonnic, *Célébration de la poésie* (Verdier Poche, 2001). Also in the "Manifesto," as relevant to the next chapter here:

> As to the poem, I'm holding a major role for rhythm in the constitution of subjects-in-language. ... Because rhythm is a form-subject. The form-subject. ... And if the rhythm-poem is a form-subject, rhythm isn't any longer a soft notion of fusion as the phenomenologists affectionately say ... isn't a notion purely formal ... as in [the notion of] the sign, but rather a form of historicization, a form of individuation. (294-95; translation mine).

they might be used in the practice of reading, did it become evident that all the terms also exhibit, within each, the core attribute of a relation of interference.

Across the several books in their careers, Husserl and Merleau-Ponty are explaining the hard work of phenomenology as a labor of specification, to explain just what an embodied mind does when it encounters things and persons in the world. They wish to rouse all the Powers of Attention, first to find what questions to ask in order to *interrogate* what happens when it happens in actual living experience; then to *describe* the results that come from the phase of questioning; finally to *disclose* provisional results, organizing so as to place a highlight upon ideas of spontaneity and freedom that point toward future, better understanding of how humAnimals make of the world a home. Since the reduction is a circling spiral, down to the soil, never complete, what's been hidden and disclosed leads to further study, new questions.

Merleau-Ponty occasionally speaks of this kind of foray as an *adventure*, aware of that word's strength of diction: literally a happening, but more usually an exciting and dangerous undertaking, with roots in Latin *advenire*, and relation to Advent or the four Sundays before Christmas: time of probation before The Coming. What is coming for a materialist like him? The possibility that a dangerous unconventional thought that descends to the soil of perception can dwell entirely within philosophy, can renew philosophy by finding the right relation between perceiving-thinking-writing. Everywhere in Merleau-Ponty's writings a reader is aware of his excitement at finding and revealing his own ideas, and of his realization of his own power at expressing them.

What entities are being interrogated? Simple cognition already questions what turns up unexpected in experience. After that the assumptions behind appearances are suspended to see what perceiving and thinking might be without the overlay of concept, idea, mind, and representation. After that the *opinio communis* behind science is open to challenge, along with the rational structures of perspective in art and of behavior in culture and politics. "Every question," he said, "is part of the central question that is ourselves, of that appeal for totality, to which no objective being answers" (*IPP* 104). So it is finally ourselves being interrogated, our perceptual faith, which means the way we're charmed by what we see and hear and touch and do not wonder or worry about what is coming in behind. Students of the adventures of experience know, however, that "[p]hilosophy is the perceptual faith questioning itself about itself" (103). At some level of knowing, as close as may be to conscious knowing, Merleau-Ponty also knew that this kind of interrogation is the crossing of chiasm and thus also the relation of cognitive-perceptual interference. He wrote in the late "Working Notes," in a plan for new work: "Show that philosophy as *interrogation* ... can consist only in showing how the world is *articulated* [emphasis added] starting from zero of being which is not nothingness, that is, in installing itself on the edge of being, neither in the for Itself, nor in the in Itself, at the joints, where the multiple *entries* of the world cross" (*VI* 260). On this set of statements about the questioning attitude, another paradoxical name for phenomenology will be the philosophy that never stops starting.

Description

In the lectures on Descartes that Merleau-Ponty heard in the late 1920s, Husserl gave what his French auditor would call a "fresh mutation" on the doctrine of the reduction, coming round to seeing it as less of a fixed method, and instead an "index of a multitude of problems" (*IPP* 174). Merleau-Ponty himself in the Preface to *Phenomenology of Perception*, in his brilliant feisty beginning, would say that the phenomenological attitude had to be strict in describing, but not much concerned with explaining or analyzing: first and foremost he had to make an advance on what Husserl had started in disavowal of science, in favor of a return to this world prior to knowledge. It meant avoiding whatever was "abstract, signitive, and dependent, just like geography with regard to the landscape where we first learned what a forest, a meadow, or a river is" (lxxii). In the spirit and direct line of Husserl, he returned often to specify how phenomenological descriptions might achieve their full import. In a late essay "Eye and Mind," he argued that description had to question itself about the need to find the positive in the negative and the negative in the positive—about why those incompossibles present themselves as they do. So doing, the operation of this most particular description lays the foundations of a dialectical philosophy more sophisticated than that of Hegel and Marx, where now the interrogator in depth describes relations of interference. Such a dialectician is a perpetual beginner, always looking outside herself or himself, with some delight in describing the "*Offenheit der Umwelt*," the openness of a world entangled with our embodied minds (*IPP* 124). Such a description reveals a world behind appearance, behind the science and the names that we will again require and return to. This universe of living paradoxes is strange to us. Its new meanings take their very start beyond the reflexes of sign, metaphor, symbol. One result of this second power of attention will be a reworking of concepts like those which are ordinarily used in analysis of language.

The entire *Collected Poems* of Wallace Stevens will be seen to be a working out of the premise that description reveals strangeness as an under-level, or backside, of appearance. Whether he took this from Merleau-Ponty cannot be known, but all the terms that carry and operate a phenomenology are there. "Description Without Place" is a poem in seven pages and seven sections, packed full of perceptions, that makes a green queen's mind make the world around her green, that finds "flat appearance" to be our usual state "[e]xcept for delicate clinking," and that conveys that there are "potential seemings" everywhere, even in the death of a soldier or the existences of Anne of England or of Pablo Neruda in Ceylon (296ff). The seemings of even a summer day swarm, because they are description without place—they are imagination at work loosening the strands of intentionality to render the world's odd and sounding strangeness. From them we imagine further (last lines of the poem) to what the future "must portend, / Be alive with its own seemings, seeming to be / Like rubies reddened by rubies reddening" (302). The future is also and primarily description without place. The poem extends the vocabulary of phenomenology by the capacious concept of "seeming," and extends the usual range from over-emphasis on the visual to a delight in the different-but-same of sounds of words. So not just description of description as it describes, but enactment of that through energies of attention in utterance, two-line stanza, rhyme and off-rhyme, image, arc of argument, colors, sounds, names, and sentences equal to lines and sentences draped over the ends of lines.[5]

Disclosure

Again the story begins with Husserl, for whom, Merleau-Ponty says, "the whole of philosophy . . . consists in restoring a power to signify, a birth of meaning, or a wild meaning" (*VI* 155), and who was the first to perform the "epoché of language, the suspension" (*HLP* 44), and to deliver, before Heidegger in Germany and several French followers "[t]his speech truly *dimension* or *Eröffnung* <'disclosure'> of an immense leaf <*feuillet*> of Being and across it the very Being speaking in us ('pure' expression)" (44). *Disclosure* may not be primarily of matters linguistic, but it is most certainly delivered in language and thus concerned with the powers and failures of writing. Next came Martin Heidegger, whose index in *Being and Time* has forty page-references to *disclosure*, spaced through the whole treatise. One of Heidegger's major claims is that *Dasein* must master its mood with knowledge, and yet that mood must be respected as "a primordial kind of being of Dasein in which it is disclosed to itself *before* all cognition and willing and *beyond* the scope of disclosure" (132). Another value-term is *attunement*, which is "a fundamental existential mode of the *equiprimordial disclosedness* of the world, Dasein-with and existence because this disclosure itself is essentially being-in-the-world" (133). Merleau-Ponty uses *disclosure* less often and has quite other things to do with it when, unlike Heidegger, he is taking world at the level of the soil where specific perceptions occur. (Heidegger and Merleau-Ponty do share the need to theorize states that come before cognition and willing, and both are concerned with the equivocations of words and meanings.) Among the Modes and Powers of Attention, *disclosure* is the one term that most adequately covers and represents the accepted paradoxes and lived-with interferences of Merleau-Ponty's phenomenology. It's the clarification that phenomenology delivers as the recovery of the world—together thing, feeling, thought.

---

5 For further explanations see: Philippe Hamon, *Du Descriptif* (New York: Hachette, 1993).

The three opening chapters of *The Visible and the Invisible*, all one hundred and twenty-nine draft pages, end with a long sentence by Merleau-Ponty, who then quotes a short sentence from Husserl's *Cartesian Meditations*. This is the upshot of a meditation on *interrogation*, about the question unasked because it hides in silence behind the reason for asking questions:

> These questions call not for the exhibiting of something said which would put an end to them, but for the disclosure of a Being that is not posited because it has no need to be, because it is silently behind all our affirmations, negations, and even behind all formulated questions, not that it is a matter of forgetting them in its silence, not that it is a matter of imprisoning it in our chatter, but because philosophy is the reconversion of silence and speech into one another. "It is the experience . . . still mute which we are concerned with leading to the pure expression of its own meaning." (129)

This is a draft sentence: winding its way through forward and then backward and then forward lunges to a final resolution at "but because." And the reason given at the end is once again, Merleau-Pontian, an equivalence structure that will not let one mode of energy win out. One might think that speech might triumph over silence, but that is impossible with this kind of thinking, where inner speech and exterior speech inhabit each other. As our outer dialogues are prepared by our mute interior mulling and mediation, our dialogues within ourselves are striated by the social.

Elsewhere in the same book, he speaks of "self-manifestation, disclosure in the process of forming itself" (91). Much later, with the same term, he discusses how literature, music, the passions, and our experience of the visual world "are, no less than the science of Lavoisier and Ampére the exploration of an invisible and the disclosure of a universe of ideas" (146). But in literature and the arts the disclosure cannot and should not be detached, as it is in Lavoisier, "from the sensible appearances and erected into a second positivity" (149). Here as elsewhere in this style of thinking: perception is born in the reversibility of the seeing and the visible, and there is also a reversibility of speech and what it signifies—what speech discloses. This epoché of language and literature provides the reason for Inkpin's address to the broad question of the disclosive function of language, in his book on Heidegger and Merleau-Ponty, which puts the term into its title. To introduce his plan in *Disclosing the World*, he emphasizes the close link of the ideas of *disclosure* and *revelation*: "the term *disclosure* helpfully signals both that it is the world itself we are aware of—not merely our own mental representations—and that the focus is on our basic, 'domain-opening' awareness of things rather than an intellectualized end product. . . . [The book will address the broad question] about the disclosive function of language, and will do so in a way that accords properly with the various kinds of experience speakers can come to have of language" (5). With this sense of priorities, Inkpin says explicitly, his approach will be phenomenological. So these practical definitions of *disclosure* that began with Husserl and were developed into new *kinds of experience* in Heidegger and Merleau-Ponty have been inherited, repurposed for further kinds of experience in philosophical linguistics, in Andrew Inkpin.

And this is the toolbox of terms we shall carry to do some analytical work in chapter 7.

Toward a trial of reading with the nine terms

A philosophy concerned with the body and its perceptions, the body in space and time, the body communicating with other bodies will have affinities with modern art, which also needs to rediscover the perceived world. If the role of the senses, as we've seen, is to cover their tracks and to make their role invisible to us, then modern art and phenomenological philosophy assign themselves the same work, in *disclosing and articulating* what is hidden in ordinary experience. From essays in high argument about reflection and truth, already quoted in these pages from *Phenomenology of Perception* and *The Prose of the World*, I take two extremely practical hints about how to appreciate painting and writing: 1) their action "reveals that world as strange and paradoxical" (*PP* lxxvii); and 2) "truth is . . . anticipation, repetition, and slippage of meaning" (*PW* 129). Merleau-Ponty's aesthetic theory here converges on what we can admire in the environmental program of environmental artist Olafur Eliasson, where "art, by goosing the senses, can make us more conscious of our positions in time, space, hierarchy, society, culture, the planet" (qtd. in Beauman). I like that *conscious of our positions*. When we read literary works with *dimensions, articulations, level, hinges, pivots, and configurations*, we are not generalizing or speculating, but recognizing features that are individual, characteristic of one style; we are registering in the midst of performing sentences and scenes. In this approach, position and movement from position are everything.

Perhaps no modern philosopher is as resourceful in taking one huge and underestimated idea—in this case, Corporeality—and expounding it through a career with such abundance of lines of argument, inner turns of thought, striking metaphors and condensed memorable phrasings, so many fetching examples, rebuttals of antagonists so considerate and yet definite. He thought of himself as a stylist and as part of his aesthetics he wrote about style. He launched four-page paragraphs like arias. He ended *Phenomenology of Perception* with a most moving page on freedom ("*your* freedom cannot be willed without . . . willing freedom for *all*" [456, emphases added]), and with a final quotation from a story by Antoine St. Exupéry. Favored writers Stendahl, Proust, Montaigne, Mallarmé, Valéry, Satrtre, Claude Simon are often on his mind in passing or in whole essays, because, as he said in "Metaphysics and the Novel," "[p]hilosophical expression assumes the same ambiguities as literary expression, if the world is such that it cannot be expressed except in 'stories' and, as it were, pointed at" (*PLS* 138). He thought of literature and poetry as contributions to philosophical *description*, but also as performances of essential phenomenology. "It is a long time," he wrote, "since there existed between literature and philosophy, not just differences of technique touching the mode of expression, but also a difference of object. In fact, since the end of the nineteenth century, relations between them have been tightly knotted together" (qtd. in Simon and Castin 10).[6] So, accordingly, what would it mean to read literary stories for perceptual content?

We would ask: who is speaking where? We would look for points where the story will change-up; cut; interrupt; pack in lists; specify; revel in adjectives, names, and nouns; pull out responses from the reader with hordes of sequenced emotions. In the telling and in the hearing, something about stories relishes down-and-dirty detail; stories have always been dense with perceptual content, but to read primarily for that has not been attempted in literary criticism.

The reason this way of thinking has not started a school is that phenomenology is more experiential than methodical. It resists pulling out transferrable terms, operations in logic, typical gambits, historical commitments, identities, so it makes discipleship harder than usual. (Also hard it may be to enlist oneself in a movement to describe and then practice reading for linguistic effects of quantum interference!) However, there is a certain modesty in this unwillingness to transfer a system, because the conversion-experience of catching on to the thesis of corporeality is transformative in itself, and because the creativity comes in through ordinary experience every day, not from technical mastery of a special vocabulary. As a practice, it is not a method among other methods, but we still need to figure out a way to think with it.

---

6 From *Sens et Non-Sens*, quoted in Anne Simon and Nicolas Castin, eds., *Merleau-Ponty et le littéraire*, the Avant-propos of the editors; translation mine.

Chapter 7: Reading Poems and a Novel with the Nine Terms

Sentence and scene in poems by W. C. Williams, Ange Mlinko, and Robert Burns

As Modes of Attention, *movement, depth, chiasm, reversibility, non-coincidence,* and *rhythm* are different phases of the same experience of perceiving, and their relevance and use must depend on qualities in the experience itself. Especially, I submit, the facets called *chiasm* and *reversibility* are close in meaning and tricky to separate in the actual approach to a text. This effort is a trial to assess how a philosopher's terms can be set to work on the literary side, to show how perception can lead to interpretation. Not all the modes are relevant to every text. But all the modes, as named terms that are now literary, too, share the virtue of sending us back to the body, back to the eventfulness of the senses as they perform the body's relation to changes in the surround, innering what is outer. It is typical of Merleau-Ponty, who calls the body "the animal of movements and perceptions" (*VI* 168), that his multispecies thinking is his knowledge theory and that the reverse is true, too.

Here is "The Yellow Chimney," a poem from the 1940s by William Carlos Williams:

There is a plume
of fleshpale
smoke upon the blue

sky. The silver
rings that
strap the yellow

brick stack at
wide intervals shine
in this amber

light—not
of the sun not of
the pale sun but

his born brother
the
declining season (*Collected Poems* 87)

The poem begins as description but ends, after the dash-structure, by shift to metaphor ("brother") and another framing of time ("season"). In form it is free verse, and in format it is the sight stanza, meaning that except for the opening line, syntax overruns the ends of the three-line blocks, so the stanzas are open at both ends. From these features, we might be put on alert that even a short descriptive text might resist our interpretive skills. Putting a highlight on sentencing, let us apply our terms for perception and attention to see what they might disclose.

- *Movement.* Williams begins with pale smoke upon blue sky, color on color, figure on ground, an image flat and pictorial, though the smoke implies and leads to its origin in the chimney. That is movement, but it is accomplished only with the slightly shocking break between lines 3 and 4, the first and second stanza, between the adjective "blue" and its noun "sky." This move is a break between stanzas that is immediately a break between the poem's two sentences, coming between the first and second word in the fourth line (with the poem's only full-stop period to signal a change of topic.) Before the chimneystack comes on the scene, we get the silver rings. Mental movement comes with refocusing of the image and with and across interruptions like the dash-structure followed by two complicating "not" structures. The short text begins with a sentence-structure of juxtaposition ("upon the blue / sky") and moves to end with a structure of apposition (with the tag of "the / declining season").
- *Depth.* Our terminology claims that the visible is a surface over something that is, for now, hidden. What begins as the flat still plume of smoke and continues with the silver rings at equal intervals around the brick stack, ends with the open-endedness of the seasonal metaphor. The plunge occurs with the introduction of the main verb in sentence 2, "shine / in this amber // light": everything turns on the noticing of a new quality and color of the light, a micro-perception of seasonal change. As readers we dive inward to register that the one day of the sun is now a higher category of the season; that is the turn from percept to concept.
- *Chiasm.* Chiasm refers to exchanges of several sorts, between the visible and the invisible, between consciousness and things, obverse/reverse, and so on. Here, the major shift at the dash-structure just past mid-poem is from the strict observer of phenomena in primary colors to the same human figure who has used a recognition about the quality of the amber light to imagine a new emotional tone, associated with autumn and the coming bittersweet decline of life (all this in the phrase "this amber / light"). Thus, the strong chiasmic phrasing of denial where the phenomena of the opening lines are cancelled out:

—not
of the sun not of
the pale sun but

The denials are needed, but they are subsumed by the movement of the whole poem, which as we have seen, uses exchanges and co-functioning to show that not distinct objective entity is the unknown speaker's quest, but experience before it is differentiated into entities.

- *Reversibility*. What unites the speaker's chiastic thought and the halves of the poem is the idea of light as both visual-phenomenal (lines 1 to the dash in line 10) and emotional-metaphorical (dash in line 10 to end). Light drenches the yellow chimney but also, not yellow now but *amber*, irradiates and signals the coming season of decline. Light is the reversible physical/moral medium: it still has the same physical photons, it still is another word for the sun, it still is the noun that controls the poem's main verb, *shines*. With this doubleness of light we are enabled to see the invisible behind the visible. Reversibility also means an opening-out, which is here enacted by an absence of a final period in the poem— not a mistake of the poet but, to the reader's eye/mind, the visual performance of an opening beyond closure.
- *Non-coincidence*. We get perceptual depth by having two eyes: stereoscopy. We get experiential stability by having a body that can look and also be looked at, can touch and be touched, and so on. In ourselves we are both noun and verb, so categories encroach and overlap, creating chiasm and reversibility in exchanges between inner self and outer surround. In this free-verse poem, the most prominent effect of non-coincidence is between sentence and line, the scissoring effect of phrase against line is in no place more enactive than what is just quoted in "not / of the sun not of / the pale sun but," where the careful symmetry-destroying placement of *not* and *of* create unusual divisions that result, for example, in a line that begins and ends with the traditionally weak preposition *of* and, also, formally contains this unsettling effect with a return to the usual, with a rhyme on *not-not-but*.[1] Rhymes, by the way, are also non-coincidence because of similar sound/different meaning: in this short poem, we have *plume-blue, brick-stack, not-but, strap-stack*, several repeated words and also an alliteration ("born brother"): it includes quite a lot of chiming, given that free verse was invented to deny that device.
- *Rhythm*. The brief poem, with its two sentences and its short lines, turns out to have intervals, with silences between words, everywhere. There are the "wide intervals" between "The silver / rings that / strap the yellow / brick stack," but beyond the obvious and visual there are conceptual breaks between adjective and noun, phrase and line, sentence and line, and parts of a sentence on either side of a dash. Betweenness, with divisions overridden, is the method and also the topic of this text, and all these effects are enactments of rhythm.
- *Interrogation*. Articulation, previously discussed as the linkage of elements across intervals, also means "utterance": how the world is spoken and, in this case, how the invisible is disclosed behind the visible. Betweenness is also conceptual, with inspection of the joints of the world's wild being. Here a refocusing reveals the newness of a micro-perception; the poem is about, and also performs,

---

[1] The non-coincidence of sentence and line is my main concern in *The Scissors of Meter*.

experiencing life on the cusp of the seasons. In Williams's brief utterance, we are between colors, seasons, qualities of light, literal objects, and the light that reveals them, and this positioning helps to elude the world-as-represented, or rather, to register the so-called objective reality, as with the opening lines in their simple picture, and then interrogate, in order to disclose the wildness within. Sites for questions include joints, gaps, pivots, and articulations.

- *Description.* As if to illustrate that all knowledge is opened up by perception, Williams uses "The" once in the title and six times in this short utterance, as a setup for nouns which he loves and needs. Also, ostensively, he uses "There is" and "this." And, in the world of the poem, Williams needs four colors and the adjective *pale*. He begins with this close listing of noticing, and he ends in metaphor; these techniques are chiasmic and reversible; both techniques are indispensable, and neither has priority. Description, in his signature style, pulls the poem back toward sense-perception and away from any explaining or analyzing.[2]

- *Disclosure.* The disclosive function of language is best understood as a culmination and résumé of all these Modes and Powers of Attention. It contains them. Disclosure uproots objective philosophy, brings in unfamiliar perspectives, opens awareness of other domains, and takes intelligence as a performance, not an end-product. To take just two instances from "The Yellow Chimney": it is not the chimney that matters, after the title, but "the silver / rings that / strap" the chimney, holding it up rather like a sight stanza holds up the poem and, then, catching the feeling-tone of "this amber // light" that signals the end of a season; "pale" is one word used three times for three entities in the poem, not only for the smoke (line 2) and the sun (line 12) but also for the human-like skin in the odd jammed phrase "fleshpale," which we race past at the poem's start. What is disclosed in the first instance is that poetic form (strap/stanza) has a role in focusing and emphasizing meaning. What is disclosed in the second instance is that if the same adjective can be used for human agents and physical entities, perception is always already the product of cognitive choice; even if the first-person pronoun never appears, self and scene are invisibly related.

*

The next example is Ange Mlinko's 2017 rhyme-and-meter poem, "A Horse Does Not Want to Be FedExed." In complication of person, tone, and form, this is a step up from "The Yellow Chimney." However, since the terms of a reading for disclosure are now on display, I shall be more selective in my account. The title reappears as a quotable whole line in stanza 2:

---

[2] That stylistic move is why the choice of this text by this writer is not innocent: as an early example for the teacherly trial of a disclosive kind of reading, the text suits the terms used to analyze it.

Beauty is a fight to the finish,
though you want to educate
the decorum away. Here,
in the bruised atmosphere
of a tropical storm, we wait
for the rainband to diminish,

considering horses. Your student
had one shipped from Holland.
"A horse does not want to be FedExed."
(Could one apply dressage to text?
Have it perform at one's command?
Banish felicitous accident?)
*

"You have to be a perfectionist,"
she had noted. Discipline
is stylish, but there's a grace
by which your hands displace
the eye of the storm within
the encirclement of my wrist,

and how say that, much less
transmit it? Along the coast
the tempest is elegant, like something
bred for show jumping
across state lines, almost
—no, really—over distress.
*

The scent of a broken twig
increasing a hundredfold:
the perfume of a living limb
exhaling, at the jagged enjambment, its last. All told,
the damage caused is as big

as that of any grown tree
striking the edge of the roof,
bouncing on the fence—
tripping off calls to insurance,
prayers to limbs still aloof,
and recognition of mercy.
*

A fight to the finish, "sunlight
on the garden," rain-lacquered,
hurricane-groomed.
The roses gave a start and bloomed
like silly. If we've acquired
a taste for drama, an appetite

for tropical depression follows.

—And so we clown.
I saw the fresh wood up; it awes
me to see the parasites and moss
studding the victor's crown
that brought down the house. (90-92)

This is the last poem in Ange Mlinko's book *Distant Mandate*, and as a summary and closural statement for the book, it ends with its own internal closural intent at "brought down the house," a joke made up by a cliché phrase that works two ways—as an idiom for applause, and as a reference to a hurricane crashing a tree-limb onto her roof. (The connection in this two-in-one locution: congratulations, sublime storm-threat, you have created beauty out of danger when we can discover marvels in your aftermath.) It is tedious to explain a joke, but she herself starts the thought by saying "And so we clown" (line 44). The larger point is that this author's signature method is to unify disparate perceptions and thoughts; the greater the distance between the entities brought together (*chiasm, reversibility, non-coincidence*), the greater the poet's act of imagination.

Mlinko's title is the first sign of her playful attitude, her sly indirection. The poem is not about horses; really it is about the huge outer circumstance of a Gulf Coast hurricane. The horse topic is one she and her partner-interlocutor come upon as the hurricane is still outside, raining ("we wait / for the rainband to diminish") if not rampaging.

First, to take up the Merleau-Pontian theme of *movements* and perceptions, it is essential to note that one primary story of the poem is to stage a progress from distance-perception effects of vision ("bruised" [line 4]) to interior perceptions of touch ("your hands . . . my wrist" [lines 15-18]) and scent ("the perfume of a living limb / exhaling . . . its last" [lines 27-29]), moving to vision in the images of sunlight on the garden, "rain-lacquered" (lines 37-39), another dart inward to taste and appetite (line 42), and out finally to see the "parasites and moss" (line 46)—ending at the tree-top things it is the speaker's privilege to perceive because the storm gave them to her. She moves from her body looking to her body looked at, touched; from herself-into-things to things-into-herself. This recognition is perhaps best shown by the lines "your hands displace / the eye of the storm within / the encirclement of my wrist," where the storm has a humanlike eye and its massive circle has its analogue in the circle of the speaker's wrist.[3]

There is also the I-you-I, in-out-in, dialogic *movement* from the speaker herself as interrogator and narrator, then to her partner's student whose words are quoted

---

[3] Big and little circles: storm/wrist. As to scale, this is being written in September 2018 when category 3 hurricane Florence approached North and South Carolina, with a cloud-diameter of eighty miles, swirling along a line toward the coast at 5 mph, wind-speed in rain-band at 110 mph. Slowing after landfall at Wilmington, NC, the storm increased its diameter to three hundred and fifty miles.

in two places, to the partner's hands on her wrist, and then back to a more vigorous ownership of the speaker's I-pronoun in the second half of the poem. (Such a progress is entirely absent in the poem by Williams).

Further to explain Ange Mlinko's poem as a story in motion, a planned stringing of topics and tones, is to call in the Merleau-Pontian terminology. We begin with an enigmatic statement about the meaning of Beauty, encounter a first reference to the outer storm, and come upon horses and dressage as topics of discussion, with the humorous title now turned into a quotable sentence that takes up a whole line of the poem, line 9 (*interrogation, movement, non-coincidence,* and *coincidence*). We move to a linking up of the control of horses in show jumping to the control of a writer over her verbal art and, thence, to a denial of such discipline when the speaker's partner touches her wrist (*reversibility*). The hurricane jumps like a show-horse, but now over geographies and political boundaries . . . . "almost / —no, really—over distress" (line 24; *chiasm*). In the poem's second half, lines 25-48, we return to the theme of beauty as a fight, to the destructive force of the storm with the broken limb, and then we are led to refocus on beauty as seen in what the storm leaves—a new quality of light and bloom in the garden (*depth, description*). In the final six-line stanza, suddenly the speaker can see the broken-off top of the tree, "parasites and moss," which yields a "lacquered" and "groomed" vision of reality that is only possible because of destruction, because of "tropical depression" in both meanings, climatological and psychological (*chiasm, reversibility, disclosure*). The tree's crown is that of a victor "that brought down the house." End of poem; end of book. The implied applause is Mlinko's, the result of her awe at being able to achieve new knowledge of the world: Bravo, Hurricane!

What of those explicit question-mark questions about "command" (line 11) versus a "felicitous accident" (line 12)? What of the relations between *non-coincidence* and *coincidence*? Mlinko's poem runs this story of thoughts-after-hurricane through seventeen sentences, which only rarely coincide with line-ends and stanza-ends. Grammar cuts meter and meter grammar at highly unexpected places, unlike the tidy sentence-stanzas of Robert Burns which follow next as my third example. It shows that, as a fancy symmetrical rhymer and stanza maker, she has nonetheless learnt something from free-verse poets like Williams, about interference of systems and about rhythmic intervals between articulated sounds. It is part of her humorous attitude that this text about an uncontrollable force in Earth's atmosphere is set into six-line stanzas with the unusual pattern of rhyming inward to a couplet from the two ends, thus, ABCCBA; that is a reversible sequence, with a long leap of grammar and sound for the reader to connect lines 1 and 6. And in stanzas 1, 3, 5, and 7 while the rhyme stops at the last line, the plunge-on syntax has more work to do in the next stanza. This making and breaking of symmetry in the sentencing and rhyming is matched by a meter more often trochaic than iambic, and often with mid-line anapests, but always arriving at a stressed syllable for the rhyming end of the line. The invisible, easily overlooked jest and gesture of the poem is that it is a fantastic piece of careful allocation of grammar, meter, and sounds, whose hurricane topic means the abolition of all limits, all expectations. With break-and-relate everywhere, Mlinko's stylistic signature is aural and intellectual density.

With such attention to formal symmetry and the breaking of symmetry, Mlinko is highly attentive to textuality as such and what I shall call textual emotion. This attentiveness explains her attraction to show-jumping horses through the title about living horses resisting being FedExed, that is, turned into packages for shipment, turned into "text": it is convenient that the humorous and central verb of the title and the poem should rhyme with her own text-delight in formal prosodies. That concern for formal-emotional equivalences, and their breaking, is elsewhere applied by her to the "living limb" of the tree, which is subject to the poetic technique of "jagged enjamb / ment" (here the splitting of the technical term into two lines performs the playful definition of the term).

By design, two discourses line up and clash within the poem:
- beauty-decorum-text-command-perfectionist-discipline-stylish-elegant-victor's crown

  as against
- educate-decorum-away, horse-not-want-be-FedExed, accident-grace-distress-living limb-damage-mercy-like silly, a-taste-for-drama-depression

These discourses, which might be summarized as formal versus emotional, are everywhere in interference, nowhere in easy obvious isolation. As Powers of Attention, the *interrogation-description-disclosure* of the utterance are held in abeyance, in a state of in-between. One force is set against the other, and that's why the writer twice, at the poem's start and exact mid-point, will speak of the beauty of the physical world and equally of verbal art as "a fight to the finish."

The perception-based Powers of Attention enable the Modes of Attention, and the Modes exemplify the Powers. All nine of these terms send us back to the ongoing experience of the body amidst the things, beings, and emotions of the surround. Here we might remember that Merleu-Ponty said that our own "mobility is the means of compensating for the mobility of the things" (*VI* 230). *Movement* as a mode of attention, in his scheme, is "this living unity of displacements compensated for" (230). I would speculate that in literary interpretation this scheme means, or can mean, a Mlinko-like production of two-in-one phrasings that disclose a living unity, thus:
- FedExing a horse
- "bruised atmosphere"
- "apply dressage to text"
- "perform at one's command"
- "felicitous accident"
- "the tempest is elegant"
- "show jumping / across state lines"
- "hurricane-groomed"

- "an appetite / for tropical depression"
- top of tree as "victor's crown"
- "brought down the house" in two senses

So the poem's major trope is metaphor that clamps together two meanings, uniting the visible and the invisible in one locution. It is a fight to the finish because this poet's exemplary device is a kind of oxymoron. Such phrasings are indeterminate, intension, in interference. Mlinko appears to be well suited as an example for an interrogative or negative philosophy, and Merleau-Ponty's terminology has helped to display a living unity in her way of relating to things in her *Umwelt*.

*

Robert Burns was born in 1759 into a working family in Alloway, just inland from Ayr, Scotland. He was first a farmer and ploughman, then a writer, and, in "To a Mouse, on Turning Her Up in Her Nest, with the Plough, November 1785," he is bringing the text to the field for a speech to, not with, a companion animal. Though the speaker's words may not be fully dialogic, and though there is a vulnerable surge of self-pity at the end, nonetheless, Burns is here other-directed, sympathetic, sincere, and at the last self-questioning. Also, he is aware that he is transgressing two thousand years of human exceptionalism ("Man's dominion"). And by writing in Scots, he is consciously asserting a linguistic-local claim against the dominance of the English.

Wee, sleekit, cowran, tim'rous *beastie*,	*little, sleek, cowering*
O, what a panic's in thy breastie!	
Thou need na start awa sae hasty,	*away so*
Wi' bickering brattle!	*with quarrelsome chatter*
I wad be laith to rin an' chase thee,	
Wi' murd'ring *pattle!*	*plough-staff*
I'm truly sorry Man's dominion	
Has broken Nature's social union,	
An' justifies that ill opinion,	
Which makes thee startle,	
At me, thy poor, earth-born companion,	
An' *fellow-mortal!*	
I doubt na, whyles, but thou may *thieve;*	
What then? poor beastie, thou maun live!	*must*
A *daimen-icker* in a *thrave*	*ear of corn; 24 sheaves*
'S a sma' request;	
I'll get a blessin wi' thi lave,	*rest*
An' never miss't!	
Thy wee-bit *housie*, too, in ruin!	
It's silly wa's the win's are strewin!	*walls; winds; strewing*
An' naething, now, to big a new ane,	*build; one*

O' foggage green!	grass
An bleak *December's winds* ensuin,	
Baith snell an' keen!	sharp
Thou saw the fields laid bare an' wast,	waste
An' weary *Winter* comin fast,	
An' cozie here, beneath the blast,	
Thou thought to dwell,	
Till crash! the cruel *coulter* past	ploughshare
Out thro' thy cell.	
That wee-bit heap o' leaves an' stibble,	little; stubble
Has cost thee monie a weary nibble!	
Now thou's turn'd out, for a' trouble,	
But house or hald,	without; dwelling
To thole the Winter's *sleety dribble*,	endure
An' *cranreuch* cauld!	hoar-frost cold
But Mousie, thou art no thy-lane,	not alone
In proving *foresight* may be vain:	
The best-laid schemes o' *Mice* an' *Men*,	
Gang aft agley,	go often wide of the aim
An' lea'e us nought but grief an' pain,	leave
For promis'd joy!	
Still, thou art blest, compared wi' *me*!	
The *present* only toucheth thee:	
But Och! I *backward* cast my e'e,	ah; eye
On prospects drear!	
An' *foreward*, tho' I canna *see*,	
I *guess* an' *fear*! (47-48)	

The Powers of Attention, I have said, refer to higher-level, more abstract structures in the literary text, and the Modes of Attention exemplify the Powers with local structures of interference and overlay. The modes divide and divide again the lobes of the line, creating intervals of *rhythm*. In this framework, attention is the writer's perception-and-expectation in action, attention is energies-in-motion, through the reader's space-time of his or her performance of the text. In Burns, his utterance opens with *description*, as the ploughman-destroyer begins speaking to the mouse he has disturbed, and he conveys her reaction, including her form of angry speech ("bickering brattle"). Then the middle-stanzas *interrogate* his relation to his non-human addressee; this relation is sympathetic and apologetic—also intimate if the mouse is to be a "companion / An' *fellow-mortal!*" The final stanza makes the turn to where he has been heading all along (but he needs to discover this move through the steps of thought): the poem ends with *disclosure* of the speaker's open-ended bafflement, "I *guess* an' *fear!*"—a serious admission of an underlying fragility, made to the mouse who is stealing his corn.

This speech *to* the mouse, as a companion species who deserves life, is mainly why the poem has become canonical, because it is a tender expression of a fellow-feeling with animals that is historically new in the eighteenth century.[4] That expression is consistent, genial, and worked out at length through 48 lines. (Not all post-Romantic poems need to do this, of course: Ange Mlinko, with a horse in her title, finds a joke and an art-emblem in her heraldic beast, but horse-ness, horse behavior, or horse companionship are not on her agenda.) A poem to a mouse in Scots written in 1785 and Maurice Merleau-Ponty have never before appeared in the same scholarly space, but the phenomenologist did speak, as Burns might, of the man-animality intertwining, and both writers would seem to argue that we ourselves are nature. If we are nature, then literature and philosophy in this argument would need to study the unities and not the oppositions between human/animal, speaking/writing, and dialect/standard. Merleau-Ponty would have the added presumption, after Darwin, that humans are evolved from animals.

After being surprised equally with the mouse, Burns seeks to know what he has experienced, using the resource of a mixed diction—arguing with the full range between standard English philosophical terms ("Man's dominion," "Nature's social union," "foresight," "prospect") and a rich, tongue-clacking list of Scots terms for making us feel what it is to suffer winter's cold. Here, a phenomenological reading will strive to show the content that is hidden within what the human body's animal senses pull from their engagement with the world. Also, we need to show the content that is hidden in the hollowed-out back of our speaking, writing, and reading. The *disclosure* would then be of what Burns knows of how he knows and how he shows what he knows.

I shall endeavor to read Burns for the particulars of how he puts emphasis on his emphases, how through structures of interference, of *coincidence* and *non-coincidence*, he achieves what poet Gerard Manley Hopkins (a century later) claimed he wanted for his own writing, that is, the *"overing . . .* [and] *aftering of the inscape"* (*Journals* 289), that is, heavy emphasis on the signature inner structures of a text. In this trial of the Modes and Powers, *movement* becomes the story of how each stanza is a visual-emotional refocusing of the speaker's attention, and *depth* is his progress toward an inexhaustible, last-line state of "I *guess* an' *fear!*"

To slow everything down in this trial, let us try to become more conscious of the reasons and the mechanisms of knowing. Specifically looking at the mutual scissoring of sentence and line, I would begin by pointing at those sixteen exclamation points, all but one (at "crash!" in line 29) ending a line with a sentence. That punctuation use delivers a high incidence of sentences equal to lines, and (unlike Mlinko's practice) all the stanzas are rounded-off with sentence-ends, making for extreme formal stability despite the agitation betrayed by the exclamations and by the prominence

---

[4] As David Perkins demonstrates in *Romanticism and Animal Rights* (2003).

of a crucial verb in line 10, "startle." It is worth mentioning, too, that (unlike Mlinko's irregularities of meter) Burns writes easily scannable four-stress and two-stress iambic lines. The exclamation points, conveying the speaker's extreme excitement, are *non-coincident* with the extreme regularity of sentencing, rhyming, and metering. If the poem were any longer, the punctuation-effects would become cloying and the four-square formality would oppress; but, at this length, grammar and meter interfere in a careful, pleasing way, and contribute to making a largely monologic poem seem easily conversational.

The pertinence of all nine of our categories to formal patterns, as well as argumentative-emotional patterns, helps justify a discussion on the stanza Burns has chosen. Style and technique have also to be perceived. Like Mlinko, Burns has eight six-line stanzas, but, unlike her, his are all end-stopped with emphatic punctuation. His stanza-form he inherits from earlier Scots writers like Robert Fergusson, the stanza is called the Standard Habbie, and it allocates rhymes and meters in this form: A (4-stress), A (4), A (4), B (2), A (4), B (2). Robert Crawford, in his biography of the poet (2009), has in his index no less than twenty-five references to this favored format, and it is clear that the form was most often used for satirical and topical-political commentary, where its pouncing structure, with heavy closural effects, helped slam home an argument. It is also clear that Burns puts this effect on display as a young poet to prove he can push sentences through a complex form to score points and display competence to traditionalists. However, if we are right to emphasize *movement* of speech-tones and emotional progress in relation to the mouse, and *disclosure* of personal admissions, Burns is using the Standard Habbie in an original way to reveal personal weakness. That is, after exposing his complicity in anthropocentrism, he works round to a *cri de coeur* about how "schemes" come to nothing and how humans, or at least this one, are terrified by death.

In this dense text, at a level below sentence, line, and stanza, are other effects of refocus in punctuation and diction. The adjectives are exquisite always, and not only in the dramatic first line, but in places quickly passed like the daring sequence "me, thy poor, earth-born companion, / An' *fellow-mortal!*"[5] Moreover, in this "earth-born" passage we have the italic-font emphasis on key-terms; such foregrounding may occur anywhere in a line, and it often occurs on gnarly words in dialect, with (as here) the ubiquitous exclamation-point at line-end. System within or against system, then, and emphasis upon emphasis.

There are other smaller effects, emphases that turn and refocus feeling:
- Deferential intimate personal pronouns, as spoken to a mouse: *thy, thou.*
- Diminutives, as applied to mouse, mouse-house: *beastie, wee, housie.*

---

[5] Earth-born, fellow-mortal: that, spoken to a mouse, quietly in its animal politics foreshadows Burns's affiliation with the revolutionary events of the 1780s and 1790 in lines like "The rank is but the guinea's stamp, / The Man's the gowd, for a' that" ("For a' that, & a' that").

- At key turning points, interjections to signal *deepening* of personal feeling: *O* in stanza 1 and *Och* in stanza 8.
- At the passage where farming-talk is thickest in Scots speech, an elision of the verb "is" ("'S") in order to keep regular meter: "A *daimen-icker* in a *thrave* / 'S a sma' request."
- Onomatopoeia or sound-sense equivalence in the performative verb "crash!" in line 29, where the original grave disturbance is repeated in the middle of the poem, to re-energize the speaker's regret.

All these are effects of micro-perceptual shock, and the poem has a verb for those: *startle*, and we may assume that the speaker finds this word and rhymes it with *fellow-mortal* because he too has been equally surprised with the mouse he has, not by design, mortally threatened. The surprise shook him out of complacency, started the utterance, and led to an I-thou form of address.

The likeness of man and mouse far outweighs the difference, to the point where in stanza 7 the speaker arrives at the recognition for which this poem is famous, "The best laid schemes o' *Mice* an' *Men* / Gang aft agley . . ." We have arrived at this humAnimal identity, existential and alliterative and emphasized in the local speech of the Scottish Lowlands, because of stanzas 4-6 on the meaning of a loss of shelter. These stanzas might look the least justified in the poem because three eights of the poem is given to "[t]hat wee-bit heap o' leaves an' stibble" (line 31), and I thought to omit them to save space. Then I read *Scottish Architecture* by Miles Glendinning and Aonghus MacKechnie, looked for paragraphs and images on farms, crofts, and bothies of the sort where Burns and his family lived and found only castles, churches, and mansions. Burns spent stanzas on the housies of mousies because he knew exactly how hard it was to get through the winter in rudimentary housing—that is where he comes closest to the "tim'rous *beastie*," in condition, and the details and feelings in stanzas 4-6 are what lead to the daring, quotable lines on *best laid schemes* and on how *I guess* an' *fear*. So, if this investigation is to be a trial of perception and expectation in writing, from *movement* through to *disclosure*, the whole poem ought to be quoted and analyzed.

What is being disclosed in the last stanza?

But Och! I *backward* cast my e'e,
On prospects drear!
An' *foreward*, tho' I canna *see*,
I guess an' fear!

This stanza is a direct personal confession to a mouse as a fellow-mortal. It is the personal-moral invisible—death, but not before suffering—that has been lurking beneath the surface of the visible. It is an unusual form of ending that allows-in the human flaw of lack of foresight, of no-perception: *I canna see*. Burns is strong enough to allow himself a weak closure. The last lines open out into a revelation of self, but they perform this display with two verbs of uncertainty that contradict, indeed controvert, the super-emphasis of the Standard Habbie.

Ange Mlinko also makes an admission in her poem:

there's a grace
by which your hands displace
the eye of the storm within
the encirclement of my wrist,

and how say that, much less
transmit it?

For Mlinko there is a topic too intimate for poetry, or at least for this poem, but she draws us up to the edge of it, and she admits her lack of resources. In passing, she is willing to look almost overwhelmed. *How say that?* In the working-out of her line of points and perceptions, this is very attractive, and it is evidence of a mind definite, capacious, aware of limits and the over-riding of limits. In Burns, he makes his admission to a named nearby addressee, the mouse! His admission comes as the delivery of the poem's discovery at the end of the end, and the admission *discloses* a form of suffering more existential than artistic.

There is one more invisible element under the surface of the visible, or, rather, there is a meaning within or behind the sounds of the audible. To the speaker-reader of standard English, Scots forces the recognition of difference in every syllable—in a vocabulary that uses *sleekit* and *cranreuch* and *thrave* and *thole*—but also in the assault on our perceptions of the systems of sound and orthography. There would appear to be another language within our language, or, anyway, a dialect within English because all the syntax and a lot of the vocabulary are the same. Whatever we call it, the people who use it can code-switch in and out between Scots and standard but we cannot, so the unfamiliar words are something we must learn with glossaries and, then, try on our voice-boxes. Scots is a magnificent spoken language and an exceedingly beautiful literary language, the expression of a people and, respecting the language, we also recognize the people in their difference. In his high artistic shaping of Scots, with his affectionate mode of address "To a Mouse," and his handling of sentence and line in a special stanza, Burns has *disclosed* creativity within the ordinary.

Sentence and scene in Henry James's *The Ambassadors* (1903)

"No man ever steps in the same river twice, for it's not the same river and he's not the same man" (Heraklcitos). The American Lambert Strether never steps into the French river, but the point about constant change applies to the scene in which James has him involved as observer/participant.

We already had a brief look at part of this scene in an earlier chapter; let us now complete the analysis with the advantage of nine new terms and a wider scope of vision. The plot of the novel was not necessary to know earlier when only two sentences and their perceptual content were at issue. Here, briefly, it is useful to remember that the leaders of the family have sent Strether, a friend, to France to find out why errant son Chad resists returning to America. When Strether cannot get an answer, other American ambassadors arrive, who also fail. The longer passage for analysis shows how, near novel's end, Strether actually perceives and only then knows Chad and Mme. Vionnet in their liaison, and all instantly comes clear.

The elaborate scene of discovery, at the novel's late turning point at the Inn on the river, seems like a moment frozen in time because of the minute divisions in the description. After this moment, though, the novel springs toward its ending, back into time and back into truth, because of what is seen during that seeming stasis. Up to that point all has been ruled in secret, in many conversations in many pages through eleven books of the novel, by a fantastic connivance of lies thrown out by Chad, Mme. de Vionnet, and Little Bilham. Then occurs what Merleau-Ponty would call the chiasm, and all because of the unforeseen-by-characters collision/coincidence of Strether, Chad, and Madame, who have separately planned a day trip at the same riverside inn.

In the categories listed in the last two sections, temporality is only implied in the ideas of movement and rhythm, but it is well to make more explicit the manifold of time as we consider the role of this scene in the larger plot. In his chapter on temporality in *Phenomenology of Perception*, Merleau-Ponty also refers to Herakleitos only to reject him as the source of an error general and prevalent:

> We say that time passes or flows by. We speak of the flow of time. . . . But this famous metaphor is in fact quite confused. . . . For, *examining the things themselves*, the melting of the snow and its consequences are not successive events, or rather the very notion of an event has no place in the objective world. When I say that the water currently passing by was produced by a glacier two days ago, I imply a witness fixed to a certain place in the world and I compare his successive perspectives: over there he witnessed the melting of the snow and he followed the water along its descent; or perhaps after two days of waiting he sees from the riverside the pieces of wood float by that he had tossed into the river at the source. "Events" are carved out of the spatio-temporal totality of the objective world by a finite observer. And yet, if I consider this world itself, there is but a single indivisible being that does not change. Change presupposes a certain observation post where I place myself and from where I can see things go by; there are no events without someone to whom they happen and whose finite perspective grounds their individuality. Time presupposes a view upon time. Thus, time is not like a stream; time is not a fluid substance. This metaphor has been able to survive since Heraclitus up until today because we surreptitiously place in the river a witness to its flowing. (433-34)

The position of the witness matters in relation to the visual field: Henry James, in his art, need not back up as far as a philosopher or a literary critic, in their winks at Herakleitos, to put a finite observer in the objective totality of the objective world, or to imagine events as shapes. James is not tacitly but overtly *assuming the presence of a witness tied to a certain spot in the world and comparing his successive views.* In Strether's case, his successive views are inseparably visual and moral; James so prepares the visual field that even before the actual revelation everything Strether sees has become an emblem, weighted with emotion.

The scene, like the novel, is written from Strether's point of view, as the consciousness most wide and deep and closest to the author's mind. Thus and at length, with the four sentences we inspected earlier in italics, here are the last paragraphs of section 3 and the first paragraphs of section 4, in book 11:[6]

> For this had been all day at bottom the spell of the picture—that it was essentially more than anything else a scene and a stage, that the very air of the play was in the rustle of the willows and the tone of the sky. The play and the characters had, without his knowing it till now, peopled all his space for him, and it seemed somehow quite happy that they should offer themselves, in the conditions so supplied, with a kind of inevitability. It was as if the conditions made them not only inevitable, but so much more nearly natural and right as that they were at least easier, pleasanter, to put up with. The conditions had nowhere so asserted their difference from those of Woollett as they appeared to him to assert it in the little court of the Cheval Blanc while he arranged with his hostess for a comfortable climax. They were few and simple, scant and humble, but they were *the thing*, as he would have called it, even to a greater degree than Madame de Vionnet's old high salon where the ghost of the Empire walked. "The" thing was the thing that implied the greatest number of other things of the sort he had had to tackle; and it was queer of course, but so it was— the implication here was complete. Not a single one of his observations but somehow fell into a place in it; not a breath of the cooler evening that wasn't somehow a syllable of the text. The text was simple, when condensed, that in *these* places such things were, and that if it was in them one elected to move about one had to make one's account with what one lighted on. Meanwhile at all events it was enough that they did affect one—so far as the village aspect was concerned— as whiteness, crookedness and blueness set in coppery green; there being positively, for that matter, an outer wall of the White Horse that was painted the most improbable shade. That was part of the amusement—as if to show that the fun was harmless; just as it was enough, further, that the picture and the play seemed supremely to melt together in the good woman's broad sketch of what she could do for the visitor's appetite. He felt in short a confidence, and it was general, and it was all he wanted to feel. It suffered no shock even on her mentioning that she had in fact just laid the cloth for two persons, who, unlike Monsieur, had arrived by the river—in a boat of their own; who had asked her, half an hour before, what she could do for them, and had then paddled away to look at something a little further up—from which promenade they would presently return. Monsieur might meanwhile, if he liked, pass into the garden, such as it was, where she would serve him, should he wish it—for there were tables and benches in plenty—a "bitter" before his repast. Here she would also report to him on the possibility of a conveyance to his station, and here at any rate he would have the *agrément* of the river.

---

[6] The three paragraphs from the end of book 11 and one paragraph from the opening to book 12 of *The Ambassadors* (1903) are quoted from the 1909 New York edition, which is now in the public domain (the Full Text Archive).

It may be mentioned without delay that Monsieur had the *agrément* of everything, and in particular, for the next twenty minutes, of a small and primitive pavilion, that, at the garden's edge, almost overhung the water, testifying, in its somewhat battered state, to much fond frequentation. It consisted of little more than a platform, slightly raised, with a couple of benches and a table, a protecting rail and a projecting roof; but it raked the full grey-blue stream, which, taking a turn a short distance above, passed out of sight to reappear much higher up; and it was clearly in esteemed requisition for Sundays and other feasts. Strether sat there and, though hungry, felt at peace; the confidence that had so gathered for him deepened with the lap of the water, the ripple of the surface, the rustle of the reeds on the opposite bank, the faint diffused coolness and the slight rock of a couple of small boats attached to a rough landing-place hard by. The valley on the further side was all copper-green and glazed pearly sky, a sky hatched across with screens of trimmed trees, which looked flat, like espaliers; and though the rest of the village straggled away in the near quarter the view had an emptiness that made one of the boats suggestive. Such a river set one afloat almost before one could take the oars--the idle play of which would be moreover the aid to the full impression. This perception went so far as to bring him to his feet; but that movement, in turn, made him feel afresh that he was tired, and while he leaned against a post and continued to look out he saw something that gave him a sharper arrest.

IV
What he saw was exactly the right thing—a boat advancing round the bend and containing a man who held the paddles and a lady, at the stern, with a pink parasol. It was suddenly as if these figures, or something like them, had been wanted in the picture, had been wanted more or less all day, and had now drifted into sight, with the slow current, on purpose to fill up the measure. They came slowly, floating down, evidently directed to the landing-place near their spectator and presenting themselves to him not less clearly as the two persons for whom his hostess was already preparing a meal. For two very happy persons he found himself straightway taking them—a young man in shirtsleeves, a young woman easy and fair, who had pulled pleasantly up from some other place and, being acquainted with the neighborhood, had known what this particular retreat could offer them. The air quite thickened at their approach, with further intimations; the intimation that they were expert, familiar, frequent—that this wouldn't at all events be the first time. They knew how to do it, he vaguely felt—and it made them but the more idyllic, though at the very moment of the impression, as happened, their boat seemed to have begun to drift wide, the oarsman letting it go. *It had by this time none the less come much nearer—near enough for Strether to dream the lady in the stern had for some reason taken account of his being there to watch them. She had remarked on it sharply, yet her companion hadn't turned round; it was in fact almost as if our friend had felt her bid him keep still. She had taken in something as a result of which their course had wavered, and it continued to waver while they just stood off. This little effect was sudden and rapid, so rapid that Strether's sense of it was separate only for an instant from a sharp start of his own* [italics added]. He too had within the minute taken in something, taken in that he knew the lady whose parasol, shifting as if to hide her face, made so fine a pink point in the shining scene. It was too prodigious, a chance in a million, but if he knew the lady, the gentleman, who still presented his back and kept off, the gentleman, the coatless hero of the idyll, who had responded to her start, was, to match the marvel, none other than Chad.

Chad and Madame de Vionnet were then like himself taking a day in the country—though it was as queer as fiction, as farce, that their country could happen to be exactly his; and she had been the first at recognition, the first to feel, across the water, the shock—for it appeared to come to that—of their wonderful accident. Strether became aware, with this, of what was taking place—that her recognition had been even stranger for the pair in the boat, that her immediate impulse had been to control it, and that she was quickly and intensely debating with Chad the risk of betrayal. He saw they would show nothing if they could feel sure he hadn't made them out; so that he had before him for a few seconds his own hesitation. It was a sharp fantastic crisis that had popped up as if in a dream, and it had only to last the few seconds to make him feel it as quite horrible. They were thus, on either side, *trying* the other side, and all for some reason that broke the stillness like some unprovoked harsh note. It seemed to him again, within the limit, that he had but one thing to do—to settle their common question by some sign of surprise and joy. He hereupon gave large play to these things, agitating his hat and his stick and loudly calling out—a demonstration that brought him relief as soon as he had seen it answered. The boat, in mid-stream, still went a little wild—which seemed natural, however, while Chad turned round, half springing up; and his good friend, after blankness and wonder, began gaily to wave her parasol. Chad dropped afresh to his paddles, and the boat headed round, amazement and pleasantry filling the air meanwhile, and relief, as Strether continued to fancy, superseding mere violence. Our friend went down to the water under this odd impression as of violence averted—the violence of their having "cut" him, out there in the eye of nature, on the assumption that he wouldn't know it. He awaited them with a face from which he was conscious of not being able quite to banish this idea that they would have gone on, not seeing and not knowing, missing their dinner and disappointing their hostess, had he himself taken a line to match. That at least was what darkened his vision for a moment. Afterwards, after they had bumped at the landing-place and he had assisted their getting ashore, everything found itself sponged over by the mere miracle of the encounter.

After these four immense paragraphs, stretched across two of the novel's sections, there are five more paragraphs that take us to the end of section 4, book 11: here in the after-event by almost complete lack of delivered dialogue, James summarizes the awkward conversation over dinner at the Cheval Blanc, where no word touches the exploded lie on either side, and then he takes the three of them back to Paris on the train with pointless desultory talk, and he gives Strether a sleepless night alone, mulling things over in a "vain vigil." Toughly, Strether admits to himself that he has been on the receiving end of lie after lie and, tenderly, he admits to himself as much of a word as a polite American would speak even to himself (about physical love with a mistress) in the late nineteenth century, "the deep, deep truth of the intimacy revealed" (296). After this awareness, Strether hits on something to end book 11: "He recognized at last that he had really been trying all along to suppose nothing. Verily, verily, his labour had been lost. He found himself supposing innumerable and wonderful things" (296). That supposing is the impulse that carries us to book 12, and the ending of the novel on the renewed sense of Mme. de Vionnet's magnificence in her thralldom, with the utterly new assurance that Chad is a cad who is preparing to dump his mistress. The reader is left at the last with Strether's stiff and noble turn from the promise of happiness with Maria Gostrey when he says to her his only logic has been "[n]ot, out of the whole affair, to have got anything for myself" (327).

Back we go to the four paragraphs and a scan of the perceptual content, with the Modes and Powers of Attention.

Movement. After careful preparation of the static scene with details of the inn, climate, time of day, and stationing of the witness above the river, the Impressionist painting is made to move when the boat comes on the scene, advancing and then dithering in a retrograde movement that betrays the agents, Chad and Mme. de Vionnet. Their identities are deferred and then delivered by a thunderbolt at the end of a sentence.

Chiasm. Strether/Innkeeper; Strether's sense of peace in the scene/loss of peace; Strether as against the people in the boat; man in boat/woman in boat; anguished silence/overeager greeting; coincidence of meeting/inevitability of meeting; idyll/horror of encounter; the American/what can happen in Old Europe; blissful ignorance/sober knowledge of the life based on lies.

Depth. The following scenes are surfaces: the idea of a little drama for Strether alone, based on the details of the scene at the Cheval Blanc in the first two paragraphs; the colors of the Impressionist painting in the scene, before the agents are brought on, with the color not being structural; the river itself, hiding its depth; the light of the day that is counterposed against what happens to Strether after the event: "darkened his vision." All these are shown to be deceptive in the event. Depth is gained by the denial, then the excavation, of surface meanings.

Non-coincidence. As a victim of lies, Strether is misled as an ambassador, strung along, put into self-contradiction by the pair of lovers and their helper, Little Bilham. "He [Strether] had been trying all along to suppose nothing," out of generosity. He is brought into knowledge by the startling revelation of the pair on the river, their intimacy as revealed not only in the wavering motion on the river but in the lady's face hidden by the parasol and the man appearing in shirtsleeves: if the coat is off, all is apparent, and the detail tells the story Strether is not yet ready to receive even though he has seen the evidence. It takes a dark night of the soul, in his hotel room afterward, to come back into coincidence with his own knowledge. America and Europe, past and present, Chad and one's image of Chad are non-coincident even at the novel's end; only Strether has come to knowledge, which is his only reward.

Rhythm. Rhythm is always a matter of the relation of perception to expectation in human time. In these paragraphs, there are many references to artful organization and sequencing, often with literary terminology involving scene, stage, syllable of the text, drama, climax, idyll, impression, queer as fiction, and farce. There are perhaps forty or fifty separable stages, involving delays and interruptions and remarkable extensions of syntax, that take us from and through the revelation of who is on the river, and then beyond that. The break between sections 3 and 4, and the long sentence ending paragraph 2 with the delivery of Chad's name, are dazzling effects of rhythm. Recognition is deferred through division and piling-up of perceptions, then several times delivered with a shock, using the words *start* and *sharp* and *shock*.

Interrogation. These elements are all put into question:
– The outer scene with its lure of peace, solitude, a good meal, and then its idyllic promise of a perfect couple arriving in the drift of time and the river to complete the Impressionist painting;
– Strether's role as an ambassador, a person who goes between a mother and a son, and between America and France;

- Strether's role as a potential husband for Maria Gostrey, so appropriate is she for age, friendliness, intellectual match, and understanding of his character;
- The relation of Chad and Madame de Vionnet, as presented to Strether and the world with such adult insouciance, such elaborate falsehood;
- The perversely polite behavior of characters when all the previous months have been stripped bare by an instant's recognition, as they go on maintaining the lie through conversation for the length of a country meal and a train ride;
- The elaborate details and ruses of indirection and delay, including syntax in sentences stuffed with suppositions and provisos and add-ons.

What is not in doubt, but rather validated, is Lambert Strether's ability to read a scene for moral motives and to act so as to prevent the violence of an open and declared break in civility.

Description. The first of these paragraphs is a leisurely, detail-packed (as in "crookedness and blueness set in coppery green" for the view of the village) visual field in front of an observant witness, who is making a story of what he sees, with multiple shifts in topic and point of view and, even, with the voice of the woman of the inn as free indirect discourse in "Monsieur . . . would have the *agrément* of the river." The second paragraph is a bravado presentation of the sequence of movements, where the visual details are all retrospectively turned into moral meanings, as in "waver while they just stood off" in the boat. The doubled use of the same word "start" for recognitions of both Strether and Madame de Vionnet is an effect of description that is also movement, chiasm, coincidence, rhythm, interrogation, and disclosure.

Disclosure. Surprisingly, James, with his famous self-qualifying subtlety and skill at finding hidden springs of personality, has proven to be more than a match for Merleau-Ponty in his pre-cognitive grasp of bodily experience. James, too, wishes to discern what is invisible behind things and inaudible behind sounds and hidden back of time; James, too, is able to say, and show through storytelling, that humans are not aware of what is going on when we are speaking. Once the focus of the story has become *intimacy*, through the agency of the chosen scene, the novel's meanings are suddenly evident, past all the falsehoods and meanders of Strether's search of appearance. Because of this scene, which James admits (through Strether's mind) to being his climax, we know about relation of scene and agent, where all the stationed witnesses' perceptions turn out to be both physical and moral; about why Chad has needed an American ambassador and why the mission must fail, with a harsh judgment on Chad and abiding respect for his mistress and, it seems, victim; about all the illusions on both sides, between America and Europe, and about the validity of some of the clichés of national character; about temporality, including the role of sequence in the plotting of imaginary perceptions of imaginary persons, and what happens when a plot requires coincidence. With its careful placement near the story's end, along with its density and sequencing of the observer's sense-perceptions, the scene is the novel's primary device for disclosure of moral judgments.

Much in the handling of the perceptual content of the scene is represented by the little phrase "kept off": Mme. has warned Chad that Strether was there, and he, in a flash of fear and worry, responding to her concern, has held the boat from coming in to dock. Chad's very back and his holding off are telegraphing embarrassment to Strether, and these are phases in the developing perception. All that information discovered from a verb and a preposition!

Presented, his back, kept off, coatless, responded, her start: these and other phrases are expansions of the summary term before the break for a new section 4, in Strether, a *sharper arrest*. Strether is put into prison by this vision and, also, called to attention. It would be in keeping with the larger argument now to claim that these perceptions of sight, memory, and emotion are animalist. After all, sex is the invisible of it, and art in the form of landscape painting and idyll writing are the frames of it. We want high art and the intellectually distinguished James to be an example of this animalist perception and interpretation.

Non-coincidence, essentially temporal, may be the mode of attention most pertinent to literary works. *It was too prodigious, a chance in a million*: no writer of any merit will give up the opportunity to motivate the action by the character's free choice of how to behave, but James has given it up in this scene and, not only that, he has used clichés, including the word *marvel*, to call attention to the accident of the riverside meeting.

James relapses into a conventional exaggeration for an unmotivated bit of plotting: why? In bland summary, Chad and Mme. de Vionnet went to the country to the same place outside of Paris and bumped into Strether inconveniently. It is not one in a million, just unlikely, and fiction, James might say, can do that—after all his coincidences are far fewer and less blatant than Thomas Hardy's, and Hardy always got away with it. I think Merleau-Ponty suggests an explanation for James going ahead with the coincidence and then pointing at it, in a sentence like this one from the chapter on temporality: "To analyse time is not to follow out the consequences of a pre-established conception of subjectivity, it is to gain access, through time, to its concrete structure" (*PP* 410). The concrete structure of time in this story always comes back to the social armor of the structure of lies by and about Chad and Mme., which fends off all the increasingly frantic efforts of the ambassadorial go-betweens. Logically, the only way the elaborate and strong structure of lies in the first eleven books could be broken down would be 1) to go outside Paris, where the falsehoods are plausible; 2) to go outside the routines of the characters; and 3) through validation by physical perception, not by speech. Procedurally, this breaking down can be made to occur through carefully staged descriptions that turn an impressionist painting into a script for a moving-picture film. That James is able to use the coincidence as the plot's climax, justify it logically, and then inscribe every detail in sequence to hide the coincidence in realistic credibility, makes for the highest achievement of the novel: a yet further complication, quite the opposite of an easy solution to his plot's progress.

The last word in Merleau-Ponty's chapter on temporality is "freedom," and the next chapter, the very last, is titled "Freedom." When I read the final sentence on "Temporality," I think of Lambert Strether, who has been released, by the revelation in our chosen scene, from being an ambassador: "The solution of all problems of transcendence is to be sought in the thickness of the pre-objective present, in which we find our bodily being and our social being, and the pre-existence of the world, that is, the starting point of 'explanations,' in so far as they are legitimate—and at the same time the basis of our freedom" (*PP 495*). Isn't it often forgotten that the exposé of *the thickness of the pre-objective present*, that takes four hundred and thirty-three pages of intricate argument, ends on a chapter of twenty-two pages on how we get from *bodily and social being* to freedom?

For Strether, the end of his role as America's representative in Europe, the failure with Chad and the inevitable loss of whatever relationship was possible with Chad's mother, Mrs. Newsome, means the end of all responsibilities and social ties, except his more-than-friendship with Maria Gostrey. He will carry back to America what Maria on the last page calls his "wonderful impressions" of England and France, but he will not bring her as his bride. "So then she had to take it," says James, giving her all credit for empathic understanding and stoic acceptance, but Strether has the last bit of dialogue in the novel:

> She sighed it at last all comically, all tragically away. "I can't indeed resist you."
> "Then there we are!" said Strether.

That last exclamation is James through his character sighing it all away, because the tragicomic values of the work are all embodied in the earlier doings, sayings, and perceivings of these imaginary persons. Our interpretation through categories of attention should guarantee that we mean *embodied* literally, even though the characters are imaginary.

Chapter 8: Ordinary Creativity

The birth of meaning

We will never know what is happening when perceiving is occurring. An event is unknowable.[1] Birth is private and, so we hear and indeed have seen, painful and joyous. Informed, intentional help is needed to bring forth meaning and babies; however, the origin of the help is occluded. Perhaps, though, we might speculate about what is going on beforehand and what elements enter in, and we can calculate with evidence and hunches what has happened after the event. Let us move as needed before and after the unknowable by using in-process acts of perception that are already, rudimentary as may be, cognitive and creative. Those acts are cognitive and creative because the mind is embodied, and because the mission of phenomenology is to imagine and invent what Maurice Merleau-Ponty called a secondary, laborious, rediscovered naïveté. The mission is not to downgrade rationality but to remind it to be self-critical—to place perceiving-thinking-writing into a loop of circulation, but with no priority of function. If there is a rhetorical emphasis on perception, that is because perception is what philosophy and literature have too long neglected.

Who remembers any words uttered during the moment of those acts, those that bring into the world the birth of meaning? If there are words, are they statements, exclamations, questions, grunts? Very likely there are no words, or only inner speech. If the event is wordless, perhaps some kind of *thought* is intertwined and entangled. After all, something new in the *Umwelt* is about to be named!

Words are surely there before and after the event. If I invent one of those graphics that show a thinker's words of preference, in graduated-sized circles that shift down from huge to massive to large to medium, surely only one word is huge for Merleau-Ponty, and that is perception. Other words would be massive: body, Husserl, language, speech, philosophy, phenomenology, meaning, Descartes, nature, visible. Next are words that would probably be large: creative, truth, reduction or epoché, sound or hearing, touch, Hegel, the dialectic, freedom. Then would come medium-sized words: structures, Sartre, Heidegger, Marx and Marxist, interrogate, chiasm, intertwining, animal, word, witness, "just as." (Note that the list omits seven of the nine terms of precision that I redefined and used in the previous two chapters.) In earlier chapters, I have shown how nearly all the concepts in my imaginary graphic will orbit around phenomenology's leading terms, namely, perception and body. If I have succeeded, I have shown how these words in the ensemble tend to work in synergy to strengthen

---

1 Gregory Bateson asserts: "The *processes* of perception are inaccessible; only the *products* are conscious and, of course, it is the products that are necessary" (*Mind and Nature* 32). Also, there is another relevant understanding here: "The new can only be plucked from the random" (64).

a system of thought. My own terms of emphasis, *search* and *relation of interference*, do show up in Merleau-Ponty's writings, but not often, so if we bring them forward (as the minor metaphors of our larger claim here) it is part of our own attempt to circumscribe an unthought: to make-explicit an idea, thereby to clarify, thereby to collaborate from the side of literature.

This book began with Mikhail Bakhtin speaking, in "From Notes Made in 1970-1971," on the co-creativity of a writer's readers who come after and understand the writer's utterances on the basis of art-speech that survives. Now we can add a concluding claim, namely that what Merleau-Ponty has called the realization-completion of an *unthought* in a previous writer is exactly the same thing as Bakhtin's co-creativity of those who understand. The work of perceiving-thinking-writing, Bakhtin and Merleau-Ponty knew (but Bakhtin said it), has its *homecoming* in a later era, under different social-historical conditions, but future readers—"those who understand"—know enough to adjust for that. Inevitably, yet unpredictably, since creativity contains the chaotic random, what the creative after-comer recognizes is the condition for the birth of creativity in the original work of verbal art. The knowledge required in the original writer's creativity, and in their reader's creativity, is both technical-formal and social-historical.

What is known is, in brief, that perception always already stylizes and that style always historicizes. In the act of seeing we are automatically, without even trying consciously, shaping and styling what we see. Then, because we have shaped/styled, we are (again automatically) creating a narrative. What comes next is what we do with language (written or spoken), which is to make into an artifact what we have perceived, styled, historicized.

What is known, but often forgotten or avoided, is that the body is a perceiving animal. In his lecture on "Nature and Logos," Merleau-Ponty protests that in some philosophies the actual fact of humAnimal birth is understood "as if a body instrument had received from elsewhere a thought-pilot, or inversely as if an object called the body had mysteriously produced consciousness out of itself" (*IPP* 197). For him that is a monstrous state of affairs and he would marshal against it his value-terms including the *Umwelt*, the body schema, perception as true mobility, and corporeality as something that can be seen and can see itself. Creativity—as a self-assigned problem—will, as is consonant with the phenomenological attitude, once again be studied as an instance of the core logics of the relations of interference. What is created has so much abundant detail, so striking an overlay of sentences upon scenes upon stories, such complexities of emotional and intellectual engagement, that the secret origins of the work are obscured. It is those origins that the co-creating reader can interrogate, describe, and disclose. From this interrogating, describing, and disclosing comes literary analysis, or at least enjoyable reading.

Boris Pasternak, the Cold War Russian poet-novelist who wrote and attached a poet-character's portfolio of poems to the end of his novel, said that the story every poem tells is the tale of its own coming-into-being. John Fowles said that the novel as a form is only (and all) about freedom. Maurice Merleau-Ponty has a page to speculate that Stendahl became a writer when he realized that every adult human has to try to live outside the ordained assumptions of her or his society (*IPP* 85-86). Merleau-Ponty ends another essay by quoting Proust on Proust's own necessary reading of the book of his own consciousness, so to believe himself a possible writer—reading the unwritten text of himself before writing himself into a novel for the reader. Proust titled his immense novel *Á la recherche* ... with the term for *search* or *seek*, but in an early section on involuntary memory, he produced a warning to himself that I now quote to define the arc between my own first chapter and this one: "Chercher? pas seulement: créer" ("Seek? More than that: create").[2]

Merleau-Ponty is in resonance with his favored novelist Proust, and with his second-favored philosopher Bergson, when in his later writings he is increasingly taking up what philosophy's own definition might be. *In Praise of Philosophy* has a tribute to Bergson, where he praises the earlier writer for refusing the accepted terms of a usual problem as they are—Bergson is right to want to do an authentic philosophy by creating the framework of the problem and creating the solution. To make Bergeson's unthought specific, the co-creating Merleau-Ponty adds: "Thus when [Bergson] says that well-posed problems are very close to being solved, this does not mean that we have already *found* what we are looking for, but that we have already invented it" (*IPP* 14). Seek? More than that: create. It is an aspiration for himself, first, but also for scholars and commentators, for all obsessed thinkers no less than for workers in the sister arts of music, painting, and writing.

*

The discussion ahead is a sketch of a poetics of perception, to follow on from and supplement the existing phenomenology of perception. I shall rehearse and condense Merleau-Ponty's version of the creative joining of things and words, emphasizing literary relevance and the possible quotient of unthought that (once made explicit) could lead to productive, indeed, co-creative, interference between his discipline and mine.

Before this, though, I wish to frame what is next by referring not to philosophers but to a quantum physicist, David Bohm, who has written the only truly valuable book directly on the subject of its title, *On Creativity*. Bohm defines creativity as an act of perception through the mind. As such, creativity is a particular case of perception as a whole. (Reflective thought, or perception as a whole, includes various modes in his

---

[2] In Merleau-Ponty's first book (*La Structure du Comportement*, 1942), the resistance against "pre-established apparatuses" is already in evidence. Perception is and has to be creation in the moment: "The physiological process which corresponds to the perceived color or position or to the signification of a word must be improvised, actively constituted at the very moment of perception. Thus, function has a positive and proper reality; it is not a simple consequence of the existence of organs or substrate" (*The Structure of Behavior* 88).

scheme: sense perception; emotional perception or perception through the feelings; aesthetic perception; and perception through the mind.) For Bohm, creativity is a synonym for intelligence, and intelligence does not arise principally out of thought. This view has a clear affinity with Merleau-Ponty's position, but Bohm also takes his understanding a step further to affirm that the real source of intelligence comes out of the unknown and indefinable totality from which all perception originates. (I include Bohm's additional stance to report his view; Merleau-Ponty does not mention or take that further step in his thinking.)

Bohm makes the foundational and expected move Merleau-Ponty also makes, in distinguishing between what is given (memory, training, and reactive thought) and what is created (for him, the act of perception through the mind). What is given is immense and visible and what is created is out there but usually invisible. Merleau-Ponty everywhere defines *what is given* as the natural attitude, namely, a readymade and instituted language; *what is creative* is for him a pre-speculative being, that comes prior to the logical activity of the ego.

Very promising is Bohm's statement about creation being an act of perception through the mind, where perceiving and thinking are *Ineinander*. That act is phenomenological. Even more valuable to a nascent poetics is Bohm's further statement, that what is creative is fresh views of structure. This assertion recapitulates, without citation and probably without knowledge, Merleau-Ponty's claims about how *perception* already stylizes and is already expression, about constructive deformation, about new structures of equivalence in painting and writing, about syntax in depth, and about language itself as perceptual structures at another level. The relation of interference, we can now say, is also structural, so the old opposition of form *versus* content no longer applies to the languages of art. Specifically with the art-sentence, this unit for study is non-dual part and whole, static and sequential, cognitive and aesthetic: it is the very figure for entangled indetermination.

In the phenomenology of meaning-making, perception is creative because it is relational. Even the most simple of perceptions are relational and meaning-bearing. Having a body is the necessary condition for perceiving things. As Merleau-Ponty says, the body perceives nature, which it also inhabits, and "the perceived object is the prototype of meaning and alone accomplishes the actual truth of what is understood" (*PW* 106). Since perception is the actual relation between the body and things, it enlists and performs body and things. For completeness, let me add this: Since perception is one actual relation (of several) between body and mind, it enlists and performs body and mind.

Perception is creative because it is social. Lawrence Hass rightly said that, for phenomenology "the perceptual field is social through and through" (99), and this social-ness is most evidently the case in late Husserl and late Merleau-Ponty. Self, others, and things are in synergy because in our human development others have fostered our relation with things and persons in the world; they have literally given the world to us, through emotional connection and through language. "Our relation to the true passes through others," the philosopher said (*IPP* 31). The true is, in this social sense, the new. For I am not just a body, but also a social self, rooted in contingent place and time with other humAnimal and responsive selves. The generalization of my body is the perception of the other, always contingent, always occurring in a present tense, always transitive—in the *Offenheit der Umwelt* not entirely fixed, and, thus, always bearing a matrix of possibility.

Perception is creative because it is expressive. Our simple acts of moving, looking, hearing, touching, and registering passage of time already contain the secret of expressive action. More developed expression—in social feelings conveyed to a public, in claiming our freedom and spirit, in painting and writing— is self-witnessing and also witnessed by others. Nothing in this philosophy is achieved before it has been said and, in particular, for this philosopher, freedom and spirit "must witness themselves in matter or in the body, in order to be themselves," or in other words, "they must express themselves" (*IPP* 28-29). Hass is the commentator who has best explained the centrality of this premise in Merleau-Ponty: expression is not reliance upon established fact, or delivery of the readymade or known, but rather the active passage of meaning—ongoing, copresent occurrence of meaning and also the handing over and the witnessing of meaning.

Perception is creative because it reveals what in experience is sacred and what is strange. In one of his rare comments on religion, Merleau-Ponty said that philosophy does not place the sacred "here or there, like a thing, but at the joining of things and words" (*IPP* 46). Elsewhere, on Cézanne, he said that the creative work of the painter is always a response to what the world gives. So what is creative requires as a necessity what is given: "body, life, landscapes, schools, mistresses, creditors, the police, and revolution . . . are also the bread his painting consecrates" ("ILVS" 264). The idea of not ignoring but rather searching to disclose the world's strangeness, in this kind of thinking, would seem to be the same notion as what the 1920s Russian Formalists, Viktor Shklovsky in particular, described as "defamiliarization," that self-explanatory term. Suddenly, by means pictorial or verbal, the physical scene regains its vividness, richness, an illimitable quality; once again the usual blank surfaces flush with color and meaning. Merleau-Ponty, for whom the most resolute philosophers always wish to realize whatever's contrary, can convey the mechanisms by which this occurs by using terms for the unsettlement of rhetoric such as *ambiguity, deformation, a secret principle of distortion*, and *unconcealment of a sense*. On occasion this search for the uncanny leads him to produce astounding sentences: "this speaking power, in which expression premeditates itself" (*S* 18); "the expression antedates itself and postulates that being comes towards it" (*IPP* 29); and, most impressively in the "Course Notes" on Husserl, "Speech supports itself on what it sustains; it falls toward the heights" (*HLP* 52). In such passages, the reader accepts that, blandly and briefly to make a point, he is daring to use the language of paradox within the run of his own discourse.

Perception is creative because it searches speech at just the point of the joining of things and words. Perception-in-process traces the lived coupling that is new every time, whether we are speaking, listening, writing, or reading. Speaking is a face-to-face spontaneity, and writing is (or can be) a face-to-page virtual spontaneity. Speaking and writing admit others into our "deepest singularity," says Merleau-Ponty, and in so doing they make "the universal out of singulars and meaning out of our life" (*PW* 146). The creativity of the moment can even be extended to language, that linking of self and other through speech. In the late Husserl notes, he pursues this lived and in-process coupling from the other, cognitive side by condensing everything about the relation of interference when he says that language is "not an external accident. . . . *Denken* does not envelop speech; it is entangled with it" (*HLP* 32). This idea opens the door from philosophy to the art-sentence and writing: what the "Working Notes" in *The Visible and the Invisible* describe as "the philosophy of the sensible as literature" (*VI* 252). Moving to scholar-writers, Merleau-Ponty generously allows their co-creativity, when he says these latecoming commentators "are not limited to an exercise [that is] second order and repetitive": he sounds like the literary theorists of the 1980s-90s when he says that critics and philosophers can exercise "the same powers of elliptical expression which creates the work of art" (*PW* 91). If perception is creative and expressive, that should apply equally to everyone, with no forgetting the philosophers, who are one other kind of writer.

Ordinary creativity

Wallace Stevens (d. 1955) and Mikhail Bakhtin (d. 1975) were both Merleau-Ponty's contemporaries, and like him Stevens and Bakhtin had their own homecomings as writers in the years following their deaths. A third contemporary was Shunryu Suzuki (d. 1971), whose profound and elegant book *Zen Mind, Beginner's Mind* was published in 1970. None of these other three thinkers knew of each other, or of Merleau-Ponty, who knew nothing of them. Nonetheless, all four made convergent contributions to a theory of ordinary creativity. To put all of them together is to invent a tradition, even against their radical differences in national origin, chosen discipline, chosen genre, likely politics, and likely moral intention. The other three share an attitude toward experience with Merleau-Ponty: namely, discontent with established and current significations—openness toward new meanings.[3] I will get back to Stevens and Bakhtin, but here I would start the file on ordinariness with Shunryu Suzuki of the Berkeley and San Francisco Zen Centers.

On the first page of his book Suzuki writes: "In Japan we have the phrase *shoshin*, which means 'beginner's mind.' The goal of practice is always to keep our beginner's mind . . . . 'Original mind' . . . does mean a closed mind, but actually an empty mind

---

[3] They share this attitude with many others, too, but for my purposes the invented tradition starts with them. The fact of contemporaneity has some pertinence.

and a ready mind. If your mind is empty, it is always ready for anything; it is open to everything. In the beginner's mind there are many possibilities; in the expert's mind there are few" (21). With Suzuki, and with others in his practice, the perpetual beginner begins with cranking down the attention to breathing and the body: the body in sitting practice is ordinary, sitting and counting and being aware of breathing is ordinary, and watching one's own thinking is ordinary. All these simple things lead to the resolve of compassion for oneself and all sentient beings. When the Buddha focused on his own body and mind, here and now, "[a]nd when he found himself, he found that everything that exists has Buddha nature.... The state of mind that exists when you sit in the right posture is, itself, enlightenment.... To stop your mind does not mean to stop the activities of mind. It means your mind pervades your whole body" (Suzuki 28-29, 41). Suzuki's younger Bay Area colleague Mel Weitsman died in 2021, and the tribute in *Lion's Roar* quotes him restating Suzuki's doctrine: *nothing special*. "Ordinary mind," Weitsman wrote, refers to

> something routine, like the mechanics of making it through the day.... Don't think that because you are sitting zazen early in the morning that you are doing something special.... The whole universe is sitting zazen with you, and you are sitting with the universe.... When we seek the extraordinary, we stumble past because we miss the truly extraordinary right beneath our feet. ("Dharma Dragon" 40)

Beginner's Mind shares with Merleau-Pontian Mind bodily awareness, attention to attention and, thus, to the ongoingness of perception, and the wish not to diminish thinking but to pull it back into relation with perceiving and writing.

Species creativity of *Homo erectus* from about 1.8 million years ago until around 400,000 years ago, and then species creativity among the next-in-line descendants (*Homo heidelbergensis*, the Neandertals and Denisovans, the Flores peoples, and us), is absolutely ordinary. And yet that is the creativity most momentous because it defines the thing that defines us. Beginner's mind began there! This development required the genius of the species—species exceptionality—not the individual achievement of a Shakespeare, a Goethe, a Pushkin, a Proust, a Marie Curie, or a Jennifer Doudna. We are the species that co-shaped and domesticated ourselves. Augustín Fuentes speaks on compossible cooperation in this millennia-long collective social process: "Whether it was eluding predators, making and sharing stone tools, controlling fire, telling stories, or contending with shifts in climate, our ancestors creatively collaborated to deal with the challenges the world threw at them" (4). From that anthropological narrative of the creative spark, I shall take the ideas of cooperation, evolution, the self-construction of a species, a minor edge of advantage expanded and refined, and storytelling. Plainly, the development of language enabled hominid progress by facilitating an increase of cooperation through every stage over millions of years.

Jump-cut from pre-history to a few years ago. When I had a sinovial cyst removed from my left index finger, I thought about my hand for the first time, and I gained respect for the doctors who specialize in wrists and palms and fingers and knuckles and nails and the closely packed veins and muscles. The opposable thumb started to look like a little miracle. After my doctor-surgeon removed the bump, I purchased for her and for me copies of Colin McGinn's *Prehension: The Hand and the Emergence of Humanity*, where the philosopher-author approaches his body-part "from multiple directions—anatomically, functionally, emotionally, cognitively, artistically, and philosophically" (viii). As with Fuentes, tool use is his first topic: "The tool replaced the tree as man's chief object of prehension" (30). The tool-using state of mind is creative, also teleological, pointing forward to new uses. "As the brain coevolved with tools, so the hands coevolved with tools" (35). The next stage of the argument is, by the author's admission, based on no empirical evidence: McGinn suggests that the hand is the critical variable in the emergence of syntax and semantics. He takes this idea from the research of others, and he pursues and evaluates it: one hand can act as an agent, the other can act as an object, and an action can be performed by the one on the other: so it is a performance-analogue for the Subject-Verb-Object structure. Further, "[p]rimitive gestural language ... proceeds on the basis of *three* preadaptations that are brought together organically. But all center on the hands, exploiting their capacity for combinatorial sequential structure, object prehension, and symbolic mimicry. This is quite a rich brew" (47). When used for ostension, for pointing, the hands were already the perfect organs for communication, and they "graduated by incremental steps from brachiating to tool using to talking" (49). To shorten this proposal to the basic elements: evolution moved from hand to mouth, where the tongue is like a finger and directs the airflow and therefore the variability of sounds, and eventually the hand became the instrument for writing. Prehension became comprehension, and then these two coevolved. Of course, nobody knows or can know how these skills developed and coexisted in the hominid body, but McGinn's suggestion, his analogy, has the merit of connecting, somewhat plausibly, the body with language, the structure of the sentence, and one version of ordinary creativity.

Thus, we recognize species self-invention as one form of ordinary creativity. I would mention now the creativity of readers of sentences, between ancient cultures BCE and the present day, by briefly extending three examples already discussed in passing. In moving from the anthropological facts to the literary fictions, this account adopts Merleau-Ponty's shocking renegade idea of the history of perception as creative, wherein, he says, "the mystery of the first speech is no greater than the mystery of all successful expression" (*PW* 43). From the caves at Lascaux and Chauvet to Cézanne, from ancient inscriptions incised in stone tablets to books saved in the cloud on the Internet, all that matters, in this view, is that something is transacted in the moment. "For the power of language [including painting as a language] lies neither in that future of knowledge toward which it moves nor in that mythical past from which it has emerged: it lies entirely in its present," in the real-time generation of the immediate utterance (41). All preceding experience is repeated in the living exercise of speech.⁴ Living speech is ordinary, so much so that the philosopher has to submit it, along with all things visible-audible-touchable, to the Husserlian reduction. It is the same everyday quality in writing, where we forget origins and contexts of sentences because we think them familiar. To single out sentences from the run of ordinary language, for storytelling or for study, we need to shock ourselves into their infinite variety and strangeness by practicing a kind of non-understanding. Emphatically this assertion does not mean that literary language is a special subtype—there is no literary language, there is no philosophical language, there is only ordinary language repurposed.

What does the reader need to know about sentences, better to understand the birth of meaning in the joining of words and things and better to allow language itself to help them learn to co-create? 1) The first example comes from finding a color illustration in a history of Crete: the stone tablet incised with Greek letters that make up the Great Law Code of the city of Gortyn. It is rectangular, several feet wide and a couple of feet high, consisting of rows of letters with no punctuation and no accent marks and no spaces between words or sentences and, thus, no visible words or sentences. The history book says that the sense of the Code runs left to right on the first line, then loops over in the second line to run right to left, and so on in alternation fluently to the bottom. How did readers disambiguate their tablet's moral code in the absence of so many markers? L. D. Reynolds and N. G. Wilson, in their guide to ancient documents, speak of the many risks of misinterpretation, which were especially severe with plays in meter but without breakdown into lines and without cues to which character is speaking (see *Scribes and Scholars* 4-5 and 8-9). Plainly, ancient readers knew how to read what their contemporaries had written: they disambiguated by case-endings, by word-order, and by sense. Plainly, in the absence of markers they knew where one word or one sentence ended and the next began. Yet how they must have faltered, struggled, questioned. 2) Fredric Jameson's article on time in the novels of Joseph Conrad discusses how modernist prose engages in a bewildering fragmentation of acts and objects, in a deliberate (or sometimes helpless) wish to obscure relationships and play out suspense ("Time and the Sea"). He sees a fundamental contradiction in modernism between plot and sentence, which is one mode of occluding a relation of unequal power between capital (ship-owners) and labor (sailors, small merchants). His term for the reader's act of disambiguation is "delayed decoding," a way of letting the novel's meanings rest in appearances, in winding unrevealing sentences, so to prevent easy or quick disclosures. 3) Language poetry in Lyn Hejinian, Michael Palmer, Ron Silliman, Charles Bernstein, and others

---

4   On the same page Merleau-Ponty further says: "The marvel that a finite number of signs, forms, and words should give rise to an indefinite number of uses, or that other and identical marvel that linguistic meaning directs toward something beyond language, is the very prodigy of speech, and anyone who tries to explain it in terms of its 'beginning' or its 'end' would lose sight of its 'doing'" (41).

has an explicitly stated program of empowering the reader, allowing her or him to reinterpret, break off, object, focus narrowly, resist politically, and take pleasure or anger at most any point. It is a liberal policy, but the effort may be worthwhile if the reader has the stamina to stick with a long poem where the sentence is the prosody and the topics change frequently and the speaker might be a false identity and the plan may be to drone onward at length: that is asking a lot from the reader in return for the announced or implied license to leave or to interrupt or to skip around. The sentences of Language poetry—some wild with leaping logic, some full of alliteration, some abrupt, some self-revealing, some arranging a clash of discourses—redefine what a sentence can do. Language poetry redefines what a reader must do to exercise dis-ambiguation—or, now, re-ambiguation. (In an avant-garde era, ambiguity, like irony, has its uses, in preventing the reader from quickly passing to what the sentence signifies. When that happens, we cannot slow down our thinking and perform the reduction upon language.) In all three instances of readerly constraint and freedom, the sentence is a mid-level unit that exhibits interference by containing, at any moment, two contradictory possibilities: the statement of proposition and the creative obscurity of coherent deformation. With the sentence, language finds an adaptive little animal engine for correcting the objective world.

*

We are the ones who organize the encounter when late Wallace Stevens beckons to late Merleau-Ponty, through the thirty-one sections in twenty-four pages of the long poem titled "An Ordinary Evening in New Haven." It is our choice *not* to read this poem with the nine phenomenological terms of precision that we earlier defined and put to use in a cross-disciplinary trial. Why read with those terms, when Stevens already uses equivalent terms in this poem, openly and with relevance and force, and when he comes forward as already a fully phenomenological thinker? (He is not yet enrolled in the list of members, but this could be his statement of application.) Also: why quote at length, or at all, when "An Ordinary Evening" can never receive more than a partial representation? The poem is too long, has too many themes, too many tonal shifts and register shifts, too mixed a diction: these are glories and not worries, except for one who wishes to enlist the poem for a thesis. Also, relevant here: the poem's own creative method is not to tell a story or argue a position but to keep elaborating new statements and images for a core logic only legible through those very items in the spread of inventions. My own account of the New Haven poem will be selective and keyed to the constructive interference of poetry and philosophy on the topic of ordinary creativity.[5]

---

5 Cary Wolfe considers "An Ordinary Evening" possibly Stevens's greatest achievement. He has a whole chapter on the poem in *Ecological Poetics: or, Wallace Stevens's Birds* (2020). He writes from a different point of vantage, but his take on the poem is fully resonant with mine on the role of the ordinary and on poetry's leverage on philosophy as a mode of knowing.

After the title, New Haven is invoked three times in the long poem, but not as the city of a great university or the home for powerful insurance companies; rather as it is the ground where plain men experience the times of day and the changes of seasons. "Commonplace" is the summary-word for the whole utterance in hundreds of lines because this location is the *Offenheit der Umwelt*, the common place for everyone, including the writer as subsumed into the mass. The perception of change in the world is creative precisely because it is ordinary and shared, available to all, valuable because plain, inconspicuous, and always in transition. Evening is not a point in time but an unpinnable in-between time, the evolution of a shade, a process that has a name.

My account of the terms in the title should not give the impression that "An Ordinary Evening" pursues an argument. It pursues diffusion and proliferation by repeating a rather large set of themes that all branch from and point back to the terms of the title. Stevens himself describes origin, intent, and method in this long work with as many sections as days in a month: "this endlessly elaborating poem" (section 28). Several elements that repeat here in a partial list— are: the color blue; references to earth; the new; the real; speech; "as if"; beginnings and endings; language; searching; sky, wind, moon; morning, noon, evening; hearing, seeing, touching; poems; blank, plain; appearance; the commonplace; savage; romance. These elements represent change and return, so they all play out as topical refrains within a discourse that is wary of repetition as the hardening into familiar meaning that kills everything creative. Still, as the things and persons that make up the ordinariness of experiencing, these changes of day, year, climate, light, and mindset are necessary to the birth of meaning. The regular, periodic returns that the world brings are, speaking strictly, changes. Times of day and month and season and year are always new if we search the appearance of the familiar-visible for the invisible; after the epoché, we can disclose the "inescapable romance" within the "metaphysical streets" (sections 4, 11). That image puts the phenomenological new in New Haven.

Distributed among these effects of light and shade, sun and sky, are allegorical characters who are projections of the scene. These are the man of bronze, the lion of Juda, the ephebe, Professor Eucalyptus of New Haven, the walker, the architect, the actor, the man in a room, the shepherd, the hidalgo, and the scholar. They are more like characters with speaking parts than the "[p]lain men in plain towns" who are contemporaries (section 4), but they are also not yet the poet himself who organizes this savage scene but who never claims to speak in the first person.

Merleau-Ponty, too, almost never speaks with the upright pronoun, and yet, like Stevens, manages a definite angle of vision and a deliberate personal style. In both, perception always creates and, on this basis, always stylizes. In "An Ordinary Evening," Stevens, with subtle reversible power, shows the point of relation when he states that the philosopher's search is for an interior made exterior, and the poet's search is for *the same exterior made interior* (section 22). That phrasing is the most explicit example of a relation of interference between philosophy and literature in the long poem. However, there are other places, distributed throughout, where words contain that phenomenological relation of the incompossible: "a permanence composed of impermanence"; "make gay the hallucinations in surfaces"; "in the metaphysical streets of the physical town" (sections 10-11). At another point Stevens rejects the old opposition tragedy-comedy for the genre that shapes all this experience in favor of the complex self-split dehiscence of the commonplace. Here, dawn and evening are processes of some value because there is no way to cut into a process to distinguish dark from light. In the poem's last lines, New Haven's valued state is called *shade*.

Near the poem's end, Stevens gives all 18 lines of section 29 to an allegory of the forces of convention ranged against the joining of things and words. Mariners from the land of the elm trees, whose words were mere "brown clods," sail to the land of the lemon trees, "[y]ellow-blue, yellow-green," dense with vivid perceptual content. But trapped in limits of their language, in abstractions, the mariners cannot see (or taste or hear) what is in front of them, and so " [t]heir dark-colored words . . . redescribed the citrons." This negative instance serves to highlight the need for a quick, adaptive perceiving-thinking-writing that will cut closer to the curve of reality. Readymade mindsets congealed in words are what ordinary creativity has to overcome.

At the poem's last page, elaboration (the and yet, and yet, and yet), is Stevens's topic and method. These are the "edgings and inchings of final form," Stevens says, as he launches a stanza of similes and a final stanza of new metaphors that restate the relation of interference as they remind the reader of the transitional quality of all evenings. Reality, Stevens says, may be "a force that traverses a shade." The relation of interference is a force that traverses. It is what makes for the movement of representation in painting, film, and writing—what Merleau-Ponty has discussed in a late lecture: "in the film, in the cutting, editing and changes of perception, there is a solicitation and, so to speak, a celebration of our openness to the world and to the other person" (*IPP* 78). The force that traverses is a paradox in Stevens that Merleau-Ponty also alludes to, in nearly the same words and in certainly the same idea, arrived at independently. "From the simplest perception of movement to the experience of painting, we are always faced with the same paradox of a force legible in a form, a trace or signature of time in space" (78). The force that traverses is interference is embodied mind is perception is creativity.

The co-creativity of those who understand

"Co-," the prefix of mutuality

Bakhtin speaks of co-creativity, and Merleau-Ponty speaks of "the whole of my cohumans" in the late notes on Husserl on Geometry (*HLP* 36), but elsewhere within two pages Merleau-Ponty uses convergent, constitute constituting consciousness, communicate, constructed, compresent, compossible, and configurational.

In the essay titled by his editors "From Notes Made in 1970-71," Bakhtin's paragraph on "the co-creativity of those who understand" is part of a chain of points, and just before that paragraph comes an equally significant paragraph on the "principal advantages of outsideness (spatially, temporally, and nationally)" which are understanding, that is, understanding as emotional empathy, and then being able to place oneself in the other's position (142, 141). He writes: "One cannot understand understanding as a translation from the other's language into one's own language (141)," thus opening the whole topic of dialogue as intersubjectivity, which is the heart of his communication theory.

Dialogism means we are all living on the borders of ourselves, not in some self-contained Cartesian bubble of consciousness, and the borders are permeable to the speech and emotion of other persons.

Dialogism also means: no ideas except in the utterances of persons.

In a famous passage from "Discourse in the Novel," where my book falls open due to many return visits, Bakhtin says that the word in language is "half someone else's" and becomes one's own only when the speaker populates it with his own intention and accent, "when he appropriates the word, adapting it to his own semantic and expressive intention" (294).

Intersubjectivity is also the heart of phenomenology, by direct line of transmission from Husserl to Merleau-Ponty, because embodied subjectivity is co-evolved with the subjectivity of the other person in what Merleau-Ponty called "the miracle of the perception of the other."

In the thinking of Zen, the same recognition is phrased differently, in the doctrine that each person is both dependent and independent.

Co-creativity

Elements of creativity that are already established: a fresh view of structure; emergence from the random and the chaotic; what is new needs but also seeks beyond the given; perception, always in need of replenishment, is essentially creative in perceiving-thinking-writing beings.

As a species we created ourselves, domesticated ourselves, invented our own survival.

Creativity has been reduced in its possibility by being in the general mind celebrated as individual genius, but it becomes thinkable again when we consider its ordinariness in perception and when we instead study not special personalities or languages, but rather the enabling skills of every day, and when we recognize the art-sentence as it interferes with itself in ordinary-language sentences.

Other elements of creativity that require further work are its reconfiguration of active and passive, and the way things, ideas, and materials may be repurposed for use in life and art.

The prime directive in phenomenology is to take primordial wild thinking beyond what is already constituted, and thus to put cognition into a feedback loop with perception.

The second directive is to revise and exceed the natural attitude so to get behind the familiar appearances of the world to the strangeness of the world.

The third directive is to do this revision ingeniously by tracking structurally, in detail, how perception is in relation with things and persons.

The fourth directive is to keep at it because perception and its creativity are always in process, never static.

It is necessary to attend to attention in the daily ongoing work of eye, ear, and hand; that is the search of appearance, but, in the writings of Merleau-Ponty and his commentators, it has not been sufficiently emphasized how the search is hopeful, open-ended, and forward-pointing even as it is up-to-date on new science discoveries and fixed on detail coming from the surround.

The forces that perception must contend with in order to maintain its phenomenology of genesis are the ready-made, the assumed, the abstract, the constituted, the rational as the static and the familiar, science defined as the exclusive home of all that is rational, the idea, the concept, the old theory of representation, and constraints of Renaissance perspective.

Co-creativity in the phenomenology of perception is a search beyond what is known, or constituted, to a revision of rationality and a new analysis of the understanding.

In the original "co-creativity paragraph" in the 1970-71 notes, Bakhtin said we should understand the text as the author understood it, but better because all understanding is active and creative, and our mind-in-time has the supreme yet ordinary advantages of being other and later.

His memorable sentence is, "Creative understanding continues creativity, and multiplies the artistic wealth of humanity" ("From Notes" 142).

As he himself says just below, a meeting with a great human being determines, obligates, and unites.

Those who understand

The selected paragraph and the pages before and after make heavy use of the distinction both Bakhtin and Merleau-Ponty got from their early-career training in German philosophy: the distinction between the understanding and consciousness, exemplified in the phrase "[t]hrough understanding [the text] is supplemented by consciousness, and the multiplicity of its meanings is revealed" (Bakhtin, "From Notes" 142).

I will not go into it here but will mention for the record that Heidegger devotes upwards of eighty pages of *Being and Time* to the act of understanding, understanding itself, and the state or condition of understanding.

In the case of co-creation, there are two consciousnesses, that of the author and that of the interpreter, so a dialogic relation is possible.

Bakhtin is defining understanding as a power of origination that is not limited to the making of the text, but also involves a text that is repossessed and recontextualized by later evaluation, agreement/disagreement, and active search for new elements among the repeatable ones—involving the roles, as he has it, of both witness and judge.

The co-creator, he says, cannot search exclusively for what is familiar, because that does not allow the new to reveal itself.

Merleau-Ponty has his own version of co-creativity when he says that there is a prepossession of a future thought in a contemporary thought. That idea is related to his description of the late-arriving person who comes to evoke an unthought in a previous writer, which is the French philosopher's way of phrasing the core idea behind co-creativity.

Are there grounds for worry in Bakhtin's statement that a *text* is the object of attention for co-creativity and in Merleau-Ponty's statement that it is a *thought* that is made explicit when he restates positions from the later works of Husserl?

Are these two usages impugned by the following sentence on language, from *The Prose of the World*? "The marvel that a finite number of signs, forms, and words should give rise to an indefinite number of uses, or that other and identical marvel that linguistic meaning directs toward something beyond language, is the very prodigy of speech, and anyone who tries to explain it in terms of its 'beginning' or its 'end' would lose sight of its 'doing'" (PW 41).

Merleau-Ponty there puts himself and Bakhtin right, and on "doing," he is in implied agreement with the title and first-page description of method in Erin Manning and Brian Massumi, *Thought in the Act: Passages in the Ecology of Experience* (2014): "To ask ourselves what writing can do to make thought-felt what art can do, with philosophy."

I add only to the end: "and with literary criticism."

On the basis of all this discussion let us turn to what readers of philosophy and literature can do to make thought-felt what verbal art can do.

Can we imagine the kinds of things a reader of this academic book will know—what that reader will try—if they aspire to co-creation with a previous greatness?

Answer briefly because the reader's close tracking of the writer's technical moves will already be so well understood in George Sanders's scene-by-scene accounts of seven Russian stories in *A Swim in the Pond in the Rain* (2021); refer to it for ground-level attention to the writerly and readerly mind.[6]

The reader as co-creator will strive to know the historical conditions of the birth-to-meaning of the written document, mindful of Fredric Jameson's last-page, two-word injunction in *Marxism and Form*, "Always historicize!"

The reader will ask how the work of verbal art, in its era, goes beyond the pre-established order of signification.

The reader will search the structures of the author's mind to disclose the relations of interference between body and mind, which in turn structure the writing's dealings with cognition-perception, matter-spirit, and contingency-freedom.

The reader will perform the reduction upon language, by study of the sentence as where inner speech gets outered and where the verbal art hovers between the word and the paragraph, the word and the work as a whole.

The reader will attend to her or his own attention in the middles of things, not only in the sentence but in the in-between-ness of transitional moments, where writing is like dancing in the article in *The New York Times* that complained that in filming from above a large stage "the in-between moments are lost. . . . [but transitional moments]— how you get from one step to the next—are what dancing is all about" (Sehgal).[7]

The co-creative reader will be prepared to search the work's cognitive-aesthetic contradictions, at all levels, as constructive interferences that are not merely tolerated but prized as a field of study, *Ineinander* all over the place.

On the freedom of the reader

In the myth and policy of the Language poets, who came on the scene in the 1970s, the reader co-creates the meaning and the writer is hands-off and in no way a manipulator; if any manipulation occurs, it is from language itself as it produces its own meaningful story through and in the material.

The agency of the author is in part given over to the roles, rules, and hidden imperatives of the language system, so the author is more than usually passive, and language and the reader are more active.

That dynamic is the enabling avant-garde policy of this kind of writing.

It is a valid policy and the results in fifty years of impressive innovative writing show it to have been effective for readers who will assume the burdens of freedom to gain the pleasures of understanding.

---

[6] Also, in which it is clear that style-study can be done effectively with translations from alanguage other than English.
[7] The author finds a relation of interference when she says: "choreography plays with gravity and buoyancy."

Nonetheless, we may question whether this policy, so reluctant to claim the first-person pronoun and so eager to multiply authorial agency, has not managed to install the author everywhere in every cranny of the text.

No answer is forthcoming, but asking does open the issue of readerly freedom, which is already implied in our earlier citation of Bakhtin scholar Caryl Emerson, who declared that inner speech helps characters in novels, as well as writers and readers, escape roles pre-arranged for them by social pressure.

Adam Mars-Jones is approaching the issue in a review in the *London Review of Books* when he declares it undesirable, impractical to make "the reader as powerless to contest the impact of the [novel's] narrative as the characters to resist their circumstances" (36).

Mars-Jones concludes, in words that have a Merleau-Pontian resonance, that "readerly freedom is not something for technique to overcome but the medium through which technique operates, however extreme the material" (36).

In verbal art, the writing itself, as technique or style, enacts free choice within the constraints of time, personality, language, and ideology; and the reader of writing as dialogic partner donates life, attention, freedom, daring to be vulnerable and subject to manipulation.

Only when we are open to manipulation can we resist manipulation.

Stevens in "An Ordinary Evening" specifies a New Haven life "as and where we are," and values an art that is "part of the *res* itself."

Spontaneity, truth, creativity, freedom exist only within the medium through which they operate: body, material world, contingency, perceiving-thinking-writing.

Using our freedom

A writer must be obsessed and resolute to raise an immense topic at the very end, but there is a ready example of such a predecessor in Merleau-Ponty. Even when his books and essays are not directly referring to making choices or using freedom, they often get to this concern on the last page, but four speak explicitly and manage a final turn from phenomenology to existentialism: *Phenomenology of Perception* and the essays titled "Cézanne's Doubt," "Man, the Hero," and "Indirect Language and the Voices of Silence." I select from "Cézanne's Doubt" these statements that were reserved for last: "But he himself was never at the center of himself; nine days out of ten all he saw was the wretchedness of his empirical life and of his unsuccessful attempts. . . . It is still in the world, upon a canvas with colors, that he has to realize his freedom. . . . That is why he never finished working. We never get away from our life. We never see our ideas or our freedom face to face" (84). Merleau-Ponty never invented for French the term Bakhtin put near the center of his communication theory, *unfinalizability*, but the French philosopher most certainly had the same concept for the artist's freedom that is realized only in the active, ongoing, never-conclusive need to make a choice.[8]

As to the immensity of the topic, even the Norwegian philosopher Lars Svendsen, who has recently surveyed the range of essentially contested freedom concepts, has encountered the fact that "more philosophical works have probably been written on freedom than any other subject" (11). He moves from freedom's political aspects to the domain of personal freedom, writing a narrative of fundamental ontological and anthropological questions, concluding that "the crucial issue is not whether personal freedom has its limits—those will be present in any case—but whether those limits are self-imposed" (11). In the Afterword he quotes American novelist David Foster Wallace as the culmination of the book's insights: "The really important kind of freedom involves attention, and awareness, and discipline, and effort, and being able to truly care about other people and to sacrifice for them, over and over in myriad petty little unsexy ways, every day" (qtd. in Svendsen 241). Here, too, philosophy turns to literature for condensed re-statement of its core message, and here too are themes already touched upon in this discourse: attention, awareness, sacrifice, the everyday, and, perhaps most Merleau-Pontian of all, use of our freedom for something beyond ourselves, others—who are dear to us.

Phenomenology, as it aspired to be conterminous with philosophy, instituted a range of operations and special terms, and told a story of its relation with previous systems in the history of European thought. Phenomenology did not need to be a philosophy of freedom, and it was not in Husserl. When WWI began, Husserl was already 55 and had invented the phenomenological science; when WWII began, Husserl had been dead for a year. When WWII began, Merleau-Ponty was a teacher in the provinces and a soldier, and he with the rest of France lived through five years of war and occupation. He never wrote an autobiography, but some of his most arresting pages in essays recount what a shock it was to be disillusioned, after 1939, with human evil and social breakdown during those traumatic years of unfreedom. Before '39 it was an innocent era, for him and his nation; after '39 was maturity, struggle, awareness of evil, and hard choices. From the war's end forward, he never lost the belief that one of the assignments of philosophy was a definition of freedom as a moral process, that is, a fact in oneself that required a relation of care and sacrifice with others.

Antoine de St. Exupéry's wonderful book *Flight to Arras*, half action novel and half moral treatise, tells of the stoical band of French bomber crews in 1940, when people from the north of France were refugees on the roads, the Germans were advancing with tanks and fighter planes, and out of twenty-five planes in St. Exupéry's squadron

---

8 See Eran Dorfman's essay for an argument concerning a Merleau-Pontian radical reflection, where the "the long and infinite way towards freedom" (Dorfman 151) is entered upon when phenomenology "comes into being by destroying itself as separate philosophy" (Merleau-Ponty, *PP* 456).

there were seven left to defend all of France. The book is first an account of the lead-up to three minutes of terror over Arras, in heavy flak with visible tracers, frozen rudder being manhandled by Antoine de St. Exupéry the pilot, the experience of overflight and bombing, and then the escape and return to the ground. The rest of the book is a resourceful, self-wounding set of thoughts about how one justifies sacrificing oneself and comrades for a brave unified community of the French nation. On the last page of *Phenomenology of Perception*, Merleau-Ponty, concluding the final chapter on freedom, quotes St. Exupéry on how "there is before you this person, whom you love, there are these men whose existence around you is that of slaves . . . and *your* freedom cannot be willed . . . without willing freedom *for all*" (qtd. in *PP* 456). The whole book of technical exposition of forms of consciousness ends, not with the author's words, but with the words of a literary writer who was a pilot in 1940.

The essay "Man, the Hero" ends with another reference to St. Exupéry, but also with several quotations from Hemingway's *For Whom the Bell Tolls*, a novel of the late 1930s about the American professor Robert Jordan, who is blowing up Fascist bridges in the Spanish Civil War of 1936. Wounded behind Fascist lines, he has to send the partisans away while he stays to hold off the enemy with a machine gun. Should Jordan commit suicide with his revolver? No. Merleau-Ponty approves: "The man who is still alive has only one resource but a sovereign one: he must keep on acting like a living man. We die alone, but we live with other people; we are the image which they have of us; where they are, we are too" (*SNS* 186). These choices of literary heroes place an excruciating focus upon what this kind of thinking wishes to convey: that we are free—not in spite of our hold on the world and what we are, our manner of existing, and our style—but by means of them. Can we say that the resistance (the interference) of the aesthetic itself, in the novel as a form—also in irony as attitude and in tragedy as genre—is a space in which what is destructive about reification, abstraction, and unfreedom is refused? If we can say it about literature, we can say it about philosophy, too, especially as practiced by the writer, Maurice Merleau-Ponty.

Bibliography

Merleau-Ponty, Maurice. *Adventures of the Dialectic*. Trans. Joseph Bien. Evanston, IL: Northwestern University Press, 1973.

---. "Cézanne's Doubt." *The Merleau-Ponty Reader* 69-84.

---. "Eye and Mind." *The Merleau-Ponty Reader* 351-78.

---. *Humanism and Terror: An Essay on the Communist Problem*. Trans. and notes by John O'Neill. Boston: Beacon Press, 1969.

---. *Husserl at the Limits of Phenomenology*. Ed. Leonard Lawlor and Bettina Bergo. Incl. texts by Edmund Husserl. Evanston, IL: Northwestern University Press, 2002.

---. "Husserl at the Limits of Phenomenology." *In Praise of Philosophy* 181-91.

---. *In Praise of Philosophy and Other Essays*. Trans. John Wild, James Edie, and John O'Neill. Evanston, IL: Northwestern University Press, 1970.

---. "Indirect Language and the Voices of Silence." *The Merleau-Ponty Reader* 241-82.

---. *Institution and Passivity: Course Notes from the Collège de France (1954-1955)*. Trans. Leonard Lawlor and Heath Massey. Foreword by Claude Lefort. Evanston, IL: Northwestern University Press, 2010.

---. *The Merleau-Ponty Reader*. Ed. Ted Toadvine and Leonard Lawlor. Evanston, IL: Northwestern University Press, 2007.

---. *Nature: Course Notes from the Collège de France*. 1995. Comp. and notes by Dominique Séglard. Trans. Robert Vallier. Evanston, IL: Northwestern University Press, 2003.

---. *Phenomenology, Language and Sociology: Selected Essays of Maurice Merleau-Ponty*. Ed. John O'Neill. London: Heinemann, 1974.

---. *Phenomenology of Perception*. Trans. Donald A. Landes. London and New York: Routledge, 2012.

---. "The Philosopher and His Shadow." *Signs* 159-81.

---. "The Primacy of Perception and Its Philosophical Consequences." *The Merleau-Ponty Reader* 89-118.

---. *The Primacy of Perception: And Other Essays on Phenomenological Psychology, the Philosophy of Art, History and Politics*. Ed. and intro. James M. Edie. Trans. James M. Edie et al. Evanston, IL: Northwestern University Press, 1964.

---. *Le problème de la parole: Cours au Collège de France, notes, 1953-1954* [The Problem of Speech: Lectures at the Collège de France: notes]. Ed. Lovisa Andén, Franck Robert, and Emmanuel de Saint Aubert. Intro. Lovisa Andén. Afterword by Franck Robert. Geneva: Métis Press, 2020.

---. *The Prose of the World*. Ed. Claude Lefort. Trans. John O'Neill. Evanston, IL: Northwestern University Press, 1973.

---. *Recherches sur l'usage littéraire du langage: Cours au Collège de France: Notes, 1953* [Investigations into the Literary Use of Language: Lectures at the Collège de France: notes]. Ed. Benedetta Zaccaretto and Emmanuel de Saint Aubert. Notes and intro. Benedetta Zaccaretto. Geneva: Métis Press, 2013.

---. *Sense and Non-Sense: Essays*. Trans. and preface by Hubert L. Dreyfus and Patricia Allen Dreyfus. Evanston, IL: Northwestern University Press, 1964.

---. *The Sensible World and the World of Perception: Course Notes from the Collège de France, 1953*. Trans., intro. and notes by Bryan Smyth. Evanston, IL: Northwestern University Press, 2020.

---. *Signs*. Trans. and intro. Richard C. McCleary. Evanston, IL: Northwestern University Press, 1964.

---. *The Structure of Behavior*. Trans. Alden L. Fisher. Boston: Beacon Press, 1963.

---. *Themes from the Lectures at the Collège de France, 1952-1960*. Trans. John O'Neill. Evanston, IL: Northwestern University Press, 1970.

---. *The Visible and the Invisible, Followed by Working Notes*. Trans. Alphonso Lingis. Evanston, IL: Northwestern University Press, 1968.

---. *The World of Perception* [Causeries]. 1948. Trans. Oliver Davis. London and New York: Routledge, 2004.

*

Abram, David. *Becoming Animal: An Earthly Cosmology*. New York: Vintage Books, 2010.

---. *The Spell of the Sensuous*. New York: Vintage Books, 1996.

Alferi, Pierre. "Seeking a Sentence." *Poetics Journal* 10 (June 1998). Web. 16 Jan. 2023.

Anastopoulos, Charis. *Particle or Wave: The Evolution of the Concept of Matter in Modern Physics*. Princeton and Oxford: Princeton University Press, 2008.

Bakhtin, Mikhail. "Discourse in the Novel." Trans. Michael Holquist and Caryl Emerson. *The Dialogic Imagination*. Ed. Michael Holquist and Caryl Emerson. Austin: University of Texas Press, 1981. 259-422.

---. *Speech Genres and Other Late Essays*. Trans. Vern W. McGee. Ed. Caryl Emerson and Michael Holquist. Austin: University of Texas Press, 1986.

Ball, Philip. *Beyond Weird: Why Everything You Thought You Knew About Quantum Physics Is Different*. Chicago and London: University of Chicago Press, 2018.

Barad, Karen. *Meeting the Universe Half-Way: Quantum Physics and the Entanglement of Matter and Meaning*. Durham, NC: Duke University Press, 2007.

Bateson, Gregory. *Mind and Nature: A Necessary Unity*. New York: E. P. Dutton, 1979.

Beauman, Ned. "Olafur Eliasson on How to Do Good Art." *The New York Times Magazine* 13 Nov. 2014. Web. 16 Feb. 2024.

Beilock, Sian. *How the Body Knows Its Mind: The Surprising Power of the Physical Environment to Influence How You Think and Feel*. New York, London, Toronto, Sydney, New Delhi: Atria/Simon and Schuster, 2017.

Bell, Julian. "The Body in Swooping Close-Up." *The New York Review of Books* 17 Dec. 2020. Web. 16. Aug. 2023.

Blackmore, Susan. *Consciousness: An Introduction*. New York: Oxford University Press, 2004.

Bohm, David. *On Creativity*. Ed. Lee Nichol. London and New York: Routledge, 1998.

Bollobás, Enikő. *They Aren't, Until I Call Them: Performing the Subject in American Literature*. Frankfurt am Main: Peter Lang, 2010.

Brown, Charles, and Ted Toadvine, eds. *Eco-Phenomenology: Back to the Earth Itself*. Albany: State University of New York Press, 2003.

Burns, Robert. *The Best Laid Schemes: Selected Poetry and Prose of Robert Burns*. Ed. Robert Crawford and Christopher MacLachlan. Princeton and Oxford: Princeton University Press, 2009.

Butler, Judith. *Senses of the Subject*. New York: Fordham University Press, 2015.

Carbone, Mauro. *An Unprecedented Deformaton: Marcel Proust and the Sensible Ideas*. Albany: State University of New York Press, 2010.

Carman, Taylor, and Mark B. N. Hansen, eds. *The Cambridge Companion to Merleau-Ponty*. Cambridge: Cambridge University Press, 2005.

Cataldi, Suzanne, and William S. Hamrick, eds. *Merleau-Ponty and Environmental Philosophy: Dwelling on the Landscapes of Thought*. Albany, NY: State University of New York Press, 2007.

Cave, Terence. *Thinking With Literature: Towards a Cognitive Criticism*. Oxford: Oxford University Press, 2016.

Christoff, Daniel. Introduction. *Husserl ou le retour aux choses* [Husserl, or the Return of Things]. By Edmund Husserl. Ed. Daniel Christoff. Paris: Éditions Seghers, 1966.

Clark, Andy. *Being There: Putting Brain, Body, and World Together Again*. Cambridge, MA and London: The MIT Press, 1997.

Clark, T. J. "Strange Apprentice: On Pissarro and Cézanne." *London Review of Books* 8 Oct. 2020: 15-21.

Clark, Timothy. "Phenomenology." *The Oxford Handbook of Ecocriticism*. Ed. Greg Garrard. Oxford and New York: Oxford University Press, 2014.

Claxton, Guy. *Intelligence in the Flesh*. New Haven and London: Yale University Press, 2015.

Collot, Michel. "L'Oeuvre comme paysage d'une expérience" [The Work of Art as a Landscape of Experience]. Simon and Castin 23-37.

Crawford, Robert. *The Bard: Robert Burns, A Biography*. Princeton and Oxford: Princeton University Press, 2009.

Culler, Jonathan. *Theory of the Lyric*. Cambridge, MA and London: Harvard University Press, 2015.

Davidson, Michael. *Invalid Modernism: Disability and the Missing Body of the Aesthetic*. Oxford: Oxford University Press, 2019.

----. "Review of Tobin Siebers, *Disabililty Theory* (2008)." *Disability Studies Quarterly* 28.4 (Fall 2008).

Derrida, Jacques. *Edmund Husserl's* Origin of Geometry: *An Introduction*. Trans. John P. Leavey, Jr. Lincoln and London: The University of Nebraska Press, 1989.

---. *The Problem of Genesis in Husserl's Phenomenology*. Trans. Marian Hobson. Chicago and London: University of Chicago Press, 2003.

---. *Voice and Phenomenon: Introduction to the Problem of the Sign in Husserl's Phenomenology*. Trans. Leonard Lawlor. Evanston, IL: Northwestern University Press, 2011.

Dorfman, Eran. "Freedom, Perception and Radical Reflection." *Reading Merleau-Ponty: On Phenomenology of Perception*. Ed. Thomas Baldwin. London and New York: Routledge, 2007. 139-51.

Dworkin, Craig. *Radium of the Word: A Poetics of Materiality*. Chicago and London: University of Chicago Press, 2020.

Edmond, Jacob. *A Common Strangeness: Contemporary Poetry, Cross-Cultural Encounter, Comparative Literature*. New York: Fordham University Press, 2012.

Emerson, Caryl. "The Outer Word and Inner Speech: Bakhtin, Vygotsky, and the Internalization of Language." *Bakhtin: Essays and Dialogues on His Work*. Ed. Gary Saul Morson. Chicago and London: University of Chicago Press, 1981.

Empson, William. *Seven Types of Ambiguity: A Study of Its Effects in English Verse*. 1947. New York: Meridian Books, 1955.

"The Everything Is Off-Topic Thread." *Comodo Forums*. Web. 14 Aug. 2023.

Fischer, Luke. *The Poet as Phenomenologist: Rilke and the New Poems*. New York and London: Bloomsbury Academic, 2015.

Foucault, Michel. "Theatrum Philosophicum." *Language, Counter-Memory, Practice: Selected Essays and Interviews by Michel Foucault*. Trans. Donald F. Bouchard and Sherry Simon. Ed. and intro. Donald F. Bouchard. Ithaca: Cornell University Press, 1977. 175-76.

Fuentes, Augustín. *The Creative Spark: How Imagination Made Humans Exceptional*. New York: Dutton, Penguin Random House, 2017.

Gardiner, Michael. "'A Very Understandable Horror of Dialectics': Bakhtin and Marxist Phenomenology." *Materializing Bakhtin: The Bakhtin Circle and Social Theory*. Ed. Craig Brandist and Galin Tihanov. New York: St. Martin's Press, 2000.

Gibson, James J. *The Ecological Approach to Visual Perception*. Hillsdale, NJ and London: Lawrence Erlbaum Associates, 1986.

Gilmore, Jonathan. "Between Philosophy and Art." Carman and Hansen 291-317.

Glendinning, Miles, and Aengus MacKechnie. *Scottish Architecture*. London: Thames and Hudson/World of Art, 2004.

Goehr, Lydia. "Understanding the Engaged Philosopher: On Politics, Philosophy, and Art." Carman and Hansen 318-51.

Hamon, Philippe. *Du Descriptif* [On the Descriptive]. Paris: Hachette Livre, 1993.

Hass, Lawrence. *Merleau-Ponty's Philosophy*. Bloomington and Indianapolis: Indiana University Press, 2008.

Hegel, G. W. F. *The Phenomenology of Mind*. Intro. George Lichtheim. New York and Evanston: Harper Torchbooks/Harper and Row, 1967.

Heidegger, Martin. *Being and Time*. Trans. Joan Stambaugh. Rev. and foreword by Dennis J. Schmidt. Albany: State University of New York Press, 2010.

---. *Kant and the Problem of Metaphysics*. 5th enlarged ed. Trans. Richard Taft. Bloomington and Indianapolis: Indiana University Press, 1997.

Herakleitos. *Herakleitos and Diogenes*. Trans. Guy Davenport. Eugene, OR: Wipf and Stock, 2010.

Hejinian, Lyn. *The Cold of Poetry*. Los Angeles: Sun and Moon Press, 1994.

---. *The Language of Inquiry*. Berkeley, Los Angeles, London: University of California Press, 2000.

---. *My Life*. Los Angeles: Sun and Moon Press, 1987.

---. *Tribunal*. Oakland, CA: Omnidawn Press, 2019.

Herder, Johann Gottfried. "Essay on the Origin of Language." 1772. *On the Origin of Language*. Ed., trans., and afterword by John H. Moran and Alexander Gode. Intro. Alexander Gode. New York: Frederick Ungar, 1966.

Hoffmeyer, Jesper. *Biosemiotics: An Examination into the Signs of Life and the Life of Signs*. Scranton, PA: University of Scranton Press, 2008.

Hopkins, Gerard Manly. *The Journals and Papers of Gerard Manley Hopkins*. Ed. Humphrey House. Comp. Graham Storey. London: Oxford University Press, 1959.

Husserl, Edmund. *Cartesian Meditations: An Introduction to Phenomenology*. Trans. Dorion Cairns. The Hague: Martinus Nijhoff, 1960.

---. *The Crisis of European Sciences and Transcendental Phenomenology: An Introduction to Phenomenological Philosophy*. Trans. and intro. David Carr. Evanston, IL: Northwestern University Press, 1970.

---. *The Essential Husserl: Basic Writings in Transcendental Phenomenology*. Ed. Donn Welton. Bloomington and Indianapolis: Indiana University Press, 1999.

---. *Husserl ou le retour aux choses* [Husserl, or the Return of Things]. Ed. Daniel Christoff. Paris: Éditions Seghers, 1966.

---. *The Idea of Phenomenology*. Trans. William P. Alston and George Nakhnikian. Intro. George Nakhnikian. The Hague: Martinus Nijhoff, 1964.

---. *Ideas Pertaining to a Pure Phenomenology and to a Phenomenological Philosophy*. Book 2: *Studies in the Phenomenology of Constitution*. Trans. Richard Rojcewicz and André Schuwer. Dordrecht, Boston, and London: Kluwer Academic Publishers, 1989.

---. *Logical Investigations*. Vol. 1: Investigations I, II. Trans. J. N. Findlay. New York: Humanities Press, 1970.

---. *Logical Investigations*. Vol. 2: Investigations III, IV, V, VI. Trans. J. N. Findlay. London: Routledge and Kegan Paul, 1970.

Idhe, Don. "Singing the World: Language and Perception." *The Horizons of the Flesh: Critical Perspectives on the Thought of Maurice Merleau-Ponty*. Ed. Garth Gillan. Carbondale and Edwardsville: Southern Illinois University Press, 1973.

Inkpin, Andrew. *Disclosing the World: On the Phenomenology of Language*. Cambridge, MA and London: The MIT Press, 2016.

Jackendoff, Ray. *Language, Consciousness, Culture: Essays on Mental Structures*. Cambridge, MA and London: The MIT Press, 2007.

Jaén, Isabel, and Julien Jacques Simon, eds. *Cognitive Literary Studies: Current Themes and New Directions*. Austin: The University of Texas Press, 2012.

James, Henry. *The Ambassadors*. 1903. New York, 1909. *The Full Text Archive*. Web. 4 May 2023.

Jameson, Fredric. *The Hegel Variations: On the Phenomenology of Spirit*. London: Verso, 2017.

---. *Marxism and Form: Twentieth-Century Dialectical Theories of Literature*. Princeton: Princeton University Press, 1971.

---. "Time and the Sea." *London Review of Books* 4 Apr. 2020. Web. 13 Jan. 2024.

---. *Valences of the Dialectic*. London: Verso, 2009.

Käufer, Stephan, and Anthony Chemero, eds. *Phenomenology: An Introduction*. Cambridge, UK and Malden, MA: Polity Press, 2015.

Kohák, Erazim. "An Understanding Heart: Reason, Value, and Transcendental Phenomenology." Brown and Toadvine 19-36.

Lanzoni, Susan. *Empathy: A History*. New Haven and London: Yale University Press, 2018.

Lefort, Claude. *Sur une colonne absente: Écrits autour de Merleau-Ponty* [On a Missing Column: Writings around Merleau-Ponty]. Paris: Éditions Gallimard, 1978.

Lingis, Alfonso. "Merleau-Ponty and the Primacy of Reflection." *The Horizons of the Flesh: Critical Perspectives on the Thought of Merleau-Ponty*. Ed. Garth Gillan. Carbondale and Edwardsville, IL: Southern Illinois University Press, 1973.

Longo, Mariano. *Emotions Through Literature: Fictional Narratives, Society and the Emotional Self.* London and New York: Routledge, 2020.

Mackenzie, Louisa, and Stephanie Posthumus, eds. *French Thinking About Animals.* The Animal Turn Series. East Lansing: Michigan State University Press, 2015.

Manning, Erin, and Brian Massumi. *Thought in the Act: Passages in the Ecology of Existence.* Minneapolis and London: The University of Minnesota Press, 2014.

Mars-Jones, Adam. "Muffled Barks, Muted Yelps." Review of *Hurricane Season* by Fernanda Melchor. *London Review of Books* 19 Mar. 2020. Web. 14 Mar. 2024.

McGinn, Colin. *Prehension: The Hand and the Emergence of Humanity.* Cambridge, MA and London, England: The MIT Press, 2015.

Meijer, Jan M. "Verbal Art As Interference Between a Cognitive and an Aesthetic Structure." *Structure of Texts and Semiotics of Culture.* Ed. Jan van der Eng and Mojmir Grygar. Paris, The Hague: Mouton, 1973.

Meschonnic, Henri. *Critique du rythme: Anthropologie historique du langage* [The Critique of Rhtythm: The Historical Anthropology of Language]. Lagrasse: Verdier, 1982.

---. "Manifeste Pour Une Parti du Rythme [A Rhythm Party Manifesto]." In *Célébration de la poésie.* Lagrasse: Verdier Poche, 2001.

Mieszkowski, Jan. *Crises of the Sentence.* Chicago and London: The University of Chicago Press, 2019.

Mildenberg, Ariane, ed. *Understanding Merleau-Ponty, Understanding Modernism.* New York: Bloomsbury Academic, 2019.

Mlinko, Ange. *Distant Mandate.* New York: Farrar, Straus and Giroux: 2017.

Moi, Toril. *Revolution of the Ordinary: Literary Studies After Wittgenstein, Austin, and Cavell.* Chicago and London: The University of Chicago Press, 2017.

Moran, Dermot. *Edmund Husserl: Founder of Phenomenology.* Cambridge: Polity Press, 2005.

---. *Introduction to Phenomenology.* London and New York: Routledge, 2000.

Natanson, Maurice. *Edmund Husserl: Philosopher of Infinite Tasks.* Evanston, IL: Northwestern University Press, 1973.

Newland, Guy. *Appearance and Reality: The Two Truths in the Four Buddhist Tenet Systems.* Ithaca, NY: Snow Lion, 1999.

Noë, Alva. *Action in Perception.* Cambridge, MA and London: The MIT Press, 2004.

Oliver, Kelly. "Beyond Recognition: Merleau-Ponty and an Ethics of Vision." *Intertwinings: Interdisciplinary Encounters with Merleau-Ponty.* Ed. Gail Weiss. Albany: The State University of New York Press, 2008. 131-52.

Painter, Corinne, and Christian Lotz. *Phenomenology and the Non-Human Animal: At the Limits of Experience.* Dordrecht: Springer, 2007.

Palmer, Michael, ed. *Code of Signals: Recent Writings in Poetics.* Berkeley: North Atlantic Books, 1983.

Perkins, David. *Romanticism and Animal Rights.* Cambridge: Cambridge University Press, 2003.

Perloff, Marjorie. *Unoriginal Genius: Poetry by Other Means in the New Century.* Chicago and London: The University of Chicago Press, 2010.

Prynne, Jeremy. *Concepts and Conception in Poetry*. Critical Documents. Cambridge: Queen's College, 2014.

Rajan, Tilottama. *Deconstruction and the Remainders of Phenomenology: Sartre, Derrida, Foucault, Baudrillard*. Stanford: Stanford University Press, 2002.

Reynolds, L. D., and N. G. Wilson. *Scribes and Scholars: A Guide to the Transmission of Greek and Latin Literature*. 2nd ed. Oxford: Oxford University Press, 1974.

Ricoeur, Paul. *A Key to Edmund Husserl's Ideas I*. Trans. Bond Harris and Jacqueline Bouchard Spurlock. Ed. rev, intro. Pol Vandevelde. Milwaukee: Marquette University Press, 1996.

Romano, Claude. *At the Heart of Reason*. Trans. Michael B. Smith and Claude Romano. Evanston, IL: Northwestern University Press, 2015.

Rorty, Richard. "Philosophy as a Kind of Writing: An Essay on Derrida." *Consequences of Pragmatism. Essays: 1972-1980*. Minneapolis: The University of Minnesota Press, 1982.

Rosen, Charles. *The Classical Style: Haydn, Mozart, Beethoven*. Exp. ed. New York and London: W. W. Norton, 1998.

Rouse, Joseph. "Merleau-Ponty's Existential Conception of Science." Carman and Hansen 265-90.

Sanders, George. *A Swim in a Pond in the Rain: In Which Four Russians Give a Master Class on Writing, Reading, and Life*. New York: Random House, 2021.

Sartre, Jean-Paul. *Portraits (Situations IV)*. Trans. Chris Turner. London, New York, and Calcutta: Seagull Books, 2009.

Sehgal, Parul. "*Temporary* Is a Debut Novel That Leans Into the Absurdity of How We Work Now." *The New York Times* 25 Feb. 2020. C6.

Serres, Michel. *Eyes*. Trans. Anne-Marie Feenberg-Dibon. London: Bloomsbury, 2015.

---. *The Five Senses: A Philosophy of Mingled Bodies*. Vol. 1. Trans. Margaret Sankey and Peter Cowley. Intro. Stephen Connor. London and New York: Continuum, 2008.

Seshadri, Kalpana Rahita. *HumAnimal: Race, Law, Language*. Minneapolis: The University of Minnesota Press, 2012.

Setiya, Kieran. "Review of *Frank Ramsey: A Sheer Excess of Powers* by Cheryl Misak." *London Review of Books* 18 Feb. 2021. Web. 14 Mar. 2024.

Siebers, Tobin. *Disability Theory*. Ann Arbor: The University of Michigan Press, 2008.

Silliman, Ron. *The New Sentence*. New York: Roof Books, 1987.

Simon, Anne, and Nicolas Castin, eds. *Merleau-Ponty et le littéraire* [Merleau-Ponty and the Literary]. Paris: Presses de l'École normale supérieure, 1997.

Sparrow, Tom. *Plastic Bodies: Rebuilding Sensation After Phenomenology*. Foreword Catherine Malabou. New Metaphysics Series. London: Open Humanities Press, 2014.

---. *The End of Phenomenology: Metaphysics and the New Realism*. Edinburgh: Edinburgh University Press, 2014.

---. "Editor's Introduction: A Philosophy of Transience." *The Alphonso Lingis Reader*. Ed. Tom Sparrow. Minneapolis and London: The University of Minnesota Press, 2018.

Stein, Edith. *On the Problem of Empathy*. Trans. Waltrut Stein. Foreword Erwin W. Straus. The Hague: Martinus Nijhoff, 1964.

Stein, Gertrude. *Writings 1932-1946*. New York: The Library of America, 1998.

Stevens, Wallace. *The Collected Poems of Wallace Stevens*. New York: Knopf, 1955.

---. "The Relations between Poetry and Painting." *The Necessary Angel: Essays on Reality and the Imagination*. New York: Vintage Books, 1951.

---. *Stevens: Collected Poetry and Prose*. New York: The Library of America, 1997.

Suzuki, Shunryu. *Zen Mind, Beginner's Mind*. Ed. Trudy Dixon. Preface by Huston Smith. Intro. Richard Baker. New York and Tokyo: Weatherhill, 1970.

Svendsen, Lars. *A Philosophy of Freedom*. London: Reaktion Books. 2014.

Taylor, Charles. *The Language Animal: The Full Shape of the Human Linguistic Capacity*. Cambridge, MA: Harvard University Press, 2016.

Toadvine, Ted. *Merleau-Ponty's Philosophy of Nature*. Evanston, IL: Northwestern University Press, 2009.

Valéry, Paul. *The Idea of Perfection: The Poetry and Prose of Paul Valéry (a Bilingual Edition)*. Trans. Nathaniel Budavsky-Brody. New York: Farrar, Strauss and Giroux, 2020.

---. *The Art of Poetry*. Trans. Denise Folliot. Intro. T. S. Eliot. New York: Vintage Books, 1958.

Verdi, Richard. *Cézanne*. New York: Thames and Hudson, 1997.

Watson, Gay. *Attention: Beyond Mindfulness*. London: Reaktion Books, 2017.

---. *A Philosophy of Emptiness*. London: Reaktion Books, 2014.

Watten, Barrett. *Total Syntax*. Carbondale and Edwardsville: Southern Illinois University Press, 1985.

Weil, Simone. "Reflections on the Right Use of School Studies with a View to the Love of God." 1942. *Waiting For God*. New York: Harper Collins, 2009. 57-64.

Weitsman, Mel. "Dharma Dragon." *Lion's Roar: Buddhism, Meditation, Life* 5 May 2021. 38-39.

Wesling, Donald. *The Scissors of Meter: Grammetrics and Reading*. Ann Arbor: The University of Michigan Press, 1995.

---. *Animal Perception and Literary Language*. New York: Palgrave Macmillan, 2019.

Westling, Louise. *The Logos of the Living World: Merleau-Ponty, Animals, and Language*. New York: Fordham University Press, 2014.

Wheeler, Wendy. *The Whole Creature: Complexity, Biosemiotics, and the Evolution of Culture*. London: Lawrence and Wishart, 2006.

Williams, William Carlos. *The Collected Poems of William Carlos Williams*. Vol. 2: 1939-1962. Ed. Christopher MacGowan. New York: New Directions, 1986.

Wiskus, Jessica. *The Rhythm of Thought: Art, Literature, and Music After Merleau-Ponty*. Chicago and London: The University of Chicago Press, 2013.

Wolfe, Cary. *Ecological Poetics: or, Wallace Stevens's Birds*. Chicago and London: The University of Chicago Press, 2020.

Wyschogrod, Edith. *Crossover Queries: Dwelling with Negatives, Embodying Philosophy's Others*. New York: Fordham University Press, 2006.

Zunshine, Lisa, Editor. *Introduction to Cognitive Literary Studies*. Baltimore, MD: Johns Hopkins University Press, 2010.

Acknowledgments

Philosophers in the modern era are necessarily writers and we who are writers need to be thinkers. Maurice Merleau-Ponty was a most quotable stylist, as I've found through preparing for this book in the time of a pandemic when libraries were closed and I marked, heavily, my own copies of the translations. Writing this book as a literary person, I did quote the French philosopher but not in the way philosophers might, rather with quite a lot of stunning translated sentences fitted into my own sentences: here the major ideas of phenomenology of perception are captured in brilliant, mostly brief, formulations that do equally well in English as they do in the original French. This practice turned out to fit perfectly with the book's derived contention, learned from phenomenology and quantum physics, namely, one-in-another, not-one-without-the-other, and, essentially, the *interference* of energies. It's appropriate that Merleau-Ponty said this long before me, in his grand idea that perception already stylizes.

For encouragement and corrections during the making of this book, thanks are due to Enikő Bollobás, John Granger, Thomas Marshall, Kenneth Martin, David Perkins, and Kim Stanley Robinson. For specific advice on argument and style after I had a draft, I wish to thank Tadeusz Rachwał, Margaret E. Van Blaricum, and Kálmán Matolcsy. Special thanks to Donald E. Morse, my editor at the University of Debrecen, Hungary, for his faith in this project and his ability to see it through to publication.

Along with my editor and publisher at the University of Debrecen, Hungary, I would like to thank the following publishers for permission to quote from books in English and from Merleau-Ponty's original French books in the listed English translations.

Quotations from Maurice Merleau-Ponty in this book refer to the English translations from two publishers, Northwestern University Press (USA) and Taylor and Francis/Routledge (UK). The translations themselves rely on books first published in French by Gallimard Editions Ltd. (Paris), whom we thank for their judicious sponsorship of a major thinker.

Thank you to Taylor and Francis/Routledge for the use of quoted passages from Maurice Merleau-Ponty, *Phenomenology of Perception*, translated by Donald A. Landes (London and New York: Routledge, 2012).

My thanks to Northwestern University Press for generous permission to use quotations from the following volumes, as translated from the original French books by Maurice Merleau-Ponty:

- Excerpts from *The Merleau-Ponty Reader*, edited by Ted Toadvine and Leonard Lawlor (Evanston, IL: Northwestern University Press, 2007). Copyright © 2007 by Northwestern University Press. Published 2007. All rights reserved.
- Excerpts from *The Prose of the World*, translated by John O'Neill and edited by Claude Lefort (Evanston, IL: Northwestern University Press, 1973). Originally published in French as *La Prose du monde*. Copyright © 1969 by Editions

Gallimard. English translation copyright © 1973 by Northwestern University Press. First published 1973 by Northwestern University Press. First paperback edition 1981. All rights reserved.
- Excerpts from *The Visible and the Invisible*, translated by Alphonso Lingis (Evanston, IL: Northwestern University Press, 1968). Originally published in French under the title *Le Visible et l'invisible*. Copyright © 1964 by Editions Gallimard, Paris. English translation © 1968 by Northwestern University Press. First printing 1968. All rights reserved.
- Excerpts from *Signs*, translated with an introduction by Richard C. McCleary (Evanston, IL: Northwestern University Press, 1964). Originally published in French under the title *Signes* in 1960 by Librarie Gallimard, Paris. Translation copyright © 1964 by Northwestern University Press. First printing 1964. All rights reserved.
- Excerpts from *In Praise of Philosophy and Other Essays*, translated by John Wild, James Edie, and John O'Neill (Evanston, IL: Northwestern University Press, 1988). *Éloge de la philosophie* was originally published by Librarie Gallimard, Paris in 1953. Translation copyright © 1963 by Northwestern University Press. *Résumés de cours: Collège de France 1952-1960* was originally published by Éditions Gallimard in 1968. Translation copyright © 1970 by John O'Neill.

Thanks are also due to University of Chicago Press, for permission to reprint short passages from Jan Mieszkowski, *Crises of the Sentence* (Chicago and London: The University of Chicago Press, 2019).

To Farrar, Straus and Giroux, subsidiary of Macmillan Publishers, for reprinting the whole poem by Ange Mlinko titled "A Horse Does Not Want to be FedExed" from *Distant Mandate* (New York: Farrar, Straus and Giroux, 2017).

To New Directions Publishing for reprinting the entire poem by William Carlos Williams titled "The Yellow Chimney" from *The Collected Poems of William Carlos Williams*, vol. 2: 1939-1962, edited by Christopher MacGowan (New York: New Directions, 1986).

To Omnidawn Press for reprinting a brief selection from Lyn Hejinian, *Tribunal* (Oakland, CA: Omnidawn Press, 2019).

To Reaktion Books for reprinting selections from Gay Watson, *Attention: Beyond Mindfulness* (London: Reaktion Books, 2017).

The landscape painting on the cover of the print version of this book is inscribed "Tihany 1954," with the painter's name, "Komlós István." Tihany is on the shore of Hungary's Lake Balaton. The painting, in the author's collection, was purchased in Budapest at an antiquary near Margit-híd on the Danube.

The chapter 2 illustrations of the child's mode of expression were drawn by the author's daughter, Molly Wesling.

Note on the author

Donald Wesling is Professor Emeritus of English Literature at University of California San Diego. He has published on Wordsworth, John Muir, Edward Dorn, and Bakhtin; on rhyme, meter, and avant-garde prosody; and on how voice and emotion get into writing. His 2019 book on *Animal Perception and Literary Language* expanded his concerns to question how humans, evolved from animals, have learned to code perception of movement into sentences and scenes. This new book, on the one-in-another of perceiving-thinking-writing, develops his study on how perceptual content gets into pigment and words. Through the metaphor of interference, this book also advances an original argument on how literature and philosophy relate to each other.

HJEAS Books are published by Debrecen University Press and Sciendo, De Gruyter Brill's electronic publishing subsidiary

Bei Fragen zur Produktsicherheit wenden Sie sich bitte an:
If you have any questions regarding product safety,
please contact:

Walter de Gruyter GmbH
Genthiner Straße 13
10785 Berlin
productsafety@degruyterbrill.com